Hooray! Here comes Tuesday

The Home-Start Story

Margaret Harrison

Founder and Life President of Home-Start

Bamaha Publishing

First published in 2003
by Bamaha Publishing
21 Elms Road, Leicester LE2 3JD
email: bamaha.publishing@ntlworld.com

Cover Photograph: Andy Goldsworthy
Japanese Maple Leaves
Ouchiyama - Mura - Japan
21-22 November 1987

Printed and bound in Great Britain by
Abbott Colour Technology,
Turnpike Close, Lutterworth,
Leicestershire LE17 4YB

Printed on paper from sustainable sources

ISBN 0-9544707-0-2

Hooray! Here Comes Tuesday

The Home-Start Story

Margaret Harrison

CONTENTS

Acknowledgments

I am immensely grateful to so very many people, who have joined me in the Home-Start journey over the years. Whilst writing this book, the memories have come flooding back – memories of individual families, volunteers, friends, colleagues, and others too numerous to mention.

The following list includes those who suggested I should write the book and have sustained me with their support, friendship, practical help and humour throughout the writing. It also includes those who have contributed in many different roles, to Home-Start over the years. Let me apologise right now, to those I have omitted. Hopefully there will be a second edition. **Thank you** to you all.

Joan Stephens, my editor, whose patience, acceptance, and thoughtful insight have encouraged me to continue with the writing, even when sections had to be re-written. I have learned so much from you.

The following friends and relatives have also contributed immeasurably with their loving support and with turning the original draft of this book, into the final manuscript.
Family members, Basil, Jane (who has been most encouraging from her own experience of writing a book), David and Clare – all for their wisdom and practical help at every stage of the writing.
Friends, Rachel and David Carmichael, Vivienne Cooke, John and Alwyne Dean, Dr Mary Hamill, Linda Hart, Margaret Howe, Dr. John Irvine, Peggy Jaycock, Mark and Erika Monger, Mary and Justin Parker, Grant and Audrey Pitches, Beryl Riley, Denis Rice, Dr Sheila Shinman, Christine Tracey.
Home-Start Leicester, Jill Perry, Anna Causier and Alison Hill, who also allowed me to plunder their archives.
Critical reading – Tony and Christine Crispin.
Photocopying – Matthew Humphries.
Printing – Gordon Carmichael at Abbott Colour Technology.

I also acknowledge with love and gratitude, the following people, and so very many others, without whom Home-Start would not exist in the way it has developed:

Rikki Adam,Gulshan Ahmed, Gill Antoniou, Elaine Appleton, Jane Arkell, Jan Aylward, Dorothy Baden Fuller, Ina Bakker, Sandra Bannerman, Pauline Bantoft, Sir Peter Barclay, Kay Barnes, Marilyn Barnes, Kate Batchelor, Jo Bickle, Clive Bate, Wendy Bateman, Daphne Bates, Sue Belcher, Sheena Bell, Agota Benko, Els Berman, Glyn Berwick, Stephanie Besbrode, Kay Bews, Julie Bezzina, Manju Bhattacharrya, Lilo Bieback-Diel, Margaret Bird, Edit Bodis, Carol Borthwick, Debbie Bowler, Deirdre Brady, Mary Brealey, Baroness (Heather) Brigstocke, Bente Brostrom, Carol Brown, Jenny Brown, Sybil Brown, Wendy Brownlee, Barbara Browse, Tina Brumhead, Dr Elizabeth Bryan, Sophie Bryson, Bob Bunting, Brenda Burgess, Joan Burns, Kathy Butler, Bobby Cameron, Jim Carmichael, Sylvia Chadwick, Carla Chaszczewski, Peggy Church, Albert Clark, Pat Clark, Raymond Clarke, Barbara Close, Barbara Cluer, Betty Cohen, Judith Colegate, Carmen Conquer, Ruth Consterdine, Clare Cooke, Pam Cooke, Vivienne Cooke, Lady (Juliet) Cooper, Gillian Corsellis, Bernard Crump, Paul Curno, Ruth Dale, Peter Dallow, Kathy and Tony Davies, Barbara Davies, Phil Davies, Vivienne Davies, Mary Dawes, Erica De'Ath, Mehru Deboo, Elaine Dilleigh, Anne Dornan, Kathleen Duncan, Jackie Dunmore, John Durben, Dr Kedar Dwivedi, Jean Elliott, Ginny and Brigadier Andy Evans, Wendy Evans, Sue Everitt, Christine Ferguson, Caroline Flint, Phyllida Flint, Gwen Flowers, Marie Forsyth, Christine Fulford, Colonel Mike Gaffney, Sue Gamwell, Judi Geggie, Ruth George, Eva Gibson, Jagdeep, Raj and Surinder Gill, Lynn Glover, Usha Gohel, Kathy Goody, Sandra Grainger, Bette Graham, Philomena Gray, Valerie Green, Chana Greenberg, Major-General Charles Grey, Heather Groves, Dr. Sylvia Gyde, Jill Haigh, Glenys Hall, Sue Hammond, Kay Hancock, Jill Hand, Charles and Elizabeth Handy, Felicity Hanson, Celia Harris, Jane Harris, Gill Harrison, Tricia Hayllar, Wendy Haynes, Helen Henry, Margaret Henry, Moira Hemmett, Ronald Higgins, Ronnie Highmore, Jill Hiscox, Rita Hodkin, Dominic and Susannah Hollamby, Edward Holloway, Valerie Howarth, Karen Hulett, Jenny Hurkett, Rob Hutchinson, Rosemary Jackson, Peggy Jaycock, Peter and Juniper Jenks, Rev. Canon Basil Jones, Margaret Jones, Lord and Lady (Yolanda) Joseph, Sheila Kataria, Grace Kay, Aliya Kedem, Sylvia Keene, Margaret Kennedy, Christopher and Charlotte King, Heather Knox, Drs Fokko Kool, Satish Kumar, Lord (Herbert) Laming, Sir Frank Lampl, Rachel Larea, Alan Laurie, Wyn Laxton, Libby Lee, Sharon Lewis, Ralph Lilburn, Mandy Lindley, Sue Long, Caroline Longhurst, Geoffrey Lord, Anna Lynch, Richard and Rosemary Macaire, Jenny MacQueen, Alasdair MacRae, Carole Maddock, Jenny Magee, Sylvia Maley, Charlotte Mannion, Valerie Markwick, Doreen Martina, Pat Mason, Pat Mattock, Jackie

McCudden, Margaret McDowell, Victor McElfatrick, Valerie McGuffin, Peter McLaughlin, Dave Milliken, Sheila Millington, Doris Mobbs, Rigmor Moe, Shelagh Moody, Marie Morehen, Marian Moss, June Mountney, Jo Moody, Barbara Mullen, Elizabeth Murray, Sir Patrick and Lady (Penny) Nairne, Bushra Nasreen, Rajvinder Nepal, Maxine Nightingale, Maria Niarchos Gouaze, Lord Northbourne, Roger Ogle, Marie Elena Orrego, Hilary Owen, Major-General John Page, Geraldine Parsons, Gill Parsons, Christine Paterson, Sue Paterson, Jill Pedley, Berwyn Peet, Ann Pemberton, Barbara Phillips, Sherri Pickles, Prof. Basil Pillay, Gill Pirt, Pat Pitcher, Lynda Pither, Angela Plowman, Kathryn Pochin, Christine Pointon, Jenny Poole, Sue Pope, Jill Powell, Ruth Procter, Dr. Gillian Pugh, Anne Purnell, Nora Quas, Ina Quig, Dr Csaba Ratay, Gloria Raven, Philip Ray, Dianne Rees, Joyce Reeve, Deania Reid, Yvonne Renouf, Prue Reynolds, Denis Rice, Sue Roberts, Julie Robertson, Linda Robinson, Wendy Rose, Eddie Ross, Anne Rowe, Maggie Rowlands, James Sainsbury, Allison Sargeant, Vivien Saunders, Joan Scarborough, Jasu Shah, Hula Schlesinger, Mark Schnebli, Anne Schonveld, Margaret Scully, Libby Searle, Kathy Shaw, Fiona Sibbick, Sally Simmonds, Hildy Simmons, Martha Simpson, Peggie Sinclair, Sari Sirkia-Weaver, Alice Sluckin, Fiona Smith, John Smith, Joy Smith, Hilary Smyth, Jane Snelling, Ruth Sonntag, Jo Speakman, Paula Spencer, Pauline Sprott, Marie and Geoff Stead, Margaret Stephenson, Alastair Stewart, Pauline Strangeway, Lady (Ruth) Strong, Judi Sutherland, Bernard Taylor, Liz Thompson, Margaret Thompson, Winifred Thomson, Marbeth Tobin, Eve Tonks, Colin Towell, Bob Travers, Maureen Trumper, David Utting, Willem van der Eyken, Annemarie van Wijman, Stefan Vanistendael, Brian Waller, Lord (Norman) Warner, Nadia Watkins, Linda Watts, Penny Webb, Pam Webster, Bernice Weissbourd, Veronica Wellman, Gaynor Wells, Sir Michael and Lady Wilkes, Chris Wilkinson, Glenys Williams, Liz Williams, Audrey Willis, Dot Willson, Sheila Withnell, Linda Wright, Mary Wright, Lord (Patrick) Wright, Stella Woodier, Christine Yarborough, Alicia Zlatar.

All my management committee members, trustees, and chairmen both individually and as part of the team which made Home-Start successful over 25 years. All the families and volunteers and organisers, too numerous to mention by name, but still on my mind and in my heart.

Hooray! Here Comes Tuesday

The Home-Start Story

FOREWORD

Friendship is the outstanding quality which has been integral to Home-Start from the beginning – and which has helped to make it the most wonderful organisation with which anyone could wish to be connected.

In the early 1980s, the Joseph Rowntree Memorial Trust, of which I was then a trustee, received an application from a voluntary organisation in Leicester. Home-Start impressed us then, with its marvellous recipe for success in the prevention of family breakdown. It involved simplicity, friendship, home-visits and local ownership through small groups – each a separate charity with its own trustees and supporters. No wonder it has earned such wide support.

I was then also chairman of the National Institute of Social Work. We had produced a report, 'Social Workers: Their Role and Tasks' (The Barclay Report). One recommendation was for the development of neighbourhood-based services. We needed a closer working relationship between the citizen and social worker. We acknowledged that the statutory sector alone could never provide all the resources necessary for a community. Home-Start fitted well alongside the wider array of services provided by the public sector.

When I became a trustee and later chairman of Home-Start UK, I experienced for myself how Home-Start enshrines all that is efficient, effective, sensitive and kind in human nature. Margaret Harrison and her staff seemed to have an inexhaustible capacity for hard work and a real concern for individual people, their problems and their joys, thus exemplifying William Blake's adage:

"He who would do good to another must do it in minute particulars."

The success of Home-Start has not always come easily. For the trustees, every

January was nail-biting time, as we acknowledged the yawning gap between what was in the kitty and the outgoings to be filled. Should we issue redundancy notices? Make cuts? No, because magically the money flowed in just in time. Margaret had managed yet again to find a grant to keep us going.

The expansion of Home-Start has required consistently good leadership and vision. It spread slowly at first, then with increasing momentum until there are today, around 500 locally based schemes in the United Kingdom and other countries.

Hooray! Here Comes Tuesday: The Home-Start Story, shows step by step how this was achieved over 25 years. It is a most impressive story and I commend it.

Sir Peter Barclay

Introduction

"Civilisation hangs suspended, from generation to generation, by the gossamer strand of memory. If only one cohort of mothers and fathers fails to convey to its children what it has learned from its parents, then the great chain of learning and wisdom snaps."

Jacob Neusner, Professor of Philosophy and Religion, N.Y. State.

Who is The Home-Start Story for? It is for all of us in Home-Start, wherever in the world it now exists. It is for everyone who has asked what sparked the idea, how we began, and where it is all leading.

"Hooray! Here Comes Tuesday" is an acknowledgement of the optimism and energy of every person who has had the courage to become involved during the formative 25 years. All have contributed their humanity, humility and humour, for the sake of parents with young children at home. It is about ordinary people, mostly women, because they far outnumber the men in Home-Start, who have shown extraordinary ability to contribute to their society in a simple, practical way.

It is my testimony of admiration and awe for the many thousands of people, who have made it happen – the volunteers, the families, the professionals, the staff. We did it together. It is *our* story.

The names of significant individuals along the way are naturally included in the text, for posterity. Two years ago I invited contributions from anyone who wished to remember the early years. Some have written, some have phoned, and some have met me to talk. Their memories alone would fill a book. For me, the experience has been a delight – a gift. As Bente Brostrom from Norway has said, *"We made the path as we walked it."*

Many others may have chosen not to contribute, or are no longer in touch. I remember only too well the few people who left Home-Start with hurt feelings. Their stories may be different. As with everything in Home-Start, choice is fundamental to the voluntary ethic. For those who have contributed to this book, the experience has clearly been a good one. Their positive attitudes and the learning we have shared, shine through.

This journey – a journey of memories, from the conception of a new way of offering support to parents and children, to the development of an evolving national and international voluntary community, demonstrates how Home-Start combines heart with a down-to-earth approach. Amazingly, two anagrams of **Home-Start** are **Most Heart** and **Most Earth** – two of my favourite concepts.

When I started this book, I sought advice from Charles Handy, whose books on voluntary organisations and leadership styles have so often reinforced the Home-Start approach. It was wonderful to find his theories reflecting what we had discovered through practice and intuition.

"Make it autobiographical" he said, at which, I laughed – uneasily. However, now, sitting in front of the computer, with Mush our cat on my lap, and with the whole project ahead of me, I really appreciate his foresight. For unless I consult everyone involved in the development of Home-Start over 25 years, in order to convey accurately their perceptions at the time, I must inevitably write from my own perspective, drawing on written materials, diaries, and the memories, for which the responsibility is mine alone. These memories come flooding back.

It is said that emotional memory is timeless, and so it is. How remarkable then, that remembering people and incidents, all of which had an emotional content and context, enables ones mind to click straight back into the situation, the event, the personalities involved at the time. They remain as poignant as if they had occurred yesterday. There is nothing quite like a heart connection.

I am not a writer. Joan Stephens, my close friend and editor, has read drafts of each chapter as they have been written. She has let it develop from stage to stage, though sometimes she has suggested gently and wisely that I should write a particular chapter again. The completed book demonstrates Joan's trust in me, to do it my way. Amazingly, yet again, this is a mirror image of the Home-Start relationship between a volunteer and family.

★★★

Looking back to the early 1970s, I am aware how much society, government, the private, public and voluntary sectors have changed. Issues of gender, equality of opportunity, safety, litigation and devolution were not overt issues in the days when Home-Start began.

Graham Murphy, who worked in the 1970s for the Leicester Family Service Unit, once wisely said to me, *"Margaret, you know it takes a generation to change attitudes"*. He was right, for nowadays it is generally acknowledged that:

- It is not just children who have needs, but their parents and the whole family;
- Professions, agencies and government departments co-operate and communicate with each other – well, *most* of the time;
- Communities have a voice in what they need and in what individuals can contribute. I still mourn the loss of community workers, but suspect they are currently being re-introduced under various other guises and initiatives.
- Ordinary people have quite extraordinary talents and compassion for others. One of my greatest joys in Home-Start has been the way so many of the parents we support - sometimes for several years - choose to become Home-Start volunteers themselves. They like to pass it on.

Home-Start offers local volunteer support, friendship and practical help in the home, parent-to-parent, to families with young children who are going through difficult times.

The families themselves were the inspiration and the motivation for the creation of Home-Start in the early 1970s, as were other volunteers during my own years of voluntary work. Parents who were isolated, out of touch with relatives, not on speaking terms with neighbours, and who felt they had no close friend, indicated that, above all, they needed someone with time to be with them at home. They needed another parent who would understand their experience, would listen, care and have fun with them – someone to share and help in a practical down-to-earth way.

It has always been clear to me that Home-Start is about attitudes, values and standards rather than a fixed method. Everything in Home-Start is secondary to the relationships established between volunteers and the families they support.

Maybe Home-Start has developed so naturally because of these connections. To sustain them, each scheme is rooted firmly in its own community, grown organically to meet local needs. The families want it, the volunteers choose to share their own time, skills and humanity within it, the professionals and funders value it.

Maybe it is because the concept is so simple, that Home-Start has now developed in most parts of the United Kingdom, and in many other countries too.

Home-Start has universal application, regardless of location or culture. Sometimes though, it has to be adapted, as when we work with service families in the army or in an Arab community like Um el Fahm, south of the Galilee, or in a specific area of inner city Bristol. Only now are we beginning to realise the wider implications of place and time.

We really value the way parents who have coped, so very often choose to take responsibility and contribute to the lives of others around them. This can be a force for irrevocable good, strengthening their community and inevitably contributing towards a better society.

Choice and autonomy are fundamental to the Home-Start approach throughout the organisation, so are trust, understanding, respect, humour and good communication. Of course it goes wrong at times, but when it goes right. . . .WOW!

The atmosphere, which pervades our organisation, builds on the opportunity for each of us to be ourselves, to identify our own weaknesses as well as our own strengths. I am convinced that each of us needs to be needed. So many people involved in Home-Start over the years have told me how much they themselves gained from their involvement. They appreciated being able to give of themselves without inhibition, releasing their creative spark. This was what had triggered their motivation, energy and enthusiasm – qualities which have the most amazing power to spread.

When relationships are established, naturally, spontaneously and informally, mutual learning can begin. In Home-Start, we are fortunate that we can focus on the family as a whole, with shared enjoyment. It is the professionals who, of necessity, have to focus on the problems.

In Home-Start, there can be a variety of people, variety of roles, variety of funding, variety of locations, various entry and exit points, activities and routes leading to a sense of well-being for the ordinary people who choose to be involved. As Margaret Mead, the social anthropologist, once said:

> ***"Never doubt that a small group of committed citizens, can change the world. Indeed it is the only thing that ever has."***

Developing an organisation though, from local to national to international level, has also been a huge privilege. People ask whether I would have started Home-Start if I had realised how big it would become. The answer is most definitely no! I would have had neither the foresight, nor the courage. But it is the same as with one's own children. The adult bears little resemblance to the child when born. There are so many other influences and opportunities along the way. I am inspired by all that our children and Home-Start itself have become, and all that each contributes.

It has been claimed that the usual process in the formation and growth of any institution, is that it develops from inspiration to communication to dogma and thence too often on to fragmentation and collapse. At every turn, we attempted to avoid the dogma. Within Home-Start, we have always been keen to keep the personal touch alive, in all aspects of the work. This has been crucial to its positive development.

Of course, structure, policy and written guidance are essential. Creating the Home-Start written guidelines – the **'Standards and Methods of Practice' Appendix III** - was a shared responsibility. That these have remained virtually unchanged over 20 years is a tribute to the colleagues who first practised the Home-Start approach, then came together to enshrine the principles into 10 points. These have been fundamental to the development of Home-Start wherever in the world it now exists. With these in place, the flexibility, mutuality and creativity of each individual within the organisation, can be released.

We always kept accurate minutes of our regular trustees, management committee and staff meetings during the first 25 formative years. These demonstrate a diary of development, not only of an organisation, but also of a concept. I have drawn heavily on these for the content of this book.

In 1980, it was John Page, retired army Major General, at the time director of a funding body, the London Law Trust, who visited us in Leicester, and suggested that Home-Start should go NATIONAL. I found this a laughable notion! But we did. He was right. Had it gone wrong we could have laid the blame on him. But it didn't. It flourished and grew. Quite simply, what we had discovered was a way of supporting families which worked, and with which most people with parenting experience could identify.

There were inevitably hiccups along the way. I vividly remember that by 1985 there were already around 60 locally-based Home-Start schemes throughout the UK, and it felt as if we had created a monster. We were really struggling.

We could no longer provide the necessary support through our small team of three, based in the national centre in Leicester, and not all could be done by schemes supporting and extending a helping hand to each other. So it was decided we should regionalise.

Again, together, we proceeded to learn, step by step. Rather than building up a chain of command with central control, we would build on lateral relationships within the regions and the four nations of the UK, relying on each other for honest feedback and support. In this way, costs could be kept low, and more could be achieved.

Indeed, our approach within the national organisation, Home-Start Consultancy/UK, as we developed relationships between staff and the schemes, attempted at all times to reflect the parent-to-parent relationships, which we were there to encourage. We were partners, doing things and learning things together - the very essence of Home-Start. It didn't *always* work, but then, as I learned early on, that is true of other methods too, however formal they are.

What follows, is the story of Home-Start, from conception towards maturity and spread! How did we begin? How does it work? How were our intuition, learning and practical approach acknowledged and endorsed? How did we cope with the gathering momentum, as we found we were developing as an organism, a community of people who care about families, locally, nationally, and even inter-nationally?

Along the way, there were issues, topics and concepts, which arose almost daily. I have addressed many of these, and they now appear in **Appendix I**. They are there for ease of identification, in alphabetical order, rather than in order of priority. They will, I hope, provoke discussion, disagreement and the glaring realisation of all that I have omitted to include in this Home-Start story.

When I retired in 1998, our Silver Jubilee year, one of the wonder-full gifts I was given by my Home-Start friends everywhere, was a new piano accordion –

an instrument I had learned as a child, but longed to take up again. Here, at the end of my Home-Start journey, I would be able to develop the joy of busking, with all it implies – the spontaneity, the freedom, the choice, the fun. Busking creates relationships of equals, where busker and listener alike can walk away.

And so it is with this book, this journey through the formative years of Home-Start. Choice and autonomy again are intrinsic. Dip in, dip out, discard, and imbibe. Perhaps insights into your own journey will vibrate and resonate with mine, like jazz, so that we might synchronize our rhythms, disc(h)ords and harmonies. But just as with jazz, ... I am left wondering whether it can indeed be written down?

Chapter 1

CONCEPTION

"Happiness lies in the joy of achievement and the thrill of creative effort."
Franklin D. Roosevelt. US President.

Naked, carrying a carving knife, the two-year-old stumbled across the busy road. He had been sent by his mother to see the community worker, who lived and worked in the house opposite. She followed close behind, yelling at him "Go and tell Alan what you done, ya lit'le bleeder!"

It was Thursday morning, so I was already there as a volunteer to look after the children in the kitchen, while their parents did group work with the community worker in the living room. "What's his name?" I asked the mother. "David" she yelled. "Oh", I said, relieved that we immediately had something in common, "I've got a David too!" "Yeah", she snarled "and I bet you've got a dad an' all!"

Well, yes, she was right. I did have a supportive husband, father to our own five-year-old David. We also had two daughters - Jane eight, happily settled at school, and Clare three, who always came with me to the Family Service Unit Drop In each week. She was the ideal little playmate for the other children, as she knew all the songs and nursery rhymes. She was very chatty, loved other children and was very accustomed to water-play in the sink. Being small like them, she related and played happily with creative ideas and language, on their level.

I knew David would be alright with us for the morning, but my heart really went out to his distraught mother, who was clearly having a very difficult time and, quite understandably, was taking it out on her two boys. "Tell me about it", I invited, "What's been happening?"

Little did I know then, that what was happening for *me* was the revelation of the huge need to give more support to **parents** – the conception of Home-Start.

As I listened intently, with a great sense of helplessness and true feelings of compassion, I realised just how much such a vulnerable young mother needed kindness, time and understanding of her intolerable situation. She told me about her own ill health, poverty, exhaustion, isolation and guilt, as she struggled to cope alone with the very basic needs of her two small sons. Throughout nights and days, week after week, there she was, without partner, parent, friend or neighbour to give her a hand, a word of encouragement, or a moment's relief from her relentless, lonely life. Everyone referred to her as 'That Family'. She really was having a terrible time.

They never told me what happened in the grown-ups' group that morning, but from then on, I found that on Thursday mornings, individual mothers would begin to come through the kitchen to use the outside toilet and stop and talk with me, one-to-one, mother-to-mother.

Their stories, their lives, touched me deeply and I found myself responding naturally from the heart, acknowledging the complexity of what they told me, but also offering practical help when I could.

One mother told me that she had been up three nights running with her Darren and did I think she should take him to the doctor, or would she be wasting his time? No, I agreed that if she felt concern, she should go, and offered to look after her three-year-old and the baby while she went.

Many of the mothers who came to chat with me, asked whether I could go and see them at home *"so we can really talk, Margaret"*. What they desperately needed was another caring, understanding parent, with time to be with them at home, to help in a practical way, and have a good laugh together from time to time.

Yes - to have a good giggle.

For some of the things they told me had a funny side to them - like hearing about the twins, who tipped the rice crispies and sugar all over the kitchen floor and then wee'd on them while their mother was at the front door. Now, handling that situation alone could bring out the most murderous instincts in an already exhausted parent. When shared with another mother though, someone who can relate to the underlying despair of the parent, yet appreciate the energetic creativity of her children, it can even be a source of humour.

So, with Alan's blessing, I did go and visit some of the parents at home, as they had requested. What a time I had!

Some were in a complete muddle. Some had no routine to the day, staying up until 3am, getting up at midday and having little idea whether it was Sunday or Monday. Well they wouldn't would they? There was no routine of going to work or going to school to differentiate one day from another. No one was coming to visit, apart from "the welfare", or a neighbour to cadge something. And it was November. There was no money and Christmas was coming up.

One mother, whose husband was in prison, leaving her with the debts and the six children, told me how jealous she was that HE had a dry bed at night, three cooked meals a day and no responsibilities!

Suddenly, what really needed to be done seemed so obvious, so simple.

There must be very many other parents like me, with time to care and time to spare. We could offer individual support, friendship and practical help at home, to other young families who were going through difficult times. These were after all, such crucial early years of family life.

This then was how the idea for Home-Start was conceived.

★ ★ ★

Between 1969 and1973, I had also been involved in two other kinds of voluntary work which had fed into my conviction that we had to find ways of preventing family breakdown and of helping parents to use the professional services more effectively.

But what had led to my own commitment to volunteering in the first place?

After A-levels at Watford Girls Grammar school, I knew that I wanted to get out and experience the wider world, meet a variety of interesting adults and, hopefully, get married and have children. Motherhood seemed immensely attractive to me then and remains so to this day.

At what to them was enormous cost at the time, my parents sent me to the Mayfair Secretarial College for Gentlewomen (yes really!) where my course included commercial Spanish. After six months I was invited for interview at the Spanish Embassy in London, for a job as private secretary to the Labour

Attaché. I was required to provide quite a lot of personal support to his non-English speaking wife and their four young daughters.

Pichuca, the three year old, used to rush into the office which was a part of the family's flat, around the corner from the Embassy. As soon as she heard my key in the door in the morning, she would come and hide in the waste-paper basket under my desk, whispering conspiratorially, *"No lo dices a Papa Marguerita!"* (don't tell Daddy!) There was always great merriment when she at last emerged, usually in the middle of some dictation about Trade Unions or Spanish Au Pair girls who were pregnant.

I remember being asked seriously by my boss, why it was that English people like their dogs more than their children? *"We see the children on leads in your parks, while the dogs run free."* That was in the late 1950s.

A real perk of working in the Spanish Embassy, was that we had a two hour lunch-break each day – siesta time. It enabled me to indulge my interest in art, visiting galleries, exhibitions and dealers in London. Art appreciation has remained a passion throughout my life, proving most useful when fundraising from the corporate sector, much, much later on.

During those happy years I met my future husband Basil. We fell in love, were married and miraculously have enjoyed a very close relationship for over 45 years. Maybe it is all due to the insistence of the Spanish family, that I should learn to cook paella before marrying.

Three months after our wedding, we sailed off to New York where Basil had a job with English Electric. I worked in the information department of the British Consulate. Then Jane, our first baby, was born. My mother back in England nearly fainted when I told her on the phone that Basil had been with me for the birth. *"Oh, the pooooor man!"* she said with feeling. How times have changed since those days!

And so there I was, a young mother with few friends, a busy travelling husband and no relatives close by. In fact, when the doctor said to me after the birth, "No relations for six weeks" I spontaneously replied that that wouldn't be difficult as they were all in England.

I met a lively, middle-aged English woman, Tess Luther, who became a good friend. Every Tuesday she caught two trains to Flushing, where we lived, to visit Janey and me for the day. She said she loved our chats, having lunch together and getting to be with the baby, as her own grandchildren were all in England. With hindsight, I now realise that Tess was the very first Home-Start volunteer ...visiting, encouraging, supporting, chattering and teasing me.

It was just so good having someone, who took an interest in us. She always praised me and my baby, came shopping or on walks together, brought a home-made cake and was generally a grandmother figure. So often Basil would come home from work and say *"I can tell Tess has been here today. You're so much brighter."*

Although we had been enticed to stay on in the States with several great job offers, we were quite clear that we wanted to have more children and be near grandparents, aunts, uncles, cousins and old friends. Such a support network was more important to us than anything else in the world. We felt very lucky to have had the opportunity to establish ourselves as parents, totally dependent on each other. But then it was time to be embraced again by our own families, back together again in England.

After a miscarriage, a difficult year while Basil searched for a suitable new niche in his old company, and several arduous months of rented accommodation and house-hunting while pregnant, our son David was born in the tiniest imaginable company flat. We then took out a mortgage on the first home of our own. Our second daughter, Clare, was born in 1966.

So it was, that with our own family complete, and casting around for some brain activity for myself, I undertook the Leicester University Certificate in Social Studies, a three-year part-time evening course. Quite simply, this changed my life.

We learnt about group dynamics by practising them in the here and now. We had lectures on developmental, social and clinical psychology, sociology, social history, social policy and administration, and social work practice. For me, the most influential part of the whole course was social ethics with Denis Rice, the Warden ofVaughan College himself. Denis was to become a great influence on me and on Home-Start.

I remember being aware at the time, that I was *thinking* more than ever before in my life! How is it that our attitudes, standards and values are formed? How and when do we become prejudiced? What is the influence of friends and family on our beliefs, passions, life-styles? How is it that a person who is an expert bank robber in peacetime, can become a hero in wartime, when he can help to gain access and crack the enemy's code? What is altruism? Does it exist, or is everyone consciously or subconsciously involved in perpetuating their own good, even if it is for a planned after life?

The course led me into extensive reading and I thoroughly enjoyed the written work too. All this was a valued contrast to my busy family life with three young children, a wide circle of friends and frequent weekend family get-togethers. After three years of studying and exams, to my great delight, I gained my qualification.

The course had left me querying though, why as parents are we not informed about the vital ages and stages of children's development after they are born?

Our health visitor used to visit me regularly, asking peremptorily how were the baby's feeding and sleeping going, before moving on to discuss our mutual love of art over a cup of tea. She never once asked whether I was encouraging the children's language, or whether they had had fresh air and fun, or even asked whether I was alright.

The course had opened my eyes wide to the role of parents, the needs of children, the statutory services and the signs of dis-ease, both in individuals and in society at large. I wanted to know why there weren't more simplified, tailor-made courses available to all parents past the ante-natal stage? "Why are parents themselves not better supported in their essential role, especially if they have few friends or close relatives of their own?" I decided to become a social worker.

Sadly, my dream was shattered by the Leicester University School of Social Work. For despite really good references from my recent lecturers, the university insisted that as I was not a university graduate, I would have to undertake the two-year rather than the one-year social work course. I was equally adamant that I did not wish to commit two years of my own family's precious lives at that stage, to indulge my own desire to undertake a full-time course.

Ironically, 15 years later, I was awarded an honorary degree – an MA by the University of Leicester - for my work in Home-Start. It coincided with the time that two of our children were immersed in obtaining their own MAs. "How come you just enjoy life and are given a higher degree, whereas we have to work for ours?" they asked.

But back to 1969 and really back to square one! My university adult education course over, the children well settled at school, I found that I had considerable time to spare. I really wanted to reach out to others beyond our family and neighbours. I decided to undertake voluntary work with families and children.

So I approached the Leicester Voluntary Workers Bureau, then only the second in the country. There Rachel Carmichael, an acquaintance who was to become a close friend and mentor, arranged for me to meet George Creighton, the Children's Officer at the Children's Department.

Together we discussed the possibility of setting up a voluntary Aunts and Uncles befriending scheme for any children in local authority care who had lost contact with their own parents.

There were 16 children's homes in Leicester in the early 70s. Today that sounds incredible. Each was a different size, had different aged children and had houseparents, whose styles of working were often idiosyncratic. In my view, there were far too many children in desperate need of a caring adult to whom they could relate, if not belong as a family. To my delight, the head of the Children's Department, the house-parents, some child-care workers and the children themselves were extremely enthusiastic about the proposed scheme. I discussed their needs with them, their ideas and the help they required to fill in the gaps.

Thus began a journey from which I learned so very much about recruiting, preparing, matching, introducing, motivating, supporting and sustaining a team of volunteers, male and female, each of whom became a social aunt or uncle to a particular child in care. They were to spend their time taking a real interest in "their" child, supporting school work, celebrating birthdays and other significant milestones, taking them on outings and generally extending their world.

I became voluntary co-ordinator of this brand new scheme, with a team of volunteers, who varied widely in age and background. It was at this stage that I began to have doubts about the verb 'to befriend', which still has oppressive connotations to me. I far prefer to talk about 'offering friendship'.

When advertising for volunteers, we used the Oxfam approach, which was about personalising the focus, so that it captured the emotion or interest of a potential recruit. ***"Can you kick a football?"*** or ***"Sally has lost all contact with her own family. Are you a parent, and could you and your family share a few hours regularly with Sally?"*** These were just two of our successful advertisements which attracted appropriate volunteers. After individual interviews, personal references, and discussion with the house-parents about the needs of individual children, each new volunteer was then matched to a suitable child.

Eventually, I had a team of 90 volunteers each linked to a child in one of the children's homes. In addition to individual support, usually by phone, we held monthly meetings to share and to learn from each other. During one of these sessions I still remember the volunteers who suggested that their time could have been better spent, had they been involved with the whole family *before* it had broken down, rather than just visiting the child in care. I wholeheartedly agreed with this sentiment – it made real sense.

We needed to find an acceptable way of supporting families, and building up their access to resources *before* their lives became irretrievably difficult. This was the *second* experience, which led to the birth of Home-Start.

There was also a *third* set of circumstances in the early 1970s, which pointed us to the need for more support for parents. A colleague in the University's Department of Extra-Mural Studies, asked me to help her with a survey of pre-school provision in the city of Leicester. This inevitably led us to realise the huge gaps, which existed in parts of the city, where many of the most vulnerable families lived.

There were few day nurseries anywhere, and certainly no mother and toddler groups or playgroups in some of the more disadvantaged communities. I had been involved in the early days of the Pre-school Playgroups Association, when a good friend, Joan Whybrow, and I had set up the first playgroup in Cosby, while our six children were still young. Now there was suddenly the challenge to launch groups for mothers and pre-school children on local council estates in Leicester, where previously none had existed.

Vivienne Cooke and I were given money by the City Council to set up a playgroup for parents and children in a brand new community centre, Kingfisher Hall, for the first time.

Beginning in an unknown area, with no established personal links, proved to be very difficult indeed.

With hindsight, we realised we had failed to consult local people. We had assumed that, by pushing leaflets through doors, not knowing where families actually lived, parents and children would flock to our newly equipped rented accommodation. How wrong we were! On the opening morning, only one brave mother and her child turned up. After six months, still only a handful of families came.

We learned some important lessons. We should have got to know local people first and enlisted their support. Rather than parachuting in, we should have grown our groups from within the communities themselves. We should have sought the help of local parents to help each other. We learned at that time, not to plan *for* people, but to think with them.

Another important lesson was that the parents who most needed an opportunity to meet others, both for their own and for their children's sake, were the very ones who lacked the confidence to come to a centre before they knew anyone else there. It was simply too big a jump into the unknown.

Several years later, I was to learn from Dr. Sheila Shinman, that "personal support precedes the effective take-up of all other services". In other words, it is a common experience that the families who most need such services and whom professionals feel would most benefit from them, are those who never make use of them.

> ***"New approaches are called for in which emphasis should be directed to the needs and attitudes of the mother . . . . .particularly those who cannot cope adequately with family responsibilities".***
>
> **A Chance for Every Child by Dr Sheila Shinman, Tavistock Publications Ltd. 1981.**

Sheila became and has remained a staunch advocate of Home-Start and a friend.

So it was that, in the late 1960s and early 1970s, I learned from parents themselves, from active volunteers, from my own experience of motherhood, and from a variety of neighbourhoods, that we needed to offer parent-to-parent support in the home. We needed to be available to parents and their children together, wherever they lived and for as long as they wished.

Chapter 2

GESTATION

"It is heart connections, not political or economic reform that will transform our society,"* said E.F. Schumacher in Small is Beautiful. *"And"* he said, *"the work begins at home."

But how did one begin a voluntary organisation? Obtain the funding? Gain credibility?

Offering support to families at home, parent-to-parent, seemed such a very obvious thing to do. After all, homes are not only shelters for bodies, but also for souls. Having someone alongside who really understands, has time and is kind, can lift the spirits and turn despair to hope. Everyone benefits – the family whose need is being met, the professionals who know there is another dimension provided, and the volunteers who, among other motivations, need to be needed themselves.

My lecturers and all the professional workers I knew, just patted me on the back when I suggested to them that it was essential to work through volunteer parents with the whole family, preferably not in an office, clinic, centre or group. Good idea, but not for them. It seemed that professionals had their own careers – as teacher, doctor, social worker, probation officer, speech therapist, psychologist, or other health professional. Their focus was on the individual – either the parent or the child. Their model was teaching, treatment, or intervention.

So how should we begin simply to offer support and encouragement – parent-to- parent, mother-to-mother?

Miraculously, two organisations came to the rescue to turn aspirations into reality. They were The Winston Churchill Memorial Trust and the Leicester Council for Voluntary Service (LCVS).

One Wednesday morning, when I arrived as a volunteer at the newly formed Social Services Department, where generic social workers had taken over from previous child care workers in the Children's Department, I was called into the office of John Dossett-Davies, the Deputy Director. *"Have you ever heard about Churchill Travelling Fellowships?"* he asked. I hadn't.

After Churchill died, a Trust was established to award Winston Churchill Travelling Fellowships enabling British citizens with a kaleidoscope of different interests to acquire knowledge overseas, 'to benefit Community and Country'. Around 100 men and women are selected each year, literally from all walks of life. In 1973 there happened to be a category for voluntary social workers. John had himself been awarded a fellowship several years earlier, so appreciated the benefits.

He told me he would strongly endorse an application from me, in recognition of what I had been doing voluntarily for the department. I had been helping social workers to find suitable volunteers to assist with their case-loads, as well as linking some to children's homes.

What an exciting opportunity! Our three children were then aged six, eight and 12, and my husband Basil had a full-time job. Nice idea, but impossible, I thought. And anyway, where would I go and what would I study?

But then, as with many things in life, if the passion to do something is there, there is usually a way forward.

By lucky chance, friends of ours had just returned from America. Wladeck Sluckin was professor of psychology at Leicester University. His wife Alice, a psychiatric social worker, had used me as a volunteer to look after children while she did group work with their parents in the child guidance clinic. Often, I had driven the whole family home afterwards, talking with the parents, learning about their difficulties. Alice thought I would benefit from spending time with different 'programs' in the States.

At the same time, Basil's sister Christine, who lived in Canada, felt cut off from the rest of her family in England and hoped to be visited.

Synchronicity? Coincidences? First John, then Alice and now Christine. Three in a row.

We put them all together, and I applied to the Winston Churchill Memorial

Trust to spend three months in America. Chris and her husband, George, said they would be delighted to have our children to go to school with their two daughters for a term if I was awarded the Fellowship. Wladeck and Alice gave me introductions to appropriate colleagues of theirs in the States.

My first short application to the Winston Churchill Memorial Trust was successful, which meant I had to submit a longer more detailed account of where I would go and what I would learn. And so I used the word "Home-Start" for the first time, based on the term Head-Start, but knowing that somehow I would want it all to lead to supporting parents and children together *at home* - a much more holistic approach.

To my complete amazement, one Saturday morning I received THE letter from the Churchill Trust offices, calling me for an interview. I screamed aloud with both excitement and fear. The children came rushing into our bedroom to see what was the matter.

Jane and David had already been told that I was applying for something special which, if successful, would mean them going to school in Canada for a term. But because I considered it so unlikely that I would go, I hadn't mentioned it to Clare who was only six. Plenty of time, I had thought, to tell her if and when it all became a reality. A bad mistake! While the rest of us were breathless with excitement, Clare just burst into tears, inconsolable, because she did not know what it was all about. She was really hurt and angry that we four big people had a secret to which she was not a party. Poor Clare - how I had misjudged her! To this day, I am acutely aware of the need to communicate openly and widely, including with children, as equals.

The interview panel at the Winston Churchill Memorial Trust, seated at the largest, most polished table ever, included Major General Lascelles, Joyce Grenfell and Sir Peter Scott. Immediately I was put at ease, found myself talking from the heart about what young families in this country really needed. It all seemed so simple. And so the interview went well . . . . until the final question.

"If you are successful and are awarded one of our Travelling Fellowships, will you be prepared to come back to this country and write and lecture on your findings?" My heart sank. Writing, yes, maybe. But lecturing *NEVER*. I'd blown it. I couldn't give them what they wanted. I knew that I would never be able to stand up in front of people and present a lecture. I just knew it.

Joyce Grenfell then leant forward, and squeezed my arm. She smiled reassuringly, just saying simply *"Oh, my dear, it is just a question of SHARING with other people you know"*. Well, I could do that! And so the interview ended, and I tripped down the top stair as I left, in my exhilarated and anguished state. Two weeks later I heard that, after all, I had been successful.

Fortunately, our children's primary school was extremely supportive when we suggested taking them to Canada for a term. They responded positively, indicating that there was much to be gained from the experience of travelling, living and learning in another country.

A major speech in Leicester, which influenced me greatly, was by David Hobman, then Director of Age Concern. His subject was the value of trusted volunteers – really a new concept altogether in those days. I remember him saying that volunteering in the 1970s, was "for the sinners and not just the saints".

He also spoke vividly about Keith Joseph's recent speech on breaking the Cycle of Deprivation. Yes, I thought, this is exactly what Home-Start will be about. Finding ways of supporting parents now, while their children are still young, so that they, in turn, will themselves become coping, caring parents for the next generation.

Around this time also, I visited the Red House, one of five government designated Education Priority Area projects in the West Riding of Yorkshire, where Lynne Poulton was creatively involving parents in their children's early learning. Mothers were sitting at tables, actually playing with children's toys - a most unusual sight in those days.

Suddenly, phrases and ideas began to become clearer. I knew that my own top priority must be to set about seeking funding for the new voluntary organisation I hoped to establish for parents and children in Leicester, soon after my return from the States.

It was the Leicester Council for Voluntary Service, which came to my aid locally. Phil Parkinson, the Director, took the trouble to come to our home one Sunday afternoon in March, with the suggestion that I should apply for Urban Aid money. This was a brand new initiative in which the Government undertook to pay 75% of the cost of a community-based project, as long as the local authority funded the other 25%. This was a wonderful opportunity for partnership, with local initiative, creativity and commitment, underpinned by central government funding. If Home-Start proved successful, this would eventually lead to full continued local authority funding.

Phil helped me to fill in the forms. We emphasised the need to find ways to break the 'cycle of deprivation'. In all subsequent applications we always included the "in" phrases of the day, such as 'preventing child abuse', or 'strengthening the community by building stronger families'.

Phil also gently persuaded me to include a salary for myself in our initial application. Somehow it seemed ethically wrong, that after so many years of voluntary work – both as a volunteer myself, and voluntary co-ordinator of volunteers, I should be paid for my work, while volunteers would receive only their out-of-pocket expenses. After all, they were to be the hub of the whole scheme.

"But what if you leave, and the scheme has to replace you?" asked Phil shrewdly. So we applied for a part-time salary, which excluded paid work during school holidays. My first funding application was completed and submitted.

Soon after I returned from America, we had the letter to say we had been successful, stating the amount and the starting date for our project. We were to launch Home-Start on 1st November 1973, with an Urban Aid Grant of £1,936 per annum. Not huge – but it felt like a big investment in the unknown. It was to stay fixed at that level, for the first three years.

A decade later, when new Home-Start schemes were beginning all over the country, we strongly advised all organisers to begin with full-time salaries. Although the first months are less hectic, it is much more difficult to increase a grant than to sustain a full-time job during part-time hours.

Three days after my 35th birthday, the Churchill Travelling Fellowship began. My parents and Basil came to see the children and me off at Heathrow airport. What an adventure it was! But why was I doing this? I was a person who would never have had the confidence to go into a café for a cup of coffee without a friend, relative or child at my side. So why ever had I undertaken this?

After a day or two handing over the children to our relatives in Ontario, I was on my way, all alone, for the first part of my Fellowship in Chicago. I put on my dark glasses and quite literally sobbed quietly throughout the flight, facing the unknown. As I alighted, following my fellow passengers to Baggage

Reclaim, I suddenly heard my name being called. Would Margaret Harrison go to the Information Desk immediately? Convinced that something was wrong with one of the children or even with family back in England, I rushed forward......to be greeted warmly by my hostess from Head-Start in Chicago.

From that minute on, my life seems to have been filled with amazing colleagues, friends and opportunities, which I simply could never have imagined possible. The Churchill Trust is right when they state that their fellowships are 'The Chance of a Lifetime'. I have never looked back.

Winston Churchill Travelling Fellowship

I spent the first four weeks of my visit, with the Chicago Committee of Urban Opportunity Head-Start Program. This involved attending their four-day initial training course for staff. Though we shared a common language, their whole approach was very different from anything I had experienced previously. I was also the only white person there.

Most days were spent in Head-Start Centers, where children from six months to six years would be brought in daily from "deprived households" and receive their food, rest periods and stimulation, rather like in a day nursery.

The previous autumn, in 1972, there had been a major national Head-Start conference on the West Coast of America, held six years after Head-Start had begun under the Johnson Presidency. Its aim was to give the most underprivileged children from disadvantaged homes and neighbourhoods, a 'head start' before their formal schooling began.

To my delight, I heard that one of the major conference conclusions was that the time had come "to give the children back to their parents!" Yes! It really did seem essential to me that the parents too were given support and opportunities for themselves. This once again reinforced my resolve to work with parents and their children together *at home*, during the crucial, formative, first few years of life.

Half way through the three months in America, Basil came out to join the children and me for a fortnight's holiday. After that, I spent a few days in Washington DC with the Department of Health, Education and Welfare, before going on for the final month of my fellowship to George Peabody College in Nashville, Tennessee.

The Demonstration and Research Center for Early Education, under the direction of Dr. Susan Grey, was just beginning to consider home-visiting as a strategy for educating parents as the first educators of their children. Paid para-professionals were used and the approach was purely cognitive. Whole bags of equipment were produced, to help para-professionals to work in the home. They would help children to recognise different shapes, sizes and colours, as well as developing their fine and gross motor skills.

When I suggested that we were also planning to do home-visiting in Leicester, England, but that we would be working through volunteer parents, providing emotional and practical support in the home to parents with their young children, I was told quite forcibly that I was naïve. Their program was costing $1m per annually. I had applied for around £2,000.

But I brought back with me many of their materials. I learned about Carkhuff's 'Art of Helping' skills - initiating, responding and communicating - for parents, teachers and counsellors. I also learned a great deal from the other DARCEE programs and research findings.

PLANNING HOME-START IN ENGLAND

With the promise of an Urban Aid grant, there were just five months to go, before embarking on what was to become the Home-Start journey of a life-time.

During those summer months, Joan Stephens, a good friend of mine, with three girls the same ages as our children, came to tea with a specific request. She had just applied for the job of Women's Page Editor on the Leicester Mercury and had to submit an article as part of the interviewing process. Could she interview me about the proposed Home-Start organisation?

Why not? Somehow from our disparate discussion, she produced an excellent article, under the pen-name Val Peters. She got the job and gave Home-Start its first publicity.

> ***"Here was my perfect story. A "first" for Leicester, a worthwhile cause, and plenty of human interest. I wrote it up. . . .and the rest is. . . .not history, but an ongoing success story."***
>
> **Joan Stephens, Leicester Mercury.**

The core message of this brand new organisation, beginning in Leicester, was that all families need a good friend during their children's early years. Were there any parents out there who would welcome another parent, a volunteer, to give them a hand at home when needed? And were there any potential volunteers with parenting experience, willing to share their spare time to support families experiencing difficulties?

In the early autumn, I had a significant and memorable meeting with Philip Ray, the new General Secretary of the Leicester Council for Voluntary Service director. He found it exciting that his local CVS would receive one of the first ever Urban Aid grants in the country, while I felt extremely motivated to make a success of this new scheme. We agreed that it would be essential to form a multi-disciplinary Support Group of people representing different professions– a very new concept in those days. As Home-Start would be functioning under the umbrella of the CVS, we needed no constitution and no formal management committee.

In order to encourage suitable people to support and guide Home-Start's early years with me, in partnership and close co-operation, I undertook to visit the Voluntary Workers' Bureau and all the relevant professionals in Social Services, Health and Education Departments, and the Probation Service, as well as people in the Marriage Guidance Council, Pre-school Playgroups Association – agencies already working with parents or children.

It was clear from the very beginning that we did not in any way wish to replicate their work. Instead, our volunteers would be alongside them to provide support, friendship and practical help for families at home – something for which they simply had neither the time nor the resources.

All were extremely co-operative, except the health visitors, with whom I had had no previous dealings. I managed to meet the Medical Officer of Health, who listened to me, as I explained about the voluntary agency we were about to establish, and why I needed the support of someone from Health. Evidently bemused, after listening without interruption, he suggested that perhaps I should work for *him* in future, to get a better deal for his health visitors, as clearly I was an enthusiast! But he had no-one who could spare the time to attend our Support Group. This was bad news as health visitors are involved with *all* pre-school children and their families. They visit at home, three or four times before each child started school, and would be ideally placed to refer families who needed the regular support of another parent.

I was advised to talk to the Royal College of Nursing, who promptly – out of trepidation, I was told later - invited me to speak at their next meeting in Leicester, one very hot evening at the beginning of September.

I was unaccustomed to delivering a talk, and had as yet, nothing practical on which I could speak knowledgeably. The assembled women fairly shredded me with their piercing questions. They were fearful that these volunteers would give parents wrong advice after only 10 sessions of preparation, whereas health visitors had had to train for six years!

I went home and sobbed. All my planning and good intentions seemed to evaporate in the hot air. But the next morning, completely out of the blue, a huge bouquet of flowers was delivered, with an attached card, which read:

> ***"We heard what you had to say. We tested you to the limit. We now intend to support you, but on our terms."***
> **Signed on behalf of the Royal College of Nursing.**

What a relief! But what were their terms? They had decided that a Senior Nursing Officer should be the filter through whom all health visitor referrals to Home-Start would be made. Similarly, she would monitor the process and progress and keep a watchful eye on all developments through her involvement on the Support Group, which, they agreed, she could attend. This arrangement was to stand for the first two years.

I decided to accept their terms.

Following meetings with all the different agencies in Leicester, we assembled the first ever Home-Start Support Group (later Management Committee), which consisted of:

Gwen Flowers, a nursery nurse tutor at South Fields College of Further Education. She gave me much time and thoughtful encouragement, and also chaired the meetings.
Maureen Shepherd, Assistant Director of Social Services, a jolly woman, for whom nothing seemed to be too much trouble.
Wyn Laxton, one of the organisers of the Voluntary Workers' Bureau, who was helpful in recruiting and interviewing volunteers.
Geraldine Parsons, Senior Nursing Officer, who was experienced and gentle. All health visitor referrals to Home-Start were to be made through her.

Margaret Stephenson, Inspector of Primary Schools for the City of Leicester Education Department, who was clever, wise and kind to me when I had feelings of self-doubt.
Philip Ray, CVS Director, who held the interface position between Home-Start and his own management committee. Nothing ever seemed to be a problem to Philip.

Good. Together we formed a 'cell of seven', the reputed number for an effective group, so all augured well. But then, a regional Inspector of the Social Work Service for the DHSS, **Gillian Corsellis**, who had been instrumental in promoting our new venture for Urban Aid funding, actually *asked* to be an Observer on the Support Group! To me, she was a large, rather formidable woman, with years of child guidance experience, who appeared to be in a rather different league and position from our other local supporters. I need not have worried. She was helpful most of the time, but when she had a particular concern, I learned to listen loudly, for she was usually right.

> ***"Officially I was there to report on Home-Start's progress, but actually because by then I was completely convinced of the worth and importance of Margaret's ideas, I wanted to support them."***
> **Gillian Corsellis, Regional Inspector, Social Work Service.**

So, we had in place the funding, the multidisciplinary Support Group, a small room and shared secretarial help in the CVS. The starting date for Home-Start was to be 1st November 1973.

Fortunately we didn't realise at the time, that it was All Saints Day.

Chapter 3

BIRTH AND THE EARLY YEARS

"As I recall the early days of Home-Start, I was thinking that trivia, the small, the inconsequential, is a lot of what Home-Start is about. Babies are associated with small things of little intrinsic importance so, by association, babies, until they grow up a bit, are of little importance. It is as though the early years are trivial. But we know otherwise!"

Alan Laurie, Marriage Guidance Counsellor and chairman of Home-Start Shrewsbury

Home-Start began in Leicester on 1st. November 1973. I worked part-time in a tiny office opposite London Road station, and had a small Urban Aid grant.

Parents with young children had filled me with an overwhelming sense of awe at how they were expected to cope, and indeed to survive at all, often in the most appalling circumstances, and against all the odds. They were my real motivation for establishing Home-Start. Regardless of where they lived, we would offer support, friendship and practical help in the home, for as long as necessary, to families in Leicester, with at least one child under school-age, needing the support of another parent.

I was clear that Home-Start would be based on human qualities, rather than qualifications. We would all be in it together, giving, learning, sharing, and receiving.

But now I actually had to get started!

Knowing we couldn't take on the world, it seemed important to focus on families at the start of family life, because the formative first years are vital to the child's future well-being. Yet it is just at this time that parents so often experience particular difficulties and frustrations of their own – a sense of isolation, exhaustion, lack of self-confidence, lower income, sleepless nights, relationship problems and the task of endlessly nurturing and giving of themselves to their young child(ren). Most need someone to help out. This might be a friend, relative or neighbour, but in the absence of any of these, then Home-Start would offer a volunteer – another parent.

I drafted some of the first leaflets sitting at the table at home, surrounded by my own family. Nearly 30 years later, much of the original wording is still in current use. It came from the heart, based on personal experience as a parent, with the voices of the young families I had visited as a volunteer, still ringing in my ears.

Developing Home-Start was done together with others at each stage. We did it step by step, doing what came naturally and logically. The masterplan evolved as we progressed.

Readers will find that this chapter echoes that process. We were involved in sustaining and running the scheme itself; sustaining and motivating a team of volunteers, and sustaining the relationships between families and their volunteers. But, like individual parts of a tapestry, the different threads – their colours, their textures - were intertwined, with each essential for the ultimate creative whole.

The following are the most significant strands in the development of the very first Home-Start scheme in Leicester, between 1973 and 1981.

THE EARLY DEVELOPMENT OF HOME-START IN LEICESTER

EARLIEST AIMS

The earliest aims were

> **"To support and encourage parents and show them how they can help their children to develop ...to build on the parent as the sustaining agent and on the home as the sustaining background ...to focus on the parent rather than on the child, so that the parent is encouraged to realise her worth as the expert for her child ....to encourage physical and verbal contact between mother and child, self-respect, language development, sensory stimulation, play, independence and outings locally ....to**

encourage the use of community resources."

Clearly I had picked up some American jargon!

We quickly learned that it was much more important to focus on the parents, (mostly mothers in those early days), their well-being and emotional needs. A sincere "How are you?" and a smile for *them,* had far greater potential to beam back on their child(ren) than any more cognitive approach. Simply sharing time, kindness, practical help, generosity and fun, we learned, can be immensely rewarding for everyone involved.

URBAN AID GRANT

It is fascinating in retrospect to track the process of Home-Start's original funding - an Urban Aid grant to support our first five years' work.

On a local level, in the autumn, Philip Ray, the newly appointed General Secretary of the Leicester Council for Voluntary Service recorded:

> ***"In a file marked 'Urban Aid Applications', bequeathed to me by my predecessor, was a local proposal for setting up a 'Leicester Home-Start scheme', which was being initiated by a young local woman, Margaret Harrison...Ministry approval of such an application meant that financial resources would be available to translate an idea on paper into a practical reality. Non-acceptance frequently resulted in the idea sinking without trace. At that moment, Home-Start's fate hung on the perception of faceless civil servants in the Whitehall maze.***
>
> ***My own reading of the proposal revealed that, like so many of the best ideas, it was both simple and uncomplicated. It recognised a basic human need and strongly argued the case that human resources within the community could be marshalled and applied to meet it, given that they were adequately supported by a central organisation. Within a few weeks Margaret visited my office with the exciting news that her project submission had been approved. Characteristically, she now wanted to get on with the job.***
>
> ***I feel that it was my good fortune to be in at the birth of Home-Start".***

Regionally:

> ***"As a regional Social Work Inspector, with Leicester on my patch, I received a submission for a scheme to support young families. With one or two reservations, I recommended the scheme and sent the application to our headquarters. It so happened that my boss, the Chief Inspector, Joan Cooper, had just been to the U.S.A. with Dr. Mia Kellmer Pringle, Director of the National Children's Bureau, and Sir Keith Joseph, Secretary of State for Health, to explore ways of breaking into the 'Cycle of Deprivation'. Too often deprivation in families continued generation after generation, and we had all been instructed to look out for anything likely to affect this 'Cycle'. Home-Start was identified as such a scheme.***
>
> **Gillian Corsellis, Social Work Service.**

Nationally:

> ***"Home-Start had notable 'Whitehall appeal' – a perfect example of a practical partnership between the voluntary and public sectors."***
>
> **Sir Patrick Nairne, Permanent Secretary at the Department of Health and Social Security.**

The Urban Aid grant spanned five years, starting with £968 for six months of 1973/74 and increasing from an annual rate of £1,936 for the following three years, to £4,015 for the years 1977 and 1978. This was to cover the salary of the project organiser (part-time for three years and full-time for two years), secretarial and administrative costs, and project expenses, which included course fees, toys and equipment, and volunteers' out-of-pocket expenses.

> ***"As I grew to know her, Margaret impressed me with her enthusiasm and single-minded commitment to the Home-Start ideal, sometimes defying convention in the pursuit of what was best for the organisation. I well recall her reluctance to accept her organiser's salary in spite of its being firmly included in the original budget forecast. She believed that the money could be much better spent!"***
>
> **Philip Ray**

THE SUPPORT GROUP/MANAGEMENT COMMITTEE

The Support Group, comprising people from a range of statutory and voluntary agencies in Leicester, as outlined previously in Chapter 2, met for the first time shortly after my appointment. It was responsible for the grant, my employment, the office and insurance, and was chaired by Gwen Flowers, senior tutor on the Nursery Nurse courses at Southfields College of Further Education. Together we quickly began to plan Home-Start.

As 'just a mother' with previous voluntary work experience, I had a healthy respect for professionally trained and experienced workers from statutory and voluntary agencies. They could help me to network within their own agencies, and encourage family referrals from a wide range of sources. They would also guide me, when necessary, on aspects of early childhood, parenthood, or on difficult issues - such as sexual abuse, or violence in the family. We, in turn, could provide families with time, and the practical and emotional support, which they also needed as a whole.

The multi-disciplinary Support Group of people would watch as the scheme developed, to ensure we were on the right track. Later, two volunteers joined the Group, to contribute their practical experience. Together, all these people gave us credibility and allayed any fears about our voluntary work approach.

Those early meetings were timed for late morning, so that immediately afterwards we could eat and talk informally together. On Support Group days our own children watched bemused, as I prepared home-made food for everyone for lunch. It was an unusual situation for senior staff from statutory and voluntary agencies to have the opportunity to talk together, informally, away from their own offices. Home-Start gained so much from them, and in turn became the forum for strong, working partnerships, with real joined-up thinking.

DECISIONS DURING THE EARLY DAYS, WHICH HAVE PROVED ESSENTIAL

Perhaps it is hardly surprising that all the early decisions about the focus and structure of Home-Start survived during the first 30 years. They were after all, simply made in response to what both the families and the professionals each needed. Home-Start was cost-effective and with available access to professional workers if needed, I was capable of making it work. Our Decisions were:

- Home-Start is a Voluntary organisation. As such, it is based firmly on the ethic of choice. Volunteers choose to work with Home-Start for as long as they wish. But perhaps above all else, families themselves have the genuine choice about whether or not they wish to accept a Home-Start volunteer into their home. Virtually all do.

- Home-Start works with the *whole* family, not just with the children or just with the parents.

- Home-Start works with families at home where they are (place) and where they are in their lives (time). Each family is unique and that uniqueness must be respected and protected.

- Home-Start has:
  a) A multi-disciplinary Management Committee (Support Group in the early days) to guide and support it.

  b) A paid Organiser, who is genuinely concerned for families, committed to working with and through motivated volunteers, and competent to work co-operatively with statutory workers.

  c) A team of volunteers who have been sensitively recruited, carefully prepared, thoughtfully matched to families, and meticulously supported by the organiser.

  d) Secure funding for at least three years if at all possible.

- Partnership (later represented in the Home-Start logo) is fundamental to the Home-Start ethos and approach. The organiser works both alongside the professionals and the volunteers in partnership; the volunteers work alongside the families, providing them with informal emotional and practical support. They are alongside families in their homes for as long as they are needed, responding to the needs expressed by the parents. And volunteers are alongside each other, sharing ideas and skills for the ultimate benefit of the families they visit.

RECRUITING THE FIRST VOLUNTEERS

During November 1973 – that first month - it had been decided to run the first course for volunteers early in the New Year, so that they could be visiting families by Easter. One of the first lessons we learned though, was that no-one volunteers *before* Christmas. There were already about five potential volunteers, some I had worked with previously, others who had responded to the first article in the Leicester Mercury in the summer.

Less successful in our quest for volunteers were a slot on Radio Leicester, leaflets delivered to parents whose children had just started primary school, and talks to women's groups. Often the prevailing attitude was *"Well I had to cope on my own, so why can't they?"*

But then the Voluntary Workers' Bureau came to our rescue in early January, when the school term had started and many parents looked forward to a worthwhile commitment in the New Year. The following advertisement elicited a good response:

> "Sue is a young mother who has just had her third baby. She has no family or friends nearby and is feeling depressed, lonely and exhausted. Have you had children and could you spare a few hours each week to visit Sue or other parents in a similar position. Telephone:..."

Of course, several people phoned immediately, asking for Sue's address *"to go round NOW!"* Others accepted that they would be interviewed and expected to attend a course of preparation, before beginning to visit a family.

Other potential volunteers responded to an advertisement in the Situations Vacant column of the local paper, stating that we were sorry we were not offering paid work, but that all out-of-pocket expenses would be paid. A course of preparation for supporting young families at home would be provided. People should have parenting experience.

We decided that being a parent was to be the only essential requirement for being a volunteer with Home-Start. We needed people who had practical experience of the ups and downs of family life, regardless of their age, social background, education or life experience.

We ended up with a team of volunteers ranging in age from 23 to 72, with a variety of life experiences to draw on. Some worked part-time; a few had full-time jobs, but they told me that voluntary work was their choice.

> ***"What has impressed me perhaps more than any other aspect of Home-Start, is that I've known and admired (and how!) several volunteers who would never have been encouraged to offer themselves (poor education; not naturally physically attractive;***

sometimes seemingly hostile and rebellious. Nevertheless, because of your insight, vision and confidence Margaret, they have truly found themselves in volunteering for Home-Start. Miracles happen not just with the families, but also with those who offer support, friendship and practical help."

Joyce Reeve, head teacher of a Special School.

"Parenthood is a great leveller and makes ordinary people out of each of us."

Anne, volunteer

Most potential volunteers were drawn to the scheme through a feeling of empathy *"I know what it is like"* and the sometimes hesitant belief that *"I think I've got something to offer, but I'm only a parent."*

Some potential volunteers expressed what they considered to be 'selfish' reasons for their interest – loneliness, boredom, the need for a challenge. We were delighted. It highlighted the mutuality of voluntary work in the 1970s, with something in it for everyone. We gladly accepted what they had to offer - themselves and their time.

"I was new to the area, so becoming a volunteer seemed a good way of getting involved in the local community. The Home-Start leaflet in our local library caught my eye. The description of the isolation of some young families rang a bell, as I had felt very cut off when I had my two children away from family and friends and my husband was working long hours."

Christine, volunteer

"Home-Start is voluntary work on your own terms. It's good to be yourself and still know you are helping out a family".

Sandra, volunteer

Interviews

We were looking for parents with humanity, humility and humour.

We wanted to work with families, through volunteers who had time to care, with understanding, experience of family life, and a flexible approach. One cannot train for creative genius, which is what most parents practise daily.

During the interviews, potential volunteers were asked about themselves, their attitudes to children, to other parents and to voluntary work. We tried to clarify their commitment to the job. They in turn needed to know more about Home-Start and our expectations.

Two members of the Voluntary Workers' Bureau staff helped with those early interviews. We did not always agree on either the method or the outcomes, but together we could channel a potentially unsuitable volunteer towards other voluntary work, so that no-one felt rejected. Eventually there were 13 volunteers for the first course.

One of my greatest lessons in Home-Start was to discover the wide variety of people who became eminently suitable volunteers. I had expected to accept women (mostly) who were articulate, energetic and capable. In practice, not all fully matched these qualities, having many problems of their own. But their motivation, tenacity and obvious sensitivity were high. They eventually made memorable contributions in families, with whom they proved to be appropriately linked.

The only potential volunteer I rejected outright, was the perfect mother, who could not remember any times when she had not enjoyed her perfect children. I felt she would have been in for too many shocks and would maybe have struggled to empathise with other parents and their very real difficulties.

Remarkably, we agonised about what to call those first volunteers. 'Home-Visitors' was unacceptable to Health Visitors – too many HVs. Then my father quite simply suggested 'Home-Start Volunteers". HSVs. Of course! The extra S made all the difference and made me smile.

When they were informed by letter that they were to be one of the first ever group of Home-Start volunteers, each was asked to confirm in writing that she would be able to attend the 10 sessions of preparation.

Taking up references

Taking up personal references was a formality. Volunteers obviously gave the names of friends, who naturally recommended them for the work.

Some potential volunteers had a history of mental fragility. Others had been in petty trouble with the law. Trusting them, knowing that they too would benefit from involvement in voluntary work by contributing to the community, seemed to be important. It was up to us, we decided, to get to know each Home-Start volunteer really well, through the process of preparation and support. In practice, we were never let down.

PREPARATION OF THE VOLUNTEERS

> ***"How different it was then – very few courses for adults in Further Education Colleges. At that time, the Principal of South Fields College was reluctant to allow a course for Home-Start volunteers".***
>
> **Gwen Flowers, NNEB Tutor.**

> ***"My reservations concerned the proposed links with the Nursery Nurse Examination Board course, which had special emphasis on the educational needs of young children. I needn't have worried! My other reservation was the use of the word 'training' being applied to the days of study offered to the volunteers. My previous association with the training of teachers and social workers made me cautious about using a term which implied two or three years' training to become a 'professional'. I felt that the relationship between volunteers and professionals, already delicate, could be adversely affected."***
>
> **Gillian Corsellis, Social Work Service.**

With help and guidance from Gwen and Gillian, both committed to the success of Home-Start, we were given a room in the College. We called our training A Course of Preparation and I was helped to think through exactly what our Home-Start volunteer parents would most need to prepare them for supporting families and young children.

My own training in group dynamics proved extremely helpful to my role of Organiser and Course Co-ordinator. The experts would be drawn in to share their professional roles and responsibilities, while I would highlight the relevance of the Home-Start approach to young families. Together, the volunteers and I would learn where and when to seek guidance from statutory workers who, by their presence on the course, would be more accessible to us, should we need them, once visiting families began.

As Home-Start is a values-based organisation, integrating attitudes, standards and values with more formal topics, was a real challenge. From the onset, we would provide our volunteers with a blueprint for the Home-Start approach of support, friendship and practical help. There would be a light touch, with humour and understanding. There were inherently very many different ideas and ways of living, which the volunteers themselves from such widely diverse backgrounds, could share with one another on the course. This in itself, would be real preparation for them for visiting families with equally varied life-styles.

> ***"I was glad to find that the social mix of volunteers really was very wide, including some mothers who would have needed Home-Start themselves. I was so impressed that the women were able, unaffectedly, to share their feelings with the rest of the group."***
>
> **Helen Henry, Marriage Guidance Counsellor.**

We would be midwives, in the Socratean sense, drawing out of the volunteers, what was already there within them, - their skills, ideas and experiences. Although knowledge can be gained on a course, a person's wisdom develops mainly from the practical experience of applying it.

There would be no formal note-taking, few written papers, with the course sessions based as far as possible on experiential learning. There would be time for intuitive, creative ideas, rather than the presentation of ready-made solutions.

> ***"The course was my motivation. It was well organised. We knew what would be expected and where we stood. We got support all the way through. I would have been put off, if it had been about gaining a certificate, but felt confident enough to go to a 'course of preparation'."***
>
> **Sandra, volunteer.**

It was important for me to learn more about each volunteer – their fears, their strengths, their attitudes – just as it was for them to know me and members of the Support Group who participated on the course. We all had the opportunity to bond together.

The new volunteers all met with me at Southfields College, one week before the course began, and together we familiarised ourselves with practical details, such as parking, college facilities and expenses, as well as with the proposed course content. This ensured that their ideas could be incorporated into the planned course outline, at the very beginning.

The course would be held each Wednesday for 10 weeks, from 10 am to 3 pm including one hour for lunch together. The opportunity to meet one another socially was important, as was the timing of the course for parents whose children were at school. We were unable to provide crêche facilities, but it meant that the volunteers with young children, who were able to make arrangements for them to be looked after during the course, would also be free eventually, to visit families on their own, if this proved appropriate.

The course included talks, discussions, films, practical sessions and participatory experience. Though I had been designated course tutor, most of the sessions were led by experts from various departments and organisations in the city, particularly from those represented on the Home-Start Support Group.

EARLY COURSES OF PREPARATION included sessions on the following:

- **Brainstorming/Wordstorming.** At the beginning of the course, after each person had introduced her/himself, we divided into groups to brainstorm the role of the Home-Start volunteer. I was always surprised at the volunteers' instinctive insight and foresight, even before visits to families began. They would, they said, be spontaneous, flexible, caring and kind. They would extend, enrich and enliven the families they would visit. They could help with practical tasks. We were off to a good start, and every one of the volunteers had spoken and contributed on the first morning.

- **The needs of parents during the early years.** These included having to manage on a low budget, relationships, isolation, mental and physical exhaustion or ill health, widening parents' horizons. We drew much from the experience of the volunteers themselves, and their own very varied backgrounds.

- **Child development.** In addition to professional input, the volunteers' ideas and personal experiences were also shared. *"My children weren't toilet trained until they were three and did it themselves." "Oh, I always held them on the potty every hour on the hour from the age of nine months and never had a wet nappy after the age of one."* It was so important at this early stage in the course, to listen to experts, but also to learn from one another that there can be many different, yet equally acceptable ways for children to develop, dependent particularly on the attitudes of the parents.

- **Abuse.** What can lead to child abuse, or to violence in the family? What are the signs of physical, emotional, sexual abuse or neglect? How should the Home-Start volunteers respond to abusive parents? What are their lines of communication? We provided the volunteers with a small booklet, which covered these questions, with the home telephone number of the Home-Start organiser (which each volunteer had anyway), the local health centres, GP surgeries and the social services duty officer.

- **Confidentiality.**

  "One mother I visited had adorable little twin boys. She was a prostitute. She talked to me about it. She knew I didn't like what she was doing, but we liked each other. Her 'boss' would call round for her earnings and once I heard him say to her "What about her (meaning me) in the other room, will she split on you?" The mum said "No, she's OK, she's my friend". I was really touched by this and I'll never know whether I did right or wrong by not reporting her, but I knew I couldn't betray her."

  Vivienne, volunteer.

  Concern about confidentiality within Home-Start was important, but we did not allow it to paralyse us.
  Where there is genuine concern, there is also respect. If confidentiality has to be breached for the safety of the children, the volunteer must face the parent openly with her concern, and offer to seek professional help together.
  Only if there is known sexual abuse, must professional help be sought first, as discussion with the family may well bring either denial or refusal to admit the volunteer to the home in future. We try to act with sensitivity at all times.
  Sometimes confidential information is known to a social worker, and the volunteer might therefore not fully recognise or appreciate the purpose behind plans made by the statutory services.

- **Labelling.** We discussed the need to own our own judgements. For example, rather than calling somebody *"manipulative"* or *"angry all the time"*, saying *"I feel she manipulates me"* or *"whenever I'm there she seems* *angry.*" This becomes a quite different dynamic, as it is acknowledged that the parent's behaviour might be reactive. For volunteers who were concerned about 'saying the right thing', we were always clear that if the attitude is right, then the words too will come out right . . . . .most of the time.

- **Listening.**

  "Sometimes I don't think I fully appreciated what I was hearing, when she told me that Johnny was her father's child".

  Christine, volunteer.

  Listening skills were role-played and discussed. We learned to be neither intrusive, nor to produce immediate solutions. Respect and genuine caring are key qualities. We learned to listen and talk in the same ratio as we have ears and mouth – i.e. listen twice as much as we talk.

- **Local visits to facilities for families in the community**. We arranged for volunteers to visit day nurseries, medical centres, mother and toddler groups, libraries and toy libraries, and many other facilities available to families. They then compiled lists of these resources for **information**. Parents who may not use written guidance, will often listen to their volunteer enthusing about what IS available for them.

- The roles and responsibilities of **Social Workers, Health Visitors, Nursery Schools,** and **Housing, Welfare and Legal Advice Centres.** We had talks on all these from people who were directly involved themselves. It was helpful to have faces and names.

- **Social Ethics.** This session really helped each of us to think about our own "bottom line" and just what we would and would not tolerate.

  "My husband is a policeman. What if I find that the family I visit is on the fiddle?" (Here, as the organiser, I made a mental note to introduce this particular volunteer to as honest a family as possible!)

  "I hope no-one ever expects me to visit a prostitute".
  "I'd be really upset to visit a family that circumcised their daughter".
  Together we faced our prejudices, our fears and our own values.

- **First Aid** in the home.

- **Play.** This was a practical session on low-cost no-cost play opportunities in the home.

- **Meals on a low budget.** Volunteers produced their best low budget recipes for each other and these were collated in a booklet to share with families when appropriate. The focus was always on the benefits of preparing and cooking food together and enjoying doing so.

  "The mother I visited said she couldn't cook. She took the kids on the bus five days a week to her favourite café, but for the other two days, they ate junk food and waited for the giro to arrive. So we started cooking really simple things together, like tuna bake with potatoes and cheese. Her boyfriend began to wait for my visit, with a recipe book in his hand, full of cheeky ideas what we could cook that morning."

  Eileen, volunteer.

- **Positive Reinforcement**. Knowing that parents are sometimes more negative with their children, than positive, we did a session I had learned in America. For ten minutes the volunteers were each asked to produce something out of newspaper. A few members of the Support Group and I walked around, making all positive comments, such as,

  "That looks lovely/fun/well-done. You're brilliant at it!"
  Then that was cleared away and the volunteers were asked to spend ten minutes finger-painting (on more newspaper!) The only change was that our comments this time round, were all negative:

  "You say that's a house but you've left off the chimney; here let me show you." (The volunteer slapped my hand!)
  "I'll get you some more paint when I've finished my cigarette." (She never did.)
  "All brown paint? You must be miserable today!" (The volunteer tore it up.)
  Then we cleared it all away and had a discussion together about the sometimes serious effects of our comments on a small child, or a delicate ego.
  After running this session twice, I lost *my* confidence, saying negative things to volunteers with whom I would have to work positively afterwards. We never repeated the sessions, but from what volunteers have remembered about the courses nearly 30 years later, they clearly

made a big impression.

- **Record Keeping.** For the first few years, volunteers used the PIE system of record keeping, which I had learned in America – Planning, Implementing and Evaluating their visits to families. But we eventually found that some volunteers with wonderful practical and personal skills found the system too arduous. Others preferred to keep a diary of their visits, so that they could be aware of changes and developments in the family. They would also record when they had helped to keep various appointments with the doctor, health clinic or the probation officer, or even when they had visited and the family was out. These were helpful for use if a case conference was called. Basic records were also kept, so that the volunteers could claim their expenses.
- **Role Play** was used particularly for our sessions on listening skills, but also when role playing family life and the role of the Home-Start volunteer. From these sessions we all gained a very clear picture of what NOT to do. It would be all too easy to focus on the children and to have fun with them, whilst leaving the parent distraught, depressed or angry, as her confidence was sapped even further.
  Our courses always aimed to illuminate, rather than to teach solutions.
- **Learning from Experienced Volunteers** was possible after the first course of preparation. Those with experience of working with families would be invited to share their feelings and to raise issues with new volunteers on the course. These were often touching, sometimes amusing, but always vivid sessions, full of insights.

(With hindsight, I wish we had done more on our courses to help volunteers to recognise signs of resilience, tenacity, gentleness and generosity in the families we support. We might have prepared them better for issues such as domestic violence, drugs and sexual diseases.)

Our courses always ended with a celebration, usually with special food and drink.

> ***"Apart from meeting new people, I feel that I have become more patient and tolerant with my own family. Not only do I wish Home-Start had been around when my own children were small, but now that I am a foster mother, the course helped me with my relationship with social workers and other foster parents. It also helped me understand the foster children better."***
>
> **Eve, volunteer.**

Our presenters were never paid, but were warmly welcomed and usually thanked with a book token or plant. Denis Rice, who led the social ethics sessions, particularly appreciated the opportunity to buy himself a book and always brought it back to be signed by the course participants.

A pattern emerged from the courses, where some volunteers came in on a high, but often, about half way through, would begin to doubt their ability to support families. This became more noticeable once experienced volunteers started to attend some of the sessions, to give actual examples of how they were getting on. But nearly always, the newest volunteers regained their own confidence, once they were linked with a family, because no parents and children ever had *all* the problems they had expected to encounter.

> ***"Margaret made every one of us feel valued. When Christine F. didn't turn up any more, we all signed a card saying we'd missed her and she came again the next week, with a big smile on her face."***
>
> **Kay, volunteer.**

We always expected to discuss issues courteously, with real respect for each other's opinions. This was a way of putting into practice ways of understanding different views and styles when visiting families too.

Frequently at the end of the course, volunteers would say,

> ***"I see life a bit differently now"***, or
> ***"I wish I'd done this course earlier while our own children were still young."***

Occasionally we had a volunteer who dominated or who always seemed to know exactly what to do in any given situation - or so she thought. Realistically, I had to face her with my concerns. Sometimes such a volunteer would be asked to help in the Home-Start Family Group, rather than visiting an individual family by herself at home.

Ronald Laing in The Divided Self, (Pelican Books) said that behaviour can be seen, while experience cannot. Yet it is our experience which influences our behaviour. We were all very aware, that our aim was to make each other's experience, as well as that of the families we visited, as happy and hopeful as possible.

We were acutely aware too that the best learning happens within a relationship; that once a volunteer began to support a young family at home, there would be much that they could learn and find out together. We knew that the Course of Preparation was only a beginning and that with on-going support and further training sessions planned, there was a steep learning curve ahead for the new Home-Start volunteers.

On the first preparation course, we had been inveigled into accepting three social services' Home-Help organisers for training alongside our new volunteers. In terms of group dynamics, this concerned me. I was flattered by the request though, and agreed, particularly as the department provided some of our funding.

Throughout the course, one of the Home Helps kept telling me firmly *"Home-Start will never work."* With her inside knowledge and experience with families, she could foresee all the pitfalls. This did nothing for my morale, but it did strengthen my resolve to make Home-Start succeed!

It was wonderful watching adults return to learning. Many of the volunteers had said in their interviews that they were "only mothers". We found we were re-connecting parent volunteers and me (!) to education. Then, very often, they and I, in turn, encouraged the parents we visited to seek further training, or adult education for themselves.

A strong feature of Home-Start has always been that many of the parents we support, later choose to become volunteers themselves. They then, in turn, attend the course of preparation and can avail themselves of all the opportunities for continuing the learning process. Many parents move on anyway, and take other courses in the community.

At the end of the course, certificates were issued to the Home-Start volunteers. They were signed and presented by the head of South Fields

College and read: **"Mary B has completed a course in preparation for Home-Start visiting."**

A general evaluation of each course was completed by the volunteers six months later, so that its relevance could be directly related to their experiences with families.

Being genuine is the key to truly helping others. Understanding, awareness, and attitudes are more important for the Home-Start volunteer than any amount of learning conceptually, during the course of preparation. So I believe there should be no set curriculum for Home-Start volunteers. Essentially, the Home-Start approach can never be taught. It can be caught from one another, when people are prepared to put their hearts and their souls into it.

It takes courage just to BE oneself, and this goes beyond anything we can learn formally.

On-Going training

On-going training, after the course had ended, became a natural process. Once Home-Start volunteers began to visit families, the gaps in their knowledge and experience became apparent. So issues, which could not be addressed during the initial course, or resolved during their support sessions, became the focus for further study.

About three times each year, we spent a morning or a day on topics such as legal aid, sanity in the summer holidays, teenagers in the family, children with special needs, mental health issues, multi-cultural opportunities, children's behaviour, parents' responsibilities and much, much more.

All volunteers were encouraged to attend these additional learning opportunities.

FAMILIES AND THEIR VOLUNTEERS

FAMILY REFERRALS

Our very first decision when starting to work with families, was what to call them in Home-Start. They are not 'clients' or 'service users', but they are what they are - parents, children and families.

Half-way through the first course of preparation, I began, with trepidation, to seek the first family referrals from statutory and voluntary agencies in Leicester, particularly from those which had a designated person on our Support Group. I decided to visit the first family referred by a social worker myself, to be a few steps ahead of the new volunteers. It was not a good experience.

> **Lucy was an 18 year-old single mother with two very young children. All Lucy really wanted to do, was to turn back the clock and regain her friends and her freedom. She told me many unhappy stories of her harsh disciplining and how she shouted at the kids for hours if necessary, until they went to sleep. After four visits, she no longer opened the door to me. When I checked this out with the social worker, I eventually heard that Lucy had misunderstood my role and had thought I could ensure that the children were taken away, into the care of the local authority. She wanted to begin again, without all the duties of parenthood.**

This story was a great inducement to the first volunteers to succeed where I hadn't. And they did!

The first social worker who really wholeheartedly referred families to Home-Start, was Barbara Browse, who worked for the Family Service Unit on the Braunstone estate in Leicester. She was quite clear that it was practical help and emotional support that these young families needed, neither of which she could provide in her professional role. Barbara's confidence in our new family support scheme really boosted my confidence. She has been a close friend ever-since.

Increasingly, I was invited to speak to groups of social workers, health visitors, probation officers, primary school teachers, magistrates, marriage guidance counsellors, child psychologists and speech therapists. Gradually, they too began to refer families. This meant that I was often able to introduce a volunteer even before the end of the courses of preparation. Those volunteers told me that the course became more meaningful once they had started to support a family themselves.

Families were referred from different parts of the city and from different cultures. It was important that referrals were not confined to a single estate or particular area. The pressures of parenthood are common to us all, irrespective of where we live, though some areas do of course bring enormous extra pressures.

One of our original objectives, had been "to be preventive rather than remedial". Since 91% of the families referred had very serious problems and needed visiting over a longer period than had originally been envisaged, we were sometimes unable to offer as much short-term support as we would have liked, to families at times of stress, or during early periods of breakdown.

For the first two years, all health visitor referrals were made through the senior nursing officer Geraldine Parsons. She was responsible for checking that volunteers were neither giving inappropriate advice nor usurping the health visitor role.

She quickly realised though, that we were in a position to help families to bring their children to health centres, to keep doctor's or hospital appointments and to help carry out simple requirements, such as weaning and going out of the home for fresh air. The health visitors also really began to appreciate the greater amount of time a volunteer could spend with a family, and the many practical things they could do together.

One health visitor said,

> ***"The volunteers are down at the base level, and that is why it is important for them to visit young families at home. They have the time and they can show they care. The problems that the professionals treat, spring from a weak base, rather like a crooked tower. We might put some of it right at the top, but it will always go wrong again unless we can tackle the fundamental issues. Home-Start volunteers do, and we depend on them."***

Housing Trusts began to refer families to Home-Start when they were re-housed, often away from family and friends. A Home-Start volunteer visiting regularly, was a great source of continuity and practical support. Sometimes she would help with furnishings through her own network of friends, or, when applicable, her place of worship. Home-Start provided a fresh start for many young parents.

One mother, who had visited her doctor when she had felt overwhelmed with responsibilities, had been offered either tranquilliser tablets, or a Home-Start volunteer. She later told us she had chosen the tablets! . . But then after another two months she approached us herself, saying *"My friend up the road's got an 'ome-Start volunteer. Can I have one now too please?"*

With hindsight, and because I subsequently had very positive experiences of supporting families myself, we learned that sometimes it is difficult for a small minority of families to benefit from the Home-Start approach. These included parents like Lucy, who really wanted to relinquish their responsibility for young children. Others included parents who were regularly in and out of prison.

Twice we were asked to support children (who previously had been fostered), and their parents after they were released from prison. Each time the children had been returned to living conditions, which were extremely squalid and the parenting neglectful. Each time the adults had quickly reverted to crime and had been re-sentenced, yet again, to several years of imprisonment. We wished we had never accepted the referrals, so that the children could have benefited from the continuous care of their foster parents.

Often though, Home-Start was able to give much needed support to a mother and children, when their dad was in prison.

The majority of parents in those early days did not refer themselves. Either they had never heard of Home-Start, or they lacked the confidence to approach us themselves and articulate their needs. We relied on professionals to refer them.

Because Home-Start is voluntary and 'on offer', there was a very high level of take-up by a very wide range of families with different needs, when they were referred to Home-Start by a professional worker.

Some years later, Dr. Maurice Hayes, Permanent Secretary at the DHSS in Northern Ireland, stated publicly:

> ***"We talk glibly about a partnership between statutory and voluntary – but with very little doubt who is the junior partner. This has to change – it is time for the statutory services to see themselves as a resource for the voluntary sector rather than the other way round. Some will see this as de-skilling and de-professionalisation of services. This is misguided. Rather it is a liberation of energy, imagination and dedication which is there in the community and which Home-Start has successfully tapped."***

The Initial Visit to a Family.

When a family was referred, (long before most of them had mobile phones), I first wrote them a straightforward letter, explaining how I had heard about them, that we had a group of volunteer parents, and that I would like to visit them to see how another mother might be able to give them a helping hand. It was important that we were not seen as an arm of the referring agency, and for that reason I nearly always visited the newly referred family alone, as soon as possible after hearing about them.

Together then, the parents and I could discuss informally, what they thought they really needed, which was often different from the expectations of their statutory workers.

> ***"The children are getting me down. All three wet the bed. I've had enough."***

> ***"I'm having my first baby. I don't feel well. My Mum lives the other side of town."***

> ***"I used to teach in primary school. I never thought parenthood would be like this."***

> ***"Living on the fourteenth floor, I never get out. He just yells all day. My health visitor said I should ignore him, my Mum says I should smack him, but I feel so bad, I just turn up the radio to drown his noise."***

> ***"My husband is a doctor. If I tell him I've had a bad day, he just tells me I should see what he's had to deal with at the surgery. I don't want to tell the health visitor I can't cope. I certainly don't want to go to a mother and toddler group, with yet MORE children. I think I'm going mad."***

> ***"My husband brought another wife from India into the home and now I'm expected to look after all five of the children. I'm not allowed money or to go out. I'm very miserable and so tired."***

> ***"My mother died when I was little and I was put into a Children's Home. I expected to live happily ever after when I had children of my own. Now I feel such a failure. They don't even like me!"***

The only records I kept after my initial visit were details which I might have forgotten, particularly recording the parents' wishes, fears and expectations.

There was no 'typical' family, but many shared similar difficulties – isolation, low income, exhaustion, feelings of depression and hopelessness, frustration, irritability, resentment, anger, guilt and feelings of aggression. We were optimistic that, with the support of a reliable, resourceful Home-Start friend, most parents would soon be coping and enjoying life again. A problem shared is indeed a problem halved.

On my initial visit to a family, I always asked the parents themselves what they would like – what kind of volunteer/other parent; where to start to give them a hand. Whatever they said, I tried to respond, because I was keen that the volunteer and family would have a good time together.

The visits were without forms or formality. Each family knew from the beginning, that we in Home-Start really cared.

If things were really bad when I first visited a family, I would pop back again the next day, if necessary. We had neither expectations nor prescriptions for how things ought to be. There was neither a plan, nor a contract about the content or the length of time visiting would last. At the very beginning though, I had expected Home-Start volunteers to visit for up to a year. But I was wrong, as it was during the second year that some of the biggest changes occurred.

I soon learned that parents respond amazingly positively to someone who really understands what a difficult patch they are going through. When I suggested that once they had had another mother to help them out, then maybe one day they might like to be a Home-Start volunteer themselves, they were usually astonished by the suggestion. But when they realised the request was genuine, they invariably began to look forward to better times ahead.

Some parents, who had every intention of becoming a Home-Start volunteer, eventually found a paid job instead. That was fine! The intention had been there, fuelling a renewed feeling of self-worth. The whole family had benefited from their sense of optimism.

Unless a health visitor had referred the family, I always told the parents that I wished to let their health visitor know that they now had a Home-Start volunteer. It was only courteous to do so, knowing that each family automatically had a health visitor allocated to them while there was a child under five years old.

MATCHING

One of the pleasures of co-ordinating Home-Start was that after getting to know each family myself from the initial visit, I could then decide which volunteer would be most suitable for them. It was rather like giving someone a present – intuitively one knew if it was right. Yet success at this stage was crucial to the success of the scheme.

Skills, interests, circumstances, experience, ages, similar/dissimilar backgrounds and geographical considerations, were all taken into account.

We offered visits once or even several times a week, depending on the volunteer's availability and the needs of the family.

Instinctively, I introduced volunteers who immediately had something in common with the parents –

- both had five children or an only child;
- both were on income support or single parents;
- a volunteer with young children herself, would visit an agoraphobic mother, whose children benefited from the opportunity to play with others at home;
- a mother with five children and three others in care, with an ex-social worker Home-Start volunteer, who admitted to understanding the realities of motherhood so much better since having two sons of her own.

Topics of common interest provided a bridge between volunteer and parent.

- ***" We both love chocolate/have a weight problem/have children the same ages/enjoy the same place of worship/the same pub/club or pets."***
- ***"Mine has fleas at the moment too."***
- ***"We enjoy Do-It-Yourself tasks/television programmes/food and drink".***

There was never any shortage of topics, allaying the fears of the new volunteers, who would ask "But what shall I say?"

Sometimes the concerns of a volunteer were a prime consideration too, for instance those who had expressed particular anxieties about psychiatric disorder, prostitution, physical violence, physical disabilities, or families with different ethnic backgrounds. These were always honoured, when matching them to referred families, though in my experience, many of the volunteers' anxieties evaporated as they became more confident themselves, eventually taking on families with a wide variety of difficulties and backgrounds. They had learned to care about them as people, rather than problems.

> ***"They like you because you're just a mum, with skills, sisterhood, sharing the good and the bad."***
>
> **Barbara, volunteer.**

Sometimes I found that opposites attracted each other. I introduced:

- a volunteer, who had two children with learning difficulties, to a mother who fussed about the normal development of her own two sons;
- a Home-Start volunteer who was a good listener, with a parent who had a great deal to talk through;
- a volunteer who spoke with authority and who knew her own mind, with a parent who was groping for direction, changing her mind and her methods daily; or
- a basically strong mother, going through a patch of insecurity, matched with an unconfident volunteer, who quickly reinforced her strengths and abilities.

It was important that the initial spark, which ignited the relationship between family and volunteer, was spontaneous and mutual, for everything in Home-Start is dependent on that relationship. Occasionally though, it took many months to build, and took a persistent demonstration of goodwill, reliability and trust.

Sometimes I had misgivings about introducing a volunteer to a family, with whom I knew I would find it difficult myself, to remain motivated. I was always honest with the volunteer about my doubts. Very often this proved to be the challenge, which encouraged potential volunteers to take on the family wholeheartedly themselves.

The intuitive judgements worked, largely because of the motivation of the volunteers and the perceptions of the families. Knowing that the volunteers had no statutory authority, were not paid, and really cared, they were able to share some of the traumas and many of the joys of their lives together.

Towards the end of the 1970s, by which time Home-Start in Leicester was large and busy, we knew we were working at full capacity. Having always enjoyed the reputation of matching families and Home-Start volunteers within a week to 10 days of referral, we were finding too often that it was taking us several weeks. This should not be allowed to happen in Home-Start.

Occasionally we simply did not have enough volunteers to go round. I would always try to visit the family myself, explaining from the beginning that it would take a little while to find a volunteer. Sometimes they were invited to attend our family group in the meantime, or I would undertake several visits myself to support them through a particularly bad patch. The referrers were always informed as soon as possible, if we were simply unable to take on the family.

In the first four years in Leicester, we supported 303 families. Each had different needs, just as each volunteer had different skills.

The Developing Relationship between Family and Volunteer at Home

> ***"I could go along as I was – no standards to reach. If I'd had standards to reach, I'd have freaked out and never done it."***
>
> **Sandra, volunteer.**

Starting slowly but building up gradually and steadily, volunteers shared their love, warmth, joy, fun, intimacy, and the expectation that the 'bad patch' would pass.

> ***"My first visit was memorable. I shall never forget the cloying, pungent "smell" of dirt, urine and poverty, as I gingerly entered the house accompanied by a smiling Margaret, who seemed totally impervious to her surroundings. But the moment I came face to face with my first mother, dejectedly sitting in this squalor with two little children of similar ages to my own, I was instantly hooked. Somehow we became kindred spirits and we soon became firm friends."***
>
> **Stephanie, volunteer.**

Attitudes, love, and humour are most significant in building a relationship with families who live in grinding, never-ending poverty. We have to support them today, whilst also endeavouring to fight for change, for a better world, in other arenas. Home-Start is not an overtly campaigning organisation.

> ***"There was no food in the house, very little heat, an inefficient cooker, virtually no furniture or floor covering, or bedding or even beds. I could go on and on. Everything was so dismal.***
> ***One of my mums ran out of terry nappies and had no money, so she tore an old tatty curtain from the window, ripped it into squares and slapped one on the baby's bottom and said 'that will have to do until my cheque comes from the social'. This was a single mum who, contrary to others' perceptions, neither smoked nor drank, but spent all her money on her children and making her home as nice as possible. Central heating and double glazing were only slowly being installed on the estate by the authorities."***
>
> **Viv, volunteer.**

Inevitably living conditions affect families both physically and emotionally. Having the basics for comfort and convenience can be life-giving. We all need essentials for a sense of well-being.

> ***"I set out with much trepidation to visit my first family. This was on one of the poorer council estates in Leicester city. I arrived at the address and, for a full five minutes dared not get out of the car. A pack of seven or eight snarling, vicious looking dogs were outside. This was before the days of 'dog catchers'.***
> ***Eventually I ventured out clutching a bag of my grandchildren's toys and books. I had been told the family had nothing. The young mother just talked and talked, while the children pounced on the bag of toys. When the time came to leave, I just hadn't the heart to take them away."***
>
> **Peggy, volunteer.**

> ***"One of my families waited until I arrived, and then proceeded to bath the children, using one coffee mug and one washing-up bowl. Five children under five years old, were bathed in the same bowl. I was then offered a cup of coffee in the same mug that was used to bath the children. Life was very varied and stimulating in those early days, as we tried to find sufficient clean and dry***

clothes for all five children at the same time! A washing machine was an unheard of luxury."

Stephanie, volunteer.

"The neighbours would come in to share their problems too, because we weren't 'official'."

Anne, volunteer.

"There was nothing nice or cared for in that family. When I gave him a toy for Christmas, he just stuffed it down his bed, to keep it out of the hands of his Mum and Dad, who would have trashed it right away."

Sylvia, volunteer.

We were able to do a lot of good through love and spontaneity, rather than inhibiting through fear or control. This was a big advantage of being a voluntary organisation.

Perhaps now is the place to be more specific about the Home-Start approach.

THE HOME-START APPROACH

The Home-Start approach is to provide support, friendship and practical help for the whole family, at home, where their difficulties exist, and where their dignity and identity can be respected and protected.

We work to the rhythm and needs of each family. "Here you are! Here I am!" The lack of pressure is in itself healing.

One of the first things a volunteer does, is to ask the parents what they think would really be helpful. So often statutory workers fail to adopt this line, which we have been told, can lead to years of unrealistic expectations on both sides.

SUPPORT

There is no set pattern to visiting, which might take place once, or several times each week. For the family it is not just the visit which is important, but the anticipation, that when the volunteer comes, good things will happen. It is a consciousness that somebody really cares about them, and will turn up regularly and reliably.

"One mother with a violent and drunken husband, had four children aged three and under. The six- month- old baby cried all the time and Mum was at the end of her tether. I found the three year old little girl running riot. Mum could not handle her and the baby just screamed and screamed. I visited every Tuesday, found lots of exciting ways for the mother to involve the children with her various activities, but also initiated lots of exciting outings. Every week the toddler's little face would be peering out of the window as I arrived and she would shout "Hooray! Here comes Tuesday."

Peggy, an early volunteer.

Peggy, a warm understanding grandmother in her late 50s at the time, had begun to turn despair into hope and chaos into order. The family lived in the back room of a damp, terraced house and most of their life was spent on and around the sofa. The mother had post-natal depression, caused partly by the birth of the fourth child, partly through deep exhaustion, and partly because her husband's only contribution to family life was to wet the bed beside her each night, creating even more washing and drudgery for her next day. On one particularly difficult morning, she had snapped *"Oh, wait until Tuesday comes"*, meaning the next occasion on which Peggy would be arriving – hence the nickname.

'Tuesday' was introduced to this family which had been referred to Home-Start simultaneously by the health visitor and the social worker. In due course, a good relationship was built with each member of the family. Initially this was achieved by just being there regularly, listening and really caring.

During some of the early visits, Tuesday took all the children out for a few hours, allowing some precious peace for the mother. However, it quickly became apparent that she also cherished the time Tuesday was with them as much as the children did. Here was a

woman with whom she could really talk – unlike most of her friends, who just arrived unexpectedly, used up valuable sofa space, proceeded to burden her with all *their* problems and expected her to make coffee for *them.*

Tuesday on the other hand, arrived regularly during the early months, on alternate mornings at 10 a.m initially, thus producing the first pattern of certainty this family had ever experienced. She didn't go with any particular task in mind, though sometimes they would do some clearing up together, or shopping or cooking. Always though, the children were involved too, and the happy atmosphere and more positive attitudes were quickly transmitted to everyone in the family. There were plenty of cuddles, which Tuesday enjoyed as much as anyone, much enthusiastic chatter, but above all, a lot of fun.

The housing was still bad, the income intolerably low, but now suddenly there was something to look forward to. Instead of living from minute to minute, or from crisis to crisis, the family began to take a whole day at a time. The new stability was transmitted to the children, who became more emotionally secure. The whining and crying stopped, and for the first time, the mother noticed and actually began to enjoy each of her own children.

Psychologist Uri Bronfenbrenner, psychologist, has said that what every child needs in order to develop his potential, is an adult who is "just crazy about that kid." In Home-Start we have to begin by being just crazy about the **parents,** so that they, in turn, can be fully involved with their children.

There is no set pattern to what a volunteer actually does. Flexibility is the keynote. Go out, stay in, amuse the children, do things together, but all the time talking and listening to each other:

- Having optimism and competence, yet humility and patience, with a family in apparently hopeless circumstances.
- Taking the children off the hands of a parent, who is badly in need of a break from them.

- Feeding the mind as well as offering support to a parent who is feeling intellectually stagnant.
- Having flair for hair and beauty care, thus giving a boost to the severely depressed mother who says she has "gone to seed".
- Being firm yet kind, with a father whose expectations of his young children are irrational and unrealistic.
- Helping to cook meals, budget, or tidying up with a parent who wants to do so, and then helping the parent to sustain the newly acquired skills.

  After visiting for three months, Gwen asked Pauline the mother, what she wanted to do together that particular afternoon. *"Clear up the kitchen"*, suggested Pauline for the first time. With three-year-old Sharon's help too, they threw away all the empty tins, cleared the sink, washed grease off the walls and work surface, washed out the cupboards and were just starting on the floor, when Billy, the teenage son returned from his Special School. *"Who's done this?"* he enquired gleefully. *"Your Mum and sister and I. Do you want to help too?"* to which he replied, *"No, but let me show you Mum's bedroom!"*

- Having a spontaneous sense of the ridiculous, laughing with a family over situations which before, or alone, would have induced panic and anger.
- Giving regular long-term daily support to a young mother suffering from severe postnatal depression, via a group of three Home-Start volunteers.

The volunteer is there because it is an open secret that all is not well, so there is no need to keep up pretences with polite and safe conversation. Often the volunteer is privileged to hear family secrets. But if a child were at risk, then the volunteer would immediately insist to the parent that together they should seek more professional help, often from a doctor or health visitor, or if necessary from a social services duty officer.

Home-Start volunteers, who have time to be with families, getting to know their tensions and anxieties, can very often avert more serious problems from developing.

"After my initial visit I wondered why the mother needed me. Then it all came tumbling out – they had a mortgage to pay, she was working from home, apparently all hours, and the simple fact was, they couldn't manage without her income. She was absolutely stressed out, the phone never seemed to stop ringing, and she was working late into the night. The baby had become a burden when he cried, and she confessed she had already treated him roughly and was afraid of what she might do to him next. Her previous job was open and it seemed the right thing for her to return and work proper hours. We found a good child minder and baby settled in straightaway. The tension was taken off Mum and everyone was happy."

Peggy, volunteer.

Another young mother sat cuddling her young baby in front of the gas fire, while two-year-old Robert struggled alone to put on his sweater, in the farthest corner of the cold, bare room. When Marie, the new Home-Start volunteer went to help him, the mother yelled *"Don't you dare! He's just like his Dad – they are both out to annoy me. I've told him to get dressed himself, even if it takes him all day!"* Knowing that Home-Start works 'with and through the parent', reluctantly Marie ignored Robert's wailing and sat down beside the mother, asking her to tell her all about why Dad was annoying her so much. After a few minutes of talking, the mother was calmer and agreed that now she would give Robert a hand with his sweater, while the volunteer could hold the baby.

One young father who had been left to cope alone with three young children, gave up his job, so that he could care for them himself. *"Housework only shows when it isn't done"*, he once told me, wisely. He really valued the support of a male volunteer, who was able to support him and the children regularly, twice each week.

Encouraging singing, which some volunteers do with pleasure, can literally re-enchant a family. It can prove psychologically, emotionally and physically healing. I have now learned from my son David, that if you liberate the voice, you so often give greater freedom to the human within.

I realised that in those early days, we had little knowledge or understanding about sexual abuse, whether inside or outside the family. It was only when psychologist, Rhoda Oppenheimer, a close colleague, alerted me to the frequent link between anorexia and sexual abuse, that we learned to be open to the possibility of its existence.

FRIENDSHIP

It is said that in the company of friends we feel most truly alive. Michael Argyle, the social psychologist, tells us in his book The Psychology of Happiness (Routledge), that a good fundamental for happiness is to have one close relationship and a network of friends. For some parents, particularly those who are alone, their volunteer can be the first close, non-demanding relationship they have ever really had.

The exchange of friendship is usually so natural that we take it for granted. Together we can express our vulnerability, disasters and triumphs. Introducing a volunteer friend to a parent who has never had a real friend, or who desperately needs one at the time, is possibly one of Home-Start's greatest gifts.

> **"Don't walk in front of me,**
> **I may not follow. Don't walk**
> **Behind me. I may not lead.**
> **Walk beside me and just be my friend."**
>
> **Anonymous.**

Real friendship, even if fostered through a voluntary organisation like Home-Start, can greatly reduce the sense of isolation, lift the spirits, engender hope and be the beginning of renewal.

> ***"They want a friend not a therapist."***
>
> **Di, social worker.**

Within Home-Start relationships, there is mutuality, kindness, playfulness, and love. Together we can build up a bond of emotional experiences and memories, which last a life-time.

> ***"The lack of formal records and the confidentiality which guaranteed freedom from being brought into some impersonal***

> ***referral network, were striking. These were important lessons, not only for Home-Start but for wider social work practice."***
>
> **Roy Wardell, Social Services Director.**

Very occasionally, a parent bursting with pent-up emotions, would be dismissive of the volunteer:

> ***"I would like to mention the volatility of some of our mums and their very unpredictable mood swings, brought on I suspect through hidden anger and frustration at the life styles they are supposed to be satisfied with. On their bad days, you can be told to F...off! and then there can be a tearful reconciliation on your next visit. As one of my mums said 'I was really awful to you last time you came. I can't think why you come back, but I knew you would'. I said I was a devil for punishment and we both had a good laugh."***
>
> **Viv, volunteer.**

Playing

When parents play with the innocence and energy of a child, then they are truly involved in playful parenting, which I believe to be vital. For some parents though, this is a whole new experience.

> ***"They're very jealous of their three and four-year-olds, if they seriously win the game".***
>
> **Barbara, volunteer.**

One Dad always sat in the room, hiding behind his newspaper when the volunteer visited. He pretended that his wife, children and the volunteer didn't exist. One day, they were playing 'hunt the matchbox'. After ten minutes or so, the volunteer, when it was her turn, popped the matchbox into the dangling heel of Dad's slipper. She probably tickled his foot as she did so. He put down the newspaper and for the first time, began to join in the fun.

Beth and Andy both had learning difficulties. When they had a son after 15 years of marriage, they over-protected him. At the age of two he was bottle-fed every four hours and nursed like a baby, unless he was strapped into

his pushchair in front of the television. A Home-Start volunteer who had been visited herself and who lived down the road, began to visit them daily. She gained their trust and they delighted in watching the volunteer playing with their son. They started to copy her and then eventually accepted her suggestion that he would enjoy the local nursery. Seven years later, the boy was attending the local school - a normal, active child.

"We do not stop playing because we grow old: we grow old because we stop playing".

Anonymous.

Playfulness can be positively infectious. We all need play-time fun-time – parents and children alike.

Mutuality

At first, when things are difficult, the volunteer naturally gives her all to the family she visits. But then usually, as things settle down and their relationship develops, it often becomes more mutual, with a parent asking *"Have you been up all night too?"* or *"I've just put the kettle on. You look as if you need a cuppa too."* This is the stage at which change for the better in a family's life can really begin – when there is giving and taking.

We found that when volunteers involved families with their own lives - their homes, their own families, friends, gardens or occasionally a farm - with shared outings and opportunities, it literally helped them to experience a different world. It could widen the parents' vision of what *is* possible and what it can really mean to have and to be a friend.

"I was just a young mother with two pre-school children, looking forward to meeting the challenge, befriending and sharing the problems of other parents. On reflection (25 years later) due to a total lack of experience, I really had no comprehension of the commitment or the difficulties that becoming a volunteer would entail, and just how much my life and future learning would become enriched by Home-Start. It was a total involvement, which would change and shape the pattern of my future life."

Stephanie, volunteer.

Having none of the trappings of the professional worker, the volunteer is just herself – another parent. It is entirely appropriate to ask her about herself, her family, her feelings; it is equally appropriate for the family to want to give something in return.

> **A volunteer asked the formally abusive mother, if she would look after HER children while she went to the dentist. It was amazing how such a jolt, could suddenly jettison a parent into unexpected altruism.**

The opportunity for mutuality, is an invaluable component of the Home-Start relationship.

> **A volunteer had three boys of her own, all with disabilities. The mother she visited cycled round to her home one day, to give her a surprise. When she discovered their living conditions, she said *"Oh, don't come to me anymore. You've got more than enough to do here. Can I come and give YOU a hand?"* It worked out well.**

> ***"Being a volunteer isn't all about giving; we get so much in return. It is so rewarding, seeing the children thrive, as their mums become happier and more confident."***
>
> **Christine, volunteer.**

> ***"We were free to make mistakes, so we would learn as two mothers growing and learning together."***
>
> **Sandra, volunteer.**

Home-Start can draw out kindness, which so often can be lying dormant.

> ***"Nowadays families aren't so materially deprived. Ours had nothing. I really used to warn them against the loan sharks and rather than lending them money, would fill up her cupboard with food. When I went next time, one mother insisted on buying me a plant. You should have seen the beam on Dad's face, as he said he wanted me to know how grateful they were. It's always a question of give and take."***
>
> **Peggy, volunteer.**

"At Christmas they gave me a lamp, which was obviously stolen. I thought, I'd better accept it, but I did say don't do it again!"

Viv, volunteer.

Patsy was overwhelmed, depressed and had no money for pet food, though it was Sandy and the cats that gave her more pleasure than the boys. Nevertheless, on my second visit she had sorted out a bag of her children's clothes *"for any poor kiddies you know Margaret."*

Rights and responsibilities are an inherent part of family life. Parents who have been visited, and become Home-Start volunteers themselves, in turn often undertake responsibility for contributing to their neighbourhood. The sense of achievement when parents who had been on the receiving end of services, sometimes for generations, began to contribute to re-energising their own community, was immeasurable. It made everyone else think they could do it too – friends, neighbours, members of the extended family. It also gave hope to the professionals.

Fun and Laughter.

Laughter really is the best medicine. When many parents begin to laugh again, we know that the real healing has begun.

One day, I turned up as planned to one of the families I visited myself. They were out. So I stuffed a note through the door, saying I'd pop back at the same time the next day. When I arrived, Paul the dad, who was six feet tall and known for his heavy hand, opened the door, and before I could get in a word, hissed *"Cor Margaret, your writing's so bad, I had to take your note down the chemist for 'im to read it to me!"*

One mother told me that she had felt so upset, she had thought of going to the church opposite, to pray. But then she said she never did that anyway, and was afraid that if she started, the church might come tumbling down on top of her.

"I'm going to divorce the lot of them."

Carol, mother.

So often, the humour of the parents we support is completely unexpected and positively infectious.

I received a delightful postcard once, depicting a scenario with a fractious child, fraught mother, and father in the armchair behind his newspaper:
Child to mother, *"What's an orgasm?"*
Mother to child, *"I dunno. Ask yer father."*
Father to child, *"I think it stands for 'Ome-start Regenerates Giggling And Supports Mums."*

Kindness

Kindness is composed of thoughtfulness, gentleness, tolerance and a respect for the dignity of others. Expressing it, is an expression of one's own value system.

> ***As*** **a Home-Start volunteer walked in the park with a young mother and her very active two-year-old one day, the mother sighed *"I really don't know what to do with her. She's got a will of her own and never does as she's told"*. To which the volunteer replied that perhaps she might try to be firm but kind. *"What is 'kind'?"* asked the parent.**

Some people cannot remember ever having experienced kindness. Some cannot remember ever having been kind to someone else. But in Home-Start there is a lot of it about, and it too is very infectious.

Language

The words we use and the images we convey, speak volumes about each of us - the person we are.

Often though, words are not needed to connect with another person. It is compassion and understanding, which can lead to a sense of hope that things really will get better.

Emotional Support/ Memories

I am touched by the number of times I meet original parents, children (often now adults), volunteers and professionals with whom we worked so closely over the years. Invariably we begin our conversation where we last left off, all those years ago. Sometimes they even begin their sentence with *"And Margaret, d'you remember when . . . ."*

Emotional memory affects us all. Recently, at Leicester station, I met a mother whose toddler used to chew the windowsills. I had to check myself from immediately enquiring about him, only doing so in the end of our chat, after we had reminisced about so much else that had been happening at the time.

Love

Quite simply, when love is genuine, it can change the world. What motivates and nurtures love, is complex. But in Home-Start there is a lot of it about. Showing love to a family, by being with them regularly, can be joyful and healing in so many ways, to family and volunteer alike.

Love creates unity, co-operation and connectedness. Within the organisation, I invariably signed my letters "with love".

Relationships

Relationships are the foundation of everything else in Home-Start.

Engaging in relationships involves motivation, emotion and action. Just how does it work, beyond intuition?

What we think and feel can affect our physical and mental health. Learning from their volunteer, to think and to act positively can so easily have a real impact on the day-to-day life of a family.

I believe we need more learning opportunities, about building strong and committed relationships throughout our organisation – adult-to-adult, staff-to-staff, parent-to-parent, parent-to-child(ren).

PRACTICAL HELP

Practical help can take many forms, including tidying up, collecting a prescription, or visiting the GP, health clinic or hospital. Sometimes when the volunteer goes with the family, she can help with explanations. For example, when Mary was suicidal and Winifred, the volunteer, accompanied her to the doctor, she was able to explain exactly what was really going on in Mary's life, rather than that she was deranged.

Similarly, when Josh went to the hospital to have his leg plaster for a clicky hip removed, Peggie, the volunteer, was available to give him and his mother a lift. She could then explain to the doctor, that Josh had used his comb to scratch the irritation down his leg, so that finding it inflamed and infested with lice, came as no surprise.

For some of us, cooking a meal can be magical, creative and practical. It can be done alone or together, involving co-operation and inter-dependence, ecology and economy. It can contribute to both physical and mental health. Often it was important to cook with a family in their home, perhaps using the only saucepan available or occasionally heating food over the fire when the gas or electricity had been disconnected.

By performing practical tasks together, the volunteer and the parent can learn to trust each other and to talk openly. They can plan, share ideas and celebrate differences.

> ***"I visited a young single Asian mother and her young child. I soon realised that she could neither read nor write, so that became the focus of my visits. She was thrilled and I was thrilled too with her progress. It made all the difference."***
>
> **Christine, volunteer.**

Although we had only a handful of male volunteers during those early years, nevertheless, there were very many other men involved in the scheme – husbands, partners, sons. Home-Start's success owed much to the close support they provided for the families too – help with transport, fixing a new door after a burglary, or putting safety catches onto cupboard doors, where there was an over-adventurous toddler. In those days we took it for granted that it was the men who helped with such practical tasks.

Together, we learned from experience that all families live family life differently. Their time clocks are different. – crack of dawn to dusk. . . midday to midnight. Their homes are different - varying from the single room with rat poison, to the cold, damp, vast vicarage. Life might be lived in a high rise, council house or flat, or in an owner-occupied home with an impossible mortgage. Life varies according to location too, whether in a rural area, coal mining community or inner city street.

> **One volunteer met the local midwife, whose leg was in plaster. Enquiring what had happened, the reply was quite natural –*"Oh, I fell out of the horse-box where I had been delivering the traveller's baby!"***

In all these varied living spaces, Home-Start could adapt. By working in the home, the volunteers saw the problems where they existed and built on what the parents had and what they really needed.

> **One parent, who simply could not cope with her extremely active toddler who pulled everything off the shelves of the supermarket as she pushed the baby in the trolley, learned a practical tip from her volunteer. *"When mine was at that stage, I used to give him two handsful of pennies to hold for me as we went in, telling him that he could help me pay for everything at the end. He felt so grown-up."***

A family accustomed to lurching from crisis to crisis could learn ways to look forward, to anticipate the new. Once their vulnerability was accepted, their self-esteem and imagination would grow in new ways. *"What shall we do next time I come?"* Together with their volunteer they would often think, imagine and plan – good T.I.P!

CASE CONFERENCES

> ***"I was aware that I had enormous influence on the mother, who talked to me very openly. I didn't realise that the professionals had to make such big decisions on such little experience of the family. Were they just covering their own backs?"***
>
> **Christine, volunteer.**

Attending case-conferences added a completely different dimension to Home-Start volunteering. I attended several courses on these, discussed them with my Support Group and we came to several conclusions.

- A Home-Start representative would only attend case conferences, if we knew we could speak positively about the family. *"Yes, I know about the bruising, but they had new tricycles for Christmas and both boys spend the day going round and round the flat on them. Yes, we know the mother is at her wits end and we try to take the family out as often as we can."*
- As parents ourselves, we were realistic about the need for most 18 month-olds to wear crash helmets most of the time. Normal tumbles and bumps were expected. Most mothers told us of their extreme aggravation at times, but few then actually acted on it. Family life is

full of tensions, frustrations, noise and anger. That is precisely why so many families need the support of a Home-Start volunteer.

- Sometimes I attended the case conference on behalf of the volunteer; occasionally they went alone and whenever possible we were there together. Occasionally we felt it would be inappropriate to go at all. We knew we could have been subpoenaed, or witness summonsed, but in practice this never happened.
- The first ever time I asked a social worker whether the parent could also attend the case conference, I was treated like someone from another planet. Yet to me it seemed such a natural request. After all, who better to present her case, than the mother herself, especially with the Home-Start volunteer at her side? This was gradually allowed more and more, even if the parent was only invited in for the last half of the conference. Most parents were amazed to find just how many professionals were actually involved with their family - from the GP, to the health visitor, social worker, police and many others. Parents often commented on how caring the professional workers were in that setting. It seemed to me that there was always a greater willingness to co-operate and help to change things, when parents could have a say, or at least a listen, themselves.
- Occasionally we were invited to the case conference of a family we were not yet visiting, knowing the likelihood that Home-Start would be invited to begin to support them. We were clear though, that we would not take on this responsibility if the family was told *"either your child will be taken into care or placed on the Child Protection Register, or you must have a Home-Start volunteer"*. Home-Start, we constantly emphasised, was 'voluntary' and 'on offer', with no force or control, - only genuine choice. The professionals were encouraged to present the possibility of having a Home-Start volunteer, to a family in a positive way.

Home-Start was always sent the notes of the case-conferences we attended, which helped us to provide realistic support for the volunteer and the family concerned.

SOME HOME-START OUTCOMES

So often, it amazed me how the volunteers, working with some of the most vulnerable families, could spin golden opportunities from everyday monochrome events.

> ***"I can't bake and have always wanted to," she said. "Right, next week we will start with scones!" She was delighted and so proud of her results. She wanted to progress to sponge cakes and a Christmas cake as the season was close. She did so well and started making birthday cakes for family and friends. Soon she was taking orders for Christmas cakes and so building up a little business, which gave her so much confidence. In turn this reflected on her children, who have all turned out so well."***
>
> **Peggy, volunteer**

Whenever families were referred, we emphasised that our task was to support them with friendship, confident that together, we could prevent more serious difficulties from developing, rather than being able to provide treatment or a cure.

In practice, in the first four years, 100% of the social workers and health visitors who had referred families, acknowledged that there had been either 'considerable change' (55% and 89% respectively) or 'some change' (45% and 11%). The volunteers and I sometimes felt we had been less successful, rating 'no change' in 13% and 10% of the families respectively. (Willem van der Eyken "Home-Start a Four Year Evaluation".)

> **Jenny was on 'nerve tablets', talked incessantly, while her three young children, without a toy in sight, sat on the bare floorboards, with frozen stares. When I introduced her, Viv the volunteer, rolled up a discarded envelope and began rolling it to each child in turn, whilst listening intently to Jenny's woes. Eventually one of the children rolled the paper ball to his mother. Jenny stopped talking, rolled it back to him, and was I thought, interacting with him for the first time ever.**

When after three months I visited Jenny again, with the volunteer, the changes were astonishing. *"We're more like sisters, Viv and me"*, beamed Jenny. She had come off her tablets, was proud of her children and had begun to respond to them and their needs. After a year of visiting, the speech therapist told us that the boys' speech had developed beyond everyone's expectations.

"One thing not often mentioned about Home-Start is its educative role: pamphlets on everything under the sun, well-intentioned, carefully prepared, glossily printed, more often than not do not reach targets. Home-Start has ways of spreading help with difficult children, overwhelmed parents, diet, housekeeping, health. Further, volunteers themselves are able to learn from their experiences of the way people live which is different from their own. So simply, this can add to mutual understanding in communities".

Alan Laurie, Marriage Guidance Counsellor.

"Watching her playing with and cuddling her two young children after months of acknowledging their existence as a burden, gave me endless pleasure".

Averil, volunteer.

Anna was a young girl who had been brought up in care. She had her first baby when she was 15. He died a cot death at 11 weeks. The distraught Anna quickly became pregnant again and a hospital social worker asked Home-Start for a motherly volunteer, to support Anna through pregnancy and after the baby was born.

Marie, a volunteer whose own children had left home and who was looking forward to being a grandmother herself, began to support Anna. Together they took her urine samples to the Infirmary, planned for the baby and got on well.

It was a surprise therefore, when one day Anna said *"I don't want you to come anymore. I've got a probation officer, social worker, doctor, midwife, health visitor and it's all too much." "Well"*, said Marie, *"you have to have the others, they are professionals who can help you, but I'm only a volunteer, so it is really your choice. I don't have to come if you don't want me."* Anna thought for a while, and then with a shy glance said, *"Oh, alright then, you can come if you want."*

What she was demonstrating, was that because we have

no authority to be there, the power to choose really was in her hands. In Home-Start we call this the power of powerlessness.

Marie was at Anna's side when the baby was born and Auntie Marie became the family's best friend.

In a very few situations, Home-Start was unable to help in the long-term. One Home-Start volunteer who had supported a young mother and her three children for almost two years, moved away from Leicester. There was no other volunteer available and within just a few weeks the co-habitee was in prison and the three children removed into care.

On another occasion the neighbour told a mother that her children must be stupid if she needed a teacher coming to her at home every week. The mother misinterpreted the volunteer's intentions and told her not to come again.

Health and Education

Creating stable, coping, happy families is an investment in their long-term future. It is now well acknowledged by primary health teams, that our mental and emotional well-being, our sense of purpose, of fun and of being needed, have a direct effect on our health.

Similarly, early education begins at home, between parents and children together.

When volunteers have high expectations of the parents, often the most amazing changes occur. *"You might want to go to teacher training college one day"*, or *"You could offer to help out **your** neighbour, when you can hear that she is at the end of her tether."* So often parents do.

The late Mia Kellmer Pringle, Director of the National Children's Bureau, said that what every child needs to develop, is love and security, praise and recognition, new experiences and responsibility. In Home-Start we are clear that it is the parents who need these first themselves, before they can even begin to meet the needs of their developing children.

Ending Family Visits

The starting and finishing points for all Home-Start work with families must be where the family wants it to be. The objectives then are their objectives, with the volunteer there as catalyst – encouraging, reassuring, praising, extending and

Gwen Flowers and early volunteers at the summer launch.

David and Gerald.

Jane with her Grandchildren.

Val and Janet and children at the Christmas party.

Vivienne and family.

Parents at the annual party.

Peggie who was asked "what is kind?"

Tony, as always full of tales to tell.

Sylvia and family.

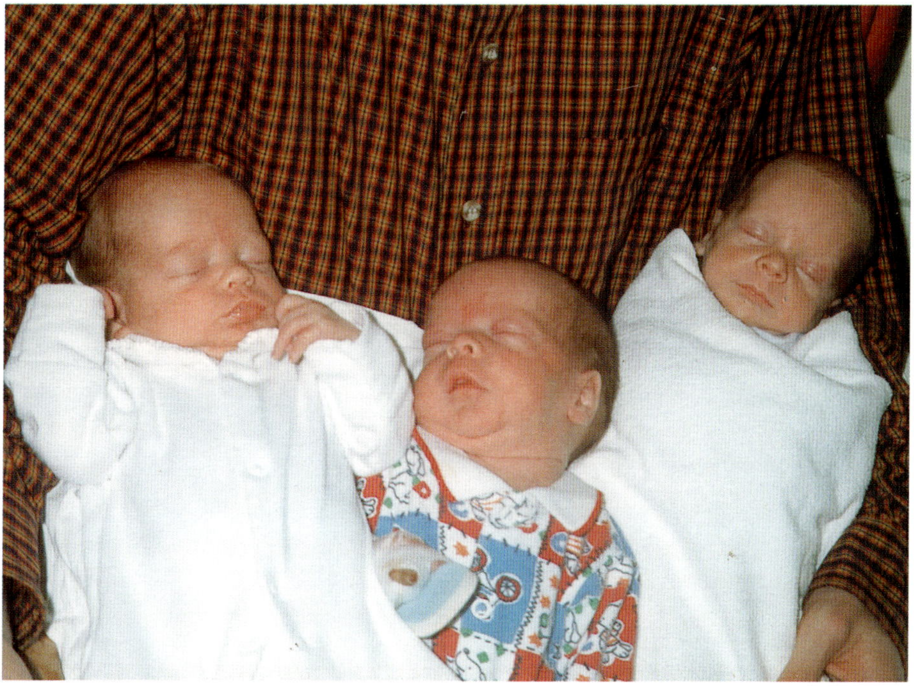

Three at once, what a handful!

Kathy at the annual party.

Face painting ....oh what fun!

Party time again.

Wendy and Barry and their family.

Early volunteers Rosemary and Tuesday (Peggy).

Marie and Geoff Stead were with Home-Start in Leicester for 25 years.

being realistic.

The volunteer's work is finished when the family members feel much more in control of their lives again, when family relationships are being worked at rather than suffered, and when the family has the confidence to use other people and resources available to them. Those who, at that stage, do not choose to become volunteers themselves, often do help their own neighbours or become involved in a responsible way within their community. *"I've joined the Child Poverty Action Group now,"* Paul told me.

The visits might end when the volunteer no longer visits 'officially' – i.e. no longer receives her expenses or support in relation to the family. But friendships may last and that is a matter between the volunteer and the family. Many of the original volunteers report still being in touch after 27 years – the next generation. On the other hand, this is certainly not a requirement.

> ***"Mehru and I are still in touch and have been friends now for 25 years. I went to Kersi's wedding recently in Reading."***
>
> **Kathryn, volunteer.**

Some volunteers (myself included), who have kept in touch with families who have become good friends over the years, are now involved with the next generation. This is an extension of our own grandparenthood – an immense privilege, watching and being with successive generations.

But realistically too . . . .

> ***"I'm afraid it would be just impossible to keep up friendships with all of the families I've visited over 25 years. We have to move on just as they do."***
>
> **Peggy, volunteer.**

Sometimes parents, for whom Home-Start support had ended, re-referred themselves months or even years later, saying that they recognised the need for another infusion of nurturing and friendship. Perhaps they had had a recent significant event in their lives, such as a birth, a death, a separation or a move. Sometimes the children had reached another significant stage in their development, proving to be unmanageable.

PATTERNS OF VISITING – The Simple and the Complex

In our 1976/77 Annual Report, written mainly for the Department of Health and Social Security and for Leicester Social Services Department, who together provided our Urban Aid Grant (75% and 25% respectively), I looked back at the varying approaches, successes and difficulties experienced in the course of visiting. Two distinct patterns had emerged.

SIMPLE

a) The Home-Start volunteer and family bond successfully, possibly because reciprocal expectations are fulfilled. *("It's so good to have someone outside the family that I can talk to."* Or *"They say I've got puerperal depression. My Mum doesn't understand, my neighbour's out at work. Now I'm on the tablets and Peggie, Dorothy and Moira each come in twice a week, I know me and the baby will be alright.")*

b) Communication is good. Problems are shared and tackled either together or by the parent alone, with the Home-Start volunteer's support and encouragement.

c) Generally the parents gain confidence and competence and the volunteer withdraws after anything between three months and three years.

d) The family can still contact Home-Start or their Home-Start volunteer if ever required for support again in the future. Some families are on their feet and launched, others have developed a real friendship and still keep in touch with one another anyway.

COMPLEX

Total Dependence

The family accepts the Home-Start volunteer, either actively or passively ("Oh alright then, she can come if she wants") and rapidly becomes totally dependent on her.

Testing Period

This might happen any time from within a few weeks of the initial visit, right up to a year later. It can take many forms:

i. The family is out when the Home-Start volunteer calls, or hurls abuse (and sometimes mattresses too).

ii. The husband/partner might decide he doesn't like a volunteer coming into the home. We are quite clear that it is our privilege to be invited in and that it has to be on the family's terms. If we are rejected, we accept this, but do inform the health visitor/original referrer, so that it is clear that we are no longer involved. Twice this led to a case conference being called, so that our respective jobs could be re- defined.

iii. One of the parents is openly hostile to the Home-Start volunteer. *"I told her to bugger off and she couldn't get out quick enough. I thought she was going through the letter box!"*

iv. Family circumstances change drastically – e.g. partners split up; children are removed into care; mental or physical health of the parent deteriorates, necessitating hospitalisation.

Mutual Disenchantment

Sometimes this coincides with a period of ill-health or extra family responsibilities in the Home-Start volunteer's own life. (One volunteer resented the warm three bed-roomed house provided by the council for the family she visited, when her own son and his new wife were struggling to cope in a small damp cottage they were renting at the same time.) Anyway, whatever the exact circumstances, disenchantment is usually mutual between the volunteer and the parents she is visiting.

Support

To cope with the above, an extra infusion of support is necessary all round.

i. It might simply be that the Home-Start volunteer needs to 'talk it out' either directly with the family, or with the Organiser or with whoever has referred the family.

ii. Maybe all that is needed is a joint visit with the Organiser to boost the Home-Start volunteer and bring some reality back into the situation.

iii. Occasionally the Home-Start volunteer might react quite spontaneously to being tested, sometimes becoming angry with the family. This honesty can be very motivating. Support for the volunteer from the original referrer or the Organiser, is always available.

iv. Sometimes the professionals are asked to give extra support. On other occasions, the Home-Start volunteer pulls out all the stops, and arranges a massive infusion of extra support.

Turning Point

Having surmounted this testing period (apart from the very few families where the Home-Start volunteer really was rejected or she herself decided not to continue visiting), this has been the turning point for innumerable families. It is at this stage that the mutual respect between parents and volunteer develops, and the ability to cope really begins.

One Home-Start volunteer, who had been with Home-Start for three years and then left to begin a three-year degree course, summed it all up beautifully, when she wrote to me:

> ***"When the honeymoon was over and I was heartily tired of the work, only the commitment to the mum helped me through the inevitable period of disenchantment. But sticking with it through this period was when the work and the growing for both, I felt, really started. Thank you Margaret for giving me the chance to gain from such memorable experiences."***
>
> **Judith, volunteer.**

Families coping again

With many families where this complex pattern of visits has emerged, it is definitely the Home-Start volunteers who have had the stickability and optimistic determination that something could be done, who have had the most dramatic results. Families who seemed to be inextricably entwined in a mesh of insoluble problems are now coping with their own lives and even in turn helping others. Some are barely aware what has wrought the change, while others say openly *"Home-Start has changed my life."*

We all learned a great deal together from these different patterns of the way visiting developed. Mutuality was significant, even if it was the Organiser helping the volunteer to identify what she was getting out of her involvement. We also learned to lower our expectations and sharpen our awareness of many different ways of doing things and of being a family.

THE VOLUNTEERS

The mother-to-mother or parent-to-parent approach, is clearly the most significant relationship in the whole of Home-Start.

Volunteers can provide six things, which are difficult or impossible for professional workers. These were as relevant in the early days as they are now:

- **Time** – on average volunteers spend four hours each week with each family they visit, with no contract and no time constraint. They are simply able to be with the family for as long as they are really needed, or for as long as they are able to stay.
- **Flexibility** – they can be responsive to what a parent feels would be most helpful on a particular day, like going back to bed for a sleep, cooking a meal, amusing the children, talking together about something other than children, getting out of the home, or just doing things together, like going for a picnic or to the park.
- **A mutual relationship** – the parent and the volunteer give and take from their relationship in a reciprocal way, which benefits both, though this does not always happen at the beginning of visiting. *"As I left, the mother took a picture off the wall and insisted I take it."* Sylvia, volunteer.
- The Home-Start volunteer **does not represent authority,** being neither paid nor formally 'trained' for her relationship with a particular family.
- There is **no other agenda,** other than to meet the needs of the family.
- The Home-Start volunteer provides **emotional support** for the whole family. A simple phrase like *"I'll come back tomorrow, because I can see you are having a difficult time"*, or just looking into the eyes of a parent with admiration and a smile can be more potent than anything else.

Many volunteers have gone on to train as counsellors, teachers, for the church, or for health and social work. They were very clear that what they provided as just another parent, was their intuition and their parenting ploys. Their patience and friendship transcended anything more formal for the families they supported. They were accepted because they were parents – not paid, no clever training, no formal qualification for their voluntary work, no PhD in psychology, no contracts, no time constraints.

> ***"Sometimes I felt frightened and bewildered, because Home-Start led me into places like Court and the Benefits Office with my family, that I'd never experienced before or since. I thought 'They're trusting me!' It's a big responsibility."***
>
> **Sylvia, volunteer.**

Volunteers report different effects on their own families:

> ***"My daughters were supportive, but my son thought I was wasting my time." "My husband always said it might be Home-Start for me, but it was certainly Home-Stop for him!"***

Unfortunately there were a few occasions when - after years of a volunteer carefully building up self-esteem in a family - a doctor, a teacher or another professional would undermine the parent or child with one quick derogatory phrase, suggesting their stupidity or worthlessness. Several excellent volunteers thought their time had been wasted, because the family took the view that the professional must be right.

> ***"We knew we were pioneers. We nearly all claimed our expenses, because Margaret was keen that our own families shouldn't be out of pocket."***
>
> **Stephanie, volunteer.**

> ***"Home-Start then was fun, friendly and supportive. We felt helpful and cheerful. The government wasn't so involved in those days, so we could be more intuitive."***
>
> **Barbara, volunteer.**

Some volunteers restricted their contact to planned regular visits; others included their families in their own daily lives.

> **When I asked Marie, our longest serving Home-Start volunteer at the time, why she was still with Home-Start in Leicester after 25 years, she replied that when you take something on, you don't expect to leave it. Home-Start for her she said, had been full of variety, insights, individual families, group work, time on the management committee, time out for her daughter's wedding and then involvement with her husband too, once he had retired.**

I gained immense respect for the qualities and skills of the Home-Start volunteers – often quite unexpected. They genuinely came from all walks of life, all backgrounds ages, stages and cultures. Some had immense problems of their own. But through their relationships with families, everyone gained and everyone grew. The few who felt they didn't, left.

Volunteers Stella and Anne had both been teachers. They felt that for them, understanding the home background was really important. They both said they learned so much from being with families at home, where their lives and their problems existed, rather than just becoming frustrated with the children at school.

SUSTAINING AND MOTIVATING VOLUNTEERS

SUPPORT FOR HOME-START VOLUNTEERS

It has been said that Home-Start visiting is possibly one of the most demanding types of voluntary work, requiring long-term commitment, energy, enthusiasm, optimism, an unfailing sense of humour and endless patience. In order to sustain these qualities, it was essential to provide each volunteer with a framework of support.

Instinctively, I dislike the word 'supervision', which encompasses a sense of superiority – a better vision – implying that one person might see more clearly than the other. A mutual exchange of support is preferable, where 'my' insight might be dependent on learning from 'your' experiences. Together the volunteer and I could discuss the reality of the situation and then both gain by releasing and realising the extraordinary possibilities, which existed.

We provided support for our Home-Start volunteers in the following ways:

Individual Formal Support

Regularly, one-to-one with the Organiser, in the office, the volunteer's home, over lunch or a drink together, or anywhere else by mutual arrangement. As my volunteers used to tell me regularly, *"We do all the work Margaret, while you just make us coffee and talk about it with us!"*
Occasionally it was expedient for a volunteer to meet with the referrer or the family's health visitor, usually in the Home-Start office, but always with the knowledge of the parents.

Group Support

Regularly once a month or so, usually with groups of up to 10 volunteers with the Organiser in the office. First names only of families visited were used. Somehow, laughter always pervaded our support sessions (and the courses of preparation). Laughter really is a great leveller when people come from very different backgrounds, with widely different experiences and expectations. Laughter can also break down barriers of fear. When a group of people come together to fulfil a common purpose – a willingness to support families - then differences recede and an amazing sense of togetherness develops. With all the inherent fun, a common spot is touched in our shared humanity.

> ***"Even though families had serious problems, we could see the funny side when we were together."***
>
> **Lynne, volunteer.**

Laughter often occurred once very difficult circumstances had been acknowledged. In so doing we were expressing our deep-rooted hope that life for the family could improve.

Collateral Support.

One-to-one support between two volunteers often developed spontaneously as friendships within the team, grew naturally. Others met each other bi-monthly in small groups of six or seven volunteers, either in a room at the office, or in each others' homes. Usually the host(ess) volunteer led the meeting. We learned that the collateral support meetings did not work when only four or less volunteers grouped together, because if one had to miss the meeting, two others invariably cancelled.
Usually, brief notes of significant issues or suggestions were recorded, to be discussed with me at our one-to-one support meetings.

Support through on-going learning opportunities.

For all volunteers, group discussions with an invited speaker were arranged periodically in response to particular problems, which arose in the course of their visiting. For example, our 1976 diary indicates that discussions were around

- ★ The essential differences between voluntary home visiting and the role of the social worker.
- ★ The role of the volunteer in visiting people diagnosed as mentally ill.

- ★ Film "Terrible Twos and Trusting Threes", followed by discussion.
- ★ A Play morning – group participation in practical play ideas.
- ★ Anxieties and feelings experienced by Home-Start volunteers when visiting families.

In addition, Home-Start volunteers were always invited to **special lectures and discussions** organised by Professor Martin Herbert at the Leicester University School of Social Work and Jill Warner/Ingles at the Leicester Royal Infirmary Student Training Unit. Some of the topics included:

- ★ The End of the Boom – Social Work in a Cold Light.
- ★ Background and Development of Children in One-Parent Families.
- ★ Prejudice – a Saturday course organised by the WEA.
- ★ The Cycle of Deprivation in Practice. Does Family History really repeat itself?
- ★ The Future of Community Medicine.
- ★ Marital/Sexual Problems.
- ★ Behaviour Modification in Family Therapy.
- ★ Behaviour Modification in Pre-school Children.

Such opportunities extended our knowledge and experience and stimulated many volunteers to go on to further learning. We all benefited and the talks were even free of charge. Their breadth and depth encouraged our best practice as well as our thinking.

Informal Support.

Every year, Home-Start volunteers had the opportunity to attend specially arranged Christmas/Summer lunches, group bookings at a restaurant, or parties in volunteers' homes. Some volunteers did not participate in the social gatherings, preferring to do their voluntary work, but clear that they had their own network of friends and family. For other volunteers, these opportunities provided a much-needed opportunity to widen their own circle of friends.

Volunteers, as well as most families, had my home phone number and the office number. This was never abused, but meant that they could make contact, when it was essential to do so.

Some volunteers gave parents their own home details, but this was left to their own discretion.

After I had run three courses of preparation, with 13 volunteers on each, I began to realise that I needed to keep my own record of when and how often I had been in touch with, or supported each of them. Quite simply, I bought an exercise book with squares, wrote the month and days across the top of each page, wrote the volunteers' names down one side, and then against each, recorded face-to-face contact, (red tick), telephone contact (blue tick), letters sent and received from volunteers, and their holiday dates. I was constantly amazed how time whizzed by and how so often when I thought I had had at least monthly contact with a volunteer, it was sometimes twice that long.

I learned to work and value each volunteer individually. Whenever a general letter was sent, inviting them to a particular meeting, I would always mention it during a support session, or phone them too, so that each felt personally invited and needed. It worked for us all, because when they turned up, I too felt validated.

Many families never acknowledge all that the involvement of another parent, a Home-Start volunteer, has meant to them. They find it hard to say thank you. So I believe it is important that the organiser shows appreciation to the volunteers, acknowledging, often after joint visits, some of the changes which have evidently occurred through her presence and perseverence.

"All volunteers need a feel-good feedback."

Peggie, organiser.

There were occasions when I was painfully aware of the responsibility of introducing a Home-Start volunteer into a shocking and seemingly intractable family situation, knowing that it would require deep, emotional commitment, which would inevitably affect the volunteer as well as the parents and children. Occasionally we sought professional advice from outside the organisation, to provide the very best support for the volunteer.

We considered it to be an advantage that each volunteer undertook to visit (at least!) two families, so that there could be contrast and balance for the volunteer. Often this would prevent her from becoming too absorbed by the problems of one particular family.

> ***"I would like to pay tribute to Margaret's leadership. She was always there for her volunteers, she never seemed impatient or angry, but would always spend time talking over our families and their problems and giving new leads for us to follow. This she did cheerfully and with great compassion."***
>
> **Vivienne, volunteer.**

A REFRESHER COURSE AND ON-GOING TRAINING FOR VOLUNTEERS

In March 1979, a series of five meetings were held for experienced Home-Start volunteers. At their request, these included talks by and discussions with:

- Willem van der Eyken – on the context and validity of Home-Start visiting.
- Helen Henry, Marriage Guidance Counsellor and chairman of our Support Group, who talked with us about approaches to counselling and sexual difficulties.
- Enid Hague, on children in care, included a visit to her Childrens' Home.
- Professor Martin Herbert, on approaches to problems and difficulties of early childhood.
- Denis Rice on interpersonal relationships.

We felt privileged in Leicester, to have friends and colleagues who combined national reputations with local knowledge.

A few Home-Start volunteers became involved in local authority Planning and Advisory Committees in different areas of the city. These were ideal opportunities to network extensively with our colleagues from other agencies, which really benefited Home-Start during those early pioneering days.

EXTENDING THE FAMILY'S WORLD

FAMILY GROUPS

Towards the end of our first full year of Home-Start, in 1974, the local Family Service Unit, which had just re-decorated and equipped its playroom, invited us to use it. Thursday mornings became Home-Start Family Group day, with parents and children brought in mostly by their volunteers. What busy, lively mornings these proved to be!

We genuinely shared joy and wonder, so that parents could be joyful and become wonderful. The original FSU social worker, Phil Cooke, who invited us in, used to joke when giving talks about the Unit, that Home-Start came in on Thursdays, and that 'our' children pissed in his files! That certainly highlighted the frequent sense of chaos!

At first we just met there. Parents and volunteers mingled, making drinks for each other, playing with groups of children or just sitting for a cigarette and a chat. After a month or so, with Christmas approaching, the parents decided it would be good to make decorations. This was followed by a Christmas party, with games and presents for each child and each adult, provided annually by the faith communities and the Voluntary Workers Bureau. Mr Bulman, a retired gentleman who drove families to the group each week, became the first Santa Claus.

We had also found a housebound elderly woman, who made the most wonderful stuffed toys if we paid for the materials, which we gladly did. She spent the next six years of her life, working to produce Christmas presents for Home-Start children.

There followed formal sessions, with speakers on keep fit, health, nutrition, make-up, and cookery. The Group produced the first ever Home-Start cookery book, with everyone pooling recipes. These had to be simple, low-cost and delicious. I still use mine to this day. We all agreed that the following Butterscotch Pudding, epitomised the Home-Start approach, including many relationships:

Butterscotch Pudding

4 oz. butter and 4 oz. sugar

Melt these together in a saucepan, until they are nearly burnt! Add most of one pint of milk, at which point it will sizzle and bubble alarmingly, but just keep stirring patiently round and round, until it all melts and blends.

Mix 11/4 rounded tablespoons cornflour with the rest of the milk.

Pour the warm milk butterscotch mixture onto the cornflour, stirring and blending.

Return it all to the pan and cook for 3 – 5 minutes more,

stirring all the time. Pour into a dish and cool. This pudding can be covered with whipped cream and toasted flaked almonds. It is sweet, delicious and comforting.

An elderly spinster lady, who lived opposite the Family Service Unit was always sweeping her steps on a Thursday morning as we arrived with the parents and children. She said she loved seeing young happy faces and that often she didn't talk to anyone else all week. After some time, we invited her in to join the group, and for a cup of coffee. She provided a cosy lap for many a child in need of a cuddle. She told us she really enjoyed the company.

More Family Groups

During the following few years, we started Family Groups in five other areas of Leicester city, where there were no other mother and toddler groups. Although I attended these sometimes, they were mostly co-ordinated by Home-Start volunteers and parents themselves, running on similar lines to our Family Service Unit group – a mixture of formality and informality. Volunteers and families were indistinguishable.

Stella, a particularly attractive volunteer, responsible for organising the Braunstone group, always wore a head scarf, tied at the nape of her neck. Within a few months, most of the mothers in the group were all wearing headscarves too.

Each of the groups held their own regular celebrations, parties, outings and had talks, with topics initiated by the parents. The Family Groups provided a stepping stone to the outside world, and a sympathetic environment in which parents and children could enjoy the company of others.

Through the Voluntary Workers' Bureau, we arranged for volunteer drivers (with specially negotiated insurance cover) to bring and return many families from home. Some of these volunteers were lonely themselves and valued the opportunity of being with us for the morning.

A difficult situation, which once arose in the group I attended, is still emblazened on my memory.

One morning, a mother asked me for money to *"buy food for the kiddies"*. She knew Home-Start did not provide money, but she also knew that in emergencies, we broke our own rules. So I gave her £5 and she gleefully popped to the shop opposite. Later that morning, without really thinking, I casually asked her what she had bought? *"Cigarettes and beer!"* . . . I was furious. She had deceived me. She could at least have told me she needed cigarettes as well as food for the children. I would have understood that. Instead, she had lied to me, which was unacceptable. We took them all back together, exchanging them for bread, honey and bananas. Then in the last minute we did also buy a packet of cigarettes. She kept saying *"sorry Margaret"* and to my relief continued coming to the Group. Some of the other mothers used to joke that *"you'd better watch out, or Margaret'll lose her rag!"*

> ***"My pet Family Group has been running for 22 years and I find such a delight in watching the children grow from babies into independent and confident school children. They love to come back too and say how they remember the happy times spent with us. They don't forget those early days."***
>
> **Peggy, volunteer and Family Group organiser.**

> ***"One of my best memories as a child was of a place I remember as the 'Family Centre'. The things I remember best were the Home-Start trips, the parties and the friends that I made during that time".***
>
> **Sheena, now a Home-Start volunteer herself.**

Divali, Eid, and Christmas were all celebrated in turn. We held celebratory parties for Home-Start parents and volunteers in a Working Men's Club each year. Some men chose to wear a tie; some women had their annual hair perm. The food was provided by a Home-Start mother, who enjoyed the infusion of cash before Christmas. The drink was paid for on the night. Some parents and volunteers organised funny games, which people still remind me of to this day, when I bump into them in Leicester.

PARENTS' EVENING MEETINGS

These developed in response to some parents saying they had no friends and never got out of the house. Generally we had evenings for parents twice each term, focussing our discussions on issues identified by the parents themselves –

- death in the family/changes in family life;
- a book a Dad had just read about a railway journey in Africa

(surprisingly popular evening, which led other parents to join the local library.);

- relationships with our children;
- coming out of clink and being a dad again.

Food and drink were important features, particularly when encouraging the men to attend. We had fish and chip suppers on our laps, or bacon butties. Beer and soft drinks were provided. Frequently the family's volunteer babysat for them, knowing the dates in advance and giving priority to the opportunity of giving the parents an evening out.

The parents' evening meetings improved understanding, communication and relationships. By providing a caring, informal environment. We found we removed barriers to learning. Some parents went on to attend literacy classes or other adult education opportunities.

HOME-START OUTINGS

The seaside at Skegness, the Farm Park at Guilsborough Grange, Twycross Zoo, Abbey Park, Victoria Park, the Co-operative College, all proved popular annual destinations for summer picnics and fun. Families visited farms belonging to volunteers or their friends. We were able literally to extend the world of many families, some of whom had never been out of Leicester. My own wish to go to the Derbyshire Dales instead of the seaside, was always outvoted.

Each year, we took large groups of children and their parents to the local Christmas pantomime. Each year, I know we annoyed other members of the public, with our Home-Start children who were intrigued by the seats which flipped up and down and who invariably unwrapped their sweets during the performance.

LIAISON WITH OTHER AGENCIES.

This was generally good. Home-Start volunteers and I talked at community lunches, the local teacher training college, had pub lunches with social workers and liaised with the Citizens' Advice Bureau, the Pre-School Playgroups Association and the Marriage Guidance Council.

In 1974/5 the National Volunteer Centre produced a report Creative

Partnerships – Between the Statutory and Voluntary Sectors in Leicester. We were told that with the active Voluntary Workers' Bureau and other voluntary organisations, including Home-Start, our city was unique in its voluntary efforts. The report was produced by Mary Bruce and Mark Rankin. Mary had been the first General Secretary of the Pre-School Playgroups Association in the early days. Subsequently, she took on many roles in Home-Start in Harrow.

From the day Home-Start began in Leicester, there was a steady flow of visitors. Many came through the DHSS, the National Children's Bureau and other national child-care organisations. Others were social workers, health visitors and other professionals, interested in this novel approach to supporting families. We also enjoyed visitors from other countries, including Australia, African countries, India, Japan, and the Netherlands. Some of these people are still in touch with me, to this day.

Three times a year, I used to meet four colleagues from other developing voluntary organisations, to compare notes and discuss ways of lobbying the government for more financial support to the voluntary sector. There were too many new initiatives, we thought, and too little endorsement of effective practice. We called ourselves the Over Fives Group, which involved Contact a Family, Crossroads Care Attendants Scheme, Carers' Association, the Alzheimers Association and Home-Start. We five women were immensely mutually supportive of each other and enjoyed our regular lunches.

EVALUATION BY WILLEM VAN DER EYKEN.

As part of the condition of our Urban Aid funding, I was to learn later, Home-Start had to undergo a formal evaluation.

> ***"As a Social Work Inspector for the region, I was asked to explore with Margaret Harrison, her willingness to take part in research. Very reluctantly she agreed, not really wanting any publicity or interference, and fearing that researchers wouldn't respect or understand the volunteers and their relationship with families. Fortunately her fears were shown to be groundless when Willem van der Eyken undertook this, and his book reveals the very promising start in Leicester, during Home-Start's first four years."***
>
> **Gillian Corsellis.**

Gillian was right. I did have to be persuaded by several people whose judgement I respected, that to allow Willem van der Eyken from the Social Science Research Council to evaluate our voluntary work would not be harmful for the families, the volunteers or our putative scheme in general.

Willem himself gently persuaded me simply to allow him to talk to referrers, families, volunteers, the Support Group and me. He would also discuss his descriptive study with the Social Services Department and with the Area Health Authority. It struck me that he was undertaking upside down research - from practice to theories and thence back again to practice. But I was also advised by the education department, that to have built in research from the beginning of our scheme, would have stunted our spontaneous and flexible approach.

Willem's concepts validated our motivation, intuition and general ways of supporting families. They gave us courage to continue. Through probing, thoughtful questions, he provoked reflection, discussion and movement. We became wiser. Our courses of preparation also improved immediately, for we gained confidence through his deeper insight. And what is more, Willem himself dared to learn from our practice.
(Home-Start: A Four-year evaluation published by Home-Start Consultancy, 1982 and 1990.)

ONGOING DEVELOPMENT OF HOME-START IN LEICESTER

The original Urban Aid Grant from November 1973, covered my part-time work as organiser until March 1977. During that time, I was brilliantly supported by many of the Home-Start volunteers, who undertook tasks beyond supporting families at home and in our Family Groups. Some of them helped regularly in the office, with mail-outs, collating and photocopying too. The Voluntary Workers' Bureau and I called them "Super Vols."

When our Urban Aid grant increased in 1977, we chose to appoint another part-time organiser, Wyn Laxton, rather than for me to work full-time. We had both expected to share the job as equals, but the reality was that I already had a long history with the scheme and it would have been more honest to acknowledge from the beginning, that I was senior in experience.

Some Facts From the First Home-Start Scheme in Leicester 1977

In May, the position was that Wyn and I were supporting 65 volunteers who were supporting 80 families at home and many others in the Family groups.

No. of Volunteers		No. of Families
38	HSVs visited one family each	38
14	HSVs visited two families each	28
4	HSVs visited three families each	12
4	HSVs were resting or helping at the Home-Start Family Group	–
3	HSVs were not matched	–
2	p/t organisers each visited a family	2
65		**80**

Two years later, in early 1979, at last all that we were undertaking to support families in Leicester, was recognised. We received local authority funding for three full-time workers and a full-time secretary. This meant that I would begin working full-time and that we could advertise the other jobs. Two long-standing and immensely able volunteers were appointed - Christine Tracey and Peggie Sinclair. Maria Brown, my husband's ex-secretary from industry before she started her own family, also joined us. Home-Start was accepted, buoyant and clearly here to stay.

Delighted that we were a staff team, we aimed at a healthy balance between our direct work with people – the referrers, volunteers, families, each other - and paperwork. Each of the three of us was responsible for a one third segment of the city of Leicester, with our own team of volunteers and families, just overlapping when appropriate. We started each week with a staff meeting, for planning and communicating together. We arranged regular one-to-one support sessions with each other, for motivation, learning and encouragement.

DEVELOPMENTS BEYOND THE LEICESTER SCHEME

Towards the end of the 1970s, other areas of Leicestershire had begun to establish Home-Start schemes of their own – Hinckley, through community worker Ken Lowles; Charnwood through Home-Start volunteer Kay Hancock, and Melton Mowbray eventually through Christine Tracey.

Another of our volunteers, Stephanie Besbrode, moved to Nottingham and initiated the first scheme there.

> ***"My time with Leicester Home-Start unfortunately only lasted a few years, as due to my husband's work we moved to Nottingham. I felt distraught at the enormous gap left by not visiting 'my' families. But urged on by Margaret's enthusiasm, I was able to discuss the possibility of setting up Home-Start in Nottingham when I got there, and the rest is history. Nottingham Home-Start celebrated its 21st. Anniversary last year."***
>
> **Stephanie, volunteer.**

In Ripley, Derbyshire, a small group of local statutory workers secured a grant from the Education department (what a coup!) and appointed Beryl Riley to organise the first scheme in their county in 1978.

By then we were also receiving many enquiries from all over the country. Huntingdon social services planned a voluntary scheme based on Home-Start, to be called Span. Gradually we found there were many exciting developments, all building on our experience of Home-Start in Leicester, working through volunteers to support families at home. Articles about our new way of offering support to families, were written in health and social work journals, as well as in women's magazines.

Then, at the end of March 1980, Major-General John Page, director of the London Law Trust, paid us a visit in our small cramped office at the back of the Leicester Council for Voluntary Service. His Trust had been approached for funding, by a man in Bristol, who envisaged launching Home-Plus. Richard Sykes' organisation would be based on Home-Start, plus additional health and education arms he told us.

At the end of the day, after John Page had talked with staff, volunteers and families, and said he had enjoyed the open sandwiches brought in from home, he suddenly made the pronouncement, which was to change my life and also that of Home-Start, irrevocably, forever:

Instead of funding the scheme in Bristol, he suggested, his London Law Trust chairman and trustees would be more inclined *"to help Home-Start to develop **nationally**"*. *"Oh! And also..."* he added, *"Home-Start could work with Service families abroad"*.

Well! Such suggestions were well beyond my vision. I remember laughing incredulously. But the next day he sent us all a bouquet of flowers, reiterating that his intentions were serious, and that we should be in touch if at anytime Home-Start wished to "go national".

By coincidence, at the very next Support Group meeting, Chris Beddoe, the social services representative expressed his concern that I was spending time assisting other areas of the country to develop Home-Start, whereas his department was providing the funding for our scheme in Leicester. Tentatively I mentioned the possible national funding from the London Law Trust, and almost in disbelief, John Page was invited to attend the very next meeting.

My world and my life changed from that moment on. Possible future models of the relationship between Home-Start in Leicester and the new national organisation were discussed. Would it be an extension of the local scheme, all under one roof, or would there be two completely separate organisations? To me it seemed so obvious that initially anyway, there should be strong and close links with our Leicester scheme, but to my complete horror the Support Group decided otherwise. There should be two separate organisations.

Immediately, I stated my belief, which I still hold to this day, that for people and other organisations seeking guidance about Home-Start, they would benefit from immediate access to the only well-established scheme at the time. They could meet and talk with the volunteers, the families, and the Support Group members, for inspiration and support. It would also be a wonderful opportunity for those in Leicester to learn about the needs of families and resources in other areas of the country, to gain a wider vision.

However, at the end of the meeting, I was given the stark options of staying with the Leicester scheme, or of running the new national organisation. Deeply upset, I expressed my shock to John Page on the way to the station. He simply replied, *"So you think you can do **three** jobs?"* *What?!* *"..continue your involvement with Leicester Home-Start, develop the national organisation **and** look after your family and home?"*

> ***"Margaret was in no way ambitious, but in effect was doing two full time jobs at the time – running Home-Start in Leicester, and also helping it to develop in other parts of the country that wanted it. We encouraged her to accept money to "go national" from the London Law Trust and her own modesty was overcome as reality broke."***
>
> **Rachel Carmichael, then the newly appointed director of the Council for Voluntary Service.**

I cried, I agonised, and finally decided that I would after all take the new national job. But, it was an immensely hard decision to make. By then, we had 100 Home-Start volunteers working with 200 families, and also six Family Groups on the main estates in Leicester. How I would miss them all!

It had been a way of life I had loved beyond all expectations. I knew I could do the job and had been privileged to live my passion for being with parents and children, for nearly eight years. Leaving it all behind would be a huge wrench. The haunting words of poet Mary Oliver played on my mind. ***"What is it that you plan to do with your one, wild and precious life?"***

> ***"Wrenching Margaret from her Leicester volunteers and families, while achieved slowly and I hope gently, was extremely difficult, especially for her. But she quickly developed new skills negotiating with those who held the purse strings, both trusts and central government. Before long, a number of key people and bodies were convinced that Home-Start was a good thing!"***
>
> **Gillian Corsellis, Social Work Adviser.**

Suddenly I was involved in new staff appointments for Leicester Home-Start, as Christine Tracey had decided to leave at the end of the year too, to develop Home-Start in Melton Mowbray. I also planned 10 induction sessions for my successors, to be run in the New Year when we would all change positions.

The door to going national was open wide and I found myself about to step forward into the unknown - all alone.

Chapter 4

TWO SPECIAL FAMILIES

"Society is not disintegrating, because of the break-up of the nuclear family, so much as because of the break-down of the tribe in which people nurtured each other."

Larry Brendtro, Reclaiming Youth International.

The Taylor Family.

The Taylor family was one of the first families ever referred to Home-Start. To all the other services that had been involved for a long time, it seemed that little had changed over many years.

Terry, the father, was in prison, where he had spent much of his adult life. He had grown up in the north east of England, one of 11 children, all sharing a few double beds.

Joan, the mother, was overwhelmed and over-weight. She had five children to cope with. Mary and Katie, eight and six years respectively, should have been at school but rarely arrived. Tina was three and the twins, Anthony and Emily, 18 months old. Three of the children wet their beds and had regular appointments at the Child Guidance Clinic.

The Taylor family was referred simultaneously to Home-Start by their social worker and their health visitor. We were told that social services had put in home-helps to "do a dig-out" regularly, but that the improvement never lasted long. Joan, though a caring mother, simply could not cope, and the social worker was keeping an eye on them.

The health visitor told us that she considered it to be a hopeless situation. The three younger children were sometimes in bed during the day with dummies in their mouths.

The local teacher was concerned about Mary and Katie's education. Too often they were not at school at all. If they did turn up on time, in the playground in the morning, they seemed to be only half dressed and had certainly not had anything to eat.

When I first met Joan, with her pale, puffy face and sad eyes, my heart reached out to her immediately. She told me she was not on speaking terms with her neighbours. Her own mother lived two bus rides away, on the other side of Leicester. She was well and truly alone.

Stella was one of our most energetic, creative volunteers at the time. She had been a school teacher, before having her own three boys, but now that they were all at school, she had a lot of time and wanted to learn about family backgrounds, so that she was better able to understand the children with obvious difficulties who had been in her classes. She would be ideal for the Taylor family, but she spoke posh! Would she and Joan ever be able to strike up a friendship?

I need not have worried. Stella's deep concern for the family cut through all the differences. She exuded kindness and unconditional acceptance.

The house was in a real mess. There were clothes everywhere – all over the sofa, on the floor, under the sink, up the stairs, hanging out of drawers. Well meaning people had often given clothes *"for poor families"*, but they were usually soiled, misshapen and didn't fit a particular child anyway. Joan and her family were given bags full of these, from the WRVS, but with five children, she never had the energy to sort them or stow them away.

On one of her early visits therefore, Stella took with her five supermarket cartons, and together she and Joan wrote a different child's name on each and began to sort clothes into respective boxes, throwing away much that was rubbish. Once the boxes had been filled with clothes, which should more or less fit each child, everyone, including the children, had a great sense of achievement. In the morning, Jean and Katie would just go to their respective boxes, choose what to wear that day, and go to school.

Stella began to visit the family on three mornings a week – EARLY, when her own boys were in school. She began by taking the two older ones to school, if they had not gone by themselves. *"Better late than never"* she told them.

Then she would return to help Joan get the three young ones out of bed, give them something to eat and drink, before going to the shops, to buy something to cook for their dinner. As they walked together, the children would kick leaves, climb on walls, pick up interesting looking rubbish, while Joan moaned her woes to Stella. She had much to moan about – the debts, the wet beds, her neighbours, her exhaustion. She felt she had too many other "workers" in her life, with demands to visit the health centre and the Child Guidance Clinic regularly.

A favourite dinner was 'Cowboy Stew', for which they bought mince, baked beans and potatoes. Back at home, the three young children were allowed to join in with the cooking, by flinging the beans and mince into a saucepan for Joan to cook. She was glad that it hadn't cost much and would feed the whole family.

Joan really began to look forward to Stella's visits, as she never criticised or cajoled. She just built on whatever seemed right on the day.

One morning she arrived, to find Joan throwing a mattress out of the bedroom window. *"I've had enough"*, she shouted to Stella. *"They've wet the beds again and this weather I can't get any of it dry."* Calmly, Stella went inside and suggested that they take all the wet bedding down to the local laundry in her car and that she would pay for the washing and drying. What a relief! The friendship, support and practical help were just what Joan needed. It was real, and she and her whole family began to settle down, knowing that when Stella came, things began to feel better.

On another occasion, Joan had cut her finger badly. Stella suggested cleaning it up and bandaging it, but if it didn't look any better by the following morning, then together they would go to the doctor. Well, according to Joan, that was the first time she felt anyone had really cared about *her*. Everyone else, she said, just used to be concerned for the children. Had they eaten? Had they been to school? Why were they still in bed? Had she taken them to the health clinic?

One day, Joan had a dental appointment at a time when it was impossible for Stella to help out with the children. Had she thought of asking her neighbour? *"But you'll have to ask her nicely, instead of your usual grumpy way, and assume she won't"* encouraged Stella realistically.

It worked and the neighbour minded the children.

She had been intrigued by this other woman visiting regularly next door, had heard them laughing and noticed that the children were more animated. She also began to get more involved and particularly enjoyed the times when she had the opportunity to chat with Stella herself too.

Six months later, Terry was discharged from prison. This last sentence, like some of the others, had been for 'grievous bodily harm'. He had been in and out of prison since the age of 17.

He was angry to find this other woman coming to his house on three mornings each week and told Stella in no uncertain terms to bugger off. *"What the bleeding hell are you doing here anyway?"* he shouted, to which she shouted back equally vehemently *"I'm bleeding well here to give your Joan a hand with the children."* Terry's version, which he told me much later, was that Stella had been terrified of him. At least Terry knew that it was his home and that he had the real choice about who to allow in, which was very important to their relationship.

Stella did not give up visiting though. Instead she wooed Terry by listening to tales of his youth and of his time in prison. He had been a cook there and was proud to teach Stella how to make suet pudding in a bag, like they had done in prison. He in turn was glad when she helped him to fill out some of his forms.

One day, Joan and Stella had made some playdough for the younger children. Terry promptly snatched it away from them, modelled a horse with it himself, and stood it on the mantlepiece, where *no-one* was allowed to touch it. He was so proud when his family marvelled at what he had produced.

Several months later, a Home-Start Family Group began to meet regularly. It was for parents and their children to be together on Tuesday mornings. Terry came to it with Joan and the three younger children. He amazed us all by responding wonderfully sensitively to Amanda, a little autistic girl, who used to follow him around. This relationship developed even more strongly when Terry decided he would start making bacon butties for the group. The smell was a great attraction and we noticed that Amanda developed real eye-contact with Terry, who was so obviously pleased to be so popular.

For the next few Christmases in a row, Terry was our Santa Claus, cast perhaps for the first time ever in his life, in the 'goodie' role. He had no teeth and we were sure the children would recognise him, but it didn't appear to matter. He was warm, funny and gentle and we all loved him. He distributed knitted toys and others given by local churches, through the Council for Voluntary Service. They were wrapped by Home-Start volunteers, and given out to each child and to each parent, by Terry.

Visits to the Taylor family lasted until the twins started school three years later, though not with the same intense frequency as in the first year. During that time, there were of course the usual ups and downs of family life. Sometimes the lows seemed insuperable. But contrary to all predictions, Terry never went back to prison again.

Eventually Joan decided that she would like to be a Home-Start volunteer herself. She had experienced and come through so much, that we were all clear she had a lot to offer other families. Much to the surprise of the Social Services Department, Joan came on our course of preparation.

As always, several other mothers who had been visited too, were on the course. But completely unexpectedly, Joan's husband Terry, turned up on the morning of Session 5. I had noticed Joan's face swollen from crying as she came in. She whispered to me that he was jealous of her attending the course and wanted to come and see for himself what it was all about.

It happened to be the session on Social Ethics, with Denis Rice, and turned out to be one of the most inspiring mornings we had ever spent. Terry contributed with vivid accounts of *his* childhood, expectations, disappointments and general perspectives on life. It made us all re-think our own prejudices, attitudes and values as we listened both to Denis and to Terry.

Joan became a really good Home-Start volunteer herself. Linda and her three children were the first she took on. Linda was a young girl, whose first two children had been in and out of local authority care, due to the violent behaviour of her husband. Her third child was born on the sofa at home, without any medical help, soon after Linda's mother had died unexpectedly. Her husband had left her and the children to cope alone. The new baby had bouts of severe diarrhoea and spent time in and out of hospital. Social Services had asked us for a volunteer, who would be acceptable to Linda, in a last attempt to keep the family together.

Joan proved to be ideal. She was very experienced with young children; lived locally so that she could pop in almost daily when necessary. She walked with the family to the health clinic at times and even met and talked with the social workers herself, to allay their fears about Linda and her family. Knowing that Joan was receiving regular and thorough support from me, as Home-Start organiser, the social worker trusted that we would let her know (with Joan and Linda's knowledge of course) if more professional help was needed. It wasn't.

Nine months later, following a case-conference, we were sent the notes, which stated that Linda and her family had settled down beyond all expectations. There was now a new co-habitee, George, to whom Terry related particularly well. He helped George to fit a fire-guard and mend the fence. He too was a really practical friend to George.

Other neighbours of the Taylor family were also influenced by their changing circumstances. They had heard that Joan (and Terry!) were now doing voluntary work with Home-Start and quite a few other local mothers volunteered for our next course of preparation. No, their lives were not all in order, any more than the rest of us, but knowing that they would be doing supported voluntary work with other families, helped to influence their own family lives in a very positive way.

This was a wonderfully encouraging example to us all, of people in a community, really beginning to help each other again.

Stella increasingly lived abroad, but the Taylor family and I have been in touch off and on over the years.

One year, Joan, her elder daughter Mary, and her first grandchild, turned up at my office on my birthday with a big bouquet of flowers. They wanted me to know that Mary's husband was earning good money clearing drains. They had a white car and Joan was proud that they were doing so well. So was I!

On one occasion, Terry asked me to give him a reference for a manual factory job, for which he had applied – the first since leaving prison many years before. I spoke to his potential employer on the phone on his behalf, feeling extremely positive that he was no longer on the fiddle and genuinely wanting to hold down a job. He got it . . . . .but! Two weeks later he walked out, saying he could make better money "on the social" with the extra pounds he could make selling items he found on the local tip. I felt let down by him and told him so.

A few years later, while walking in Leicester at dusk one winter's evening, a hunched and drunken man weaved his way towards me. As I stepped aside, I heard him mutter *"Well, bugger me if isn't our Margaret!"* I turned round to find that it was Terry. We gave each other a big hug, really glad of the reunion and he brought me up to date with all his family news.

One evening some time later, I arrived back at the Home-Start UK office after a long day away from Leicester. There was a note to say that Joan had phoned the office, to tell me that Terry had had a stroke, and would I go round to see them. I already had another commitment, so I went to see them the following lunch-time. Terry himself opened the door, looking not too bad at all. Perhaps he had just had too much to drink, I thought uncharitably to myself.

He greeted me with disdain. They had waited up, expecting me to pop in the previous evening. When I hadn't turned up, he told me that he had at least expected a card through the letter-box from me in the morning. By lunch-time they had just about given up, but then he conceded grudgingly, *"Well, alright, you're here now. Come on in!"*

One Saturday morning, I was shopping in Leicester market, when a tall dark-haired, ear-ringed youth accosted me with an unexpected hug, greeting me warmly by name. *"But remind me who you are?"* I enquired sheepishly. *"Anthony of-course,"* he replied. *Anthony!* But I had last seen him when he was about eight years old and he had fair hair then. We reminisced together, including about the time when he had phoned me at home, to tell me that his Dad now had teeth. They had been on the bathroom shelf, in a mug and he still wouldn't put them in.

When I retired, I invited some of the original families and Home-Start volunteers round for lunch in the garden one summer afternoon. Joan and Terry were among them. As we sat in the garden and reminisced, they were full of teasing and fun. I heard Terry telling one of the others *"We done a shed 'round 'ere." "Oh, did you Terry?"* I enquired. Well! Quick as a flash he said, *"Yea, the old man died and we cleared it out for 'im!"*

From time to time I still pop in to see the family. The house is full of knick-knacks, which Terry picks up at the tip where he works, when his pal gives him a lift. On one occasion, when he was proudly showing me his back garden, all paved and with gnomes and ornaments everywhere, he gave me a tiny plaster rabbit, which our grandchildren now really enjoy in our own garden.

The situation in 2002 is that, Mary and Katie, the two older girls, have broken their ties with their parents. They are choosing to run their own lives their own way. Anthony, the son, has had spells in and out of prison, but Emily and her children, and Tina and hers, are still very much in touch and doing well.

Recently our phone rang, and it was Joan. She told me that her 12th grandchild, a boy, Tyrone Phoenix Gregory, had just been born on the Queen's Jubilee. After much jubilation I told her that I was just writing the Home-Start story and could I include her family, calling her Joan? Of course I could. *"That's what you've always called me!"* I explained that sometimes names in books were changed, but offered that I'd let her read what I've written before it is published, to which she movingly replied *"You've no need to do that Margaret. I trust you!"*

Recently, Joan was 60. I baked her a cake and went round to congratulate her. She has lost weight and was looking really settled and well. She remembers our three children with affection, but tells me that David was always her favourite. She was sorry that his work was affecting his own health and advised that he should leave. I passed on her concern.

Terry continues to make me smile. He is creative, amusing and has never been back in prison.

For Joan, I have the greatest affection and admiration. She has coped throughout years of chronic ill-health herself and now has a great sense of wisdom and calm.

The Deakin Family

When we first knew her, Jane was a young mother with two children – Sheena aged four and Kenny six months. She suffered from epilepsy and was diagnosed as having severe learning difficulties.

Jane and the children had been living with her mother, but for many reasons, her professional workers, with her consent, had agreed to re-house her up the road.

It was then that they requested a Home-Start volunteer, to support Jane as much as possible while she learned to cope alone.

We introduced Dianne, herself a single parent, who lived a walk away and had had much to cope with in her own life. They got on well, but it was slow going and often very frustrating for the volunteer. She would arrive early in the morning, once her own son was in school, only to find the children in the house alone, while Jane had nipped back to her Mum's. Kenny suffered excruciating nappy rash. Sheena was under-stimulated and under-nourished.

Sometimes Dianne felt optimistic, when they had done some cooking together or had a good time with the children. At other times she felt irritated, impatient and helpless that things were not improving more quickly.

After a year of visiting, and with much support, Dianne finally told me that she had had enough. She wanted a family "that would work". So I arranged a meeting with the health visitor and social worker who had originally referred Jane to us, so that with Dianne, we could discuss the way forward. We agreed that she should just keep visiting for another six weeks, until the end of the summer holidays, when Sheena would be starting nursery school, but that she should tell Jane her plan to withdraw after that.

Jane was devastated. She had never had a real friend before and had grown to really love Dianne. She would do *anything* to keep her. And she did. Her care for Kenny improved. She gave the children regular food and promised to take Sheena to nursery school every day. At the end of the six weeks, Dianne asked me with a twinkle in her eye, whether she might be allowed to carry on visiting for a bit longer?

Well of course it was alright with me. I had wanted to protect Dianne from an undertaking, which had become so very arduous. She should continue visiting for as long as *she* chose, but be honest with Jane when she wanted to end the visits.

During that second year, things really did improve. Jane began to bring her children to the Home-Start family group. She helped me to remember and celebrate birthdays there, with the other mothers and children. One morning she offered to lock up the Centre for me, at the end of the session, because she said she knew I had lots to do back at the office. How very thoughtful.

With a gesture of great confidence in her, I handed over the keys. But then half an hour later, I popped round to make sure all was well. It was. She *had* locked up, proving that she really could take responsibility and could be trusted. What a turning point!

Sometime later, Jane told me she would like to become a Home-Start volunteer herself.

I suggested she should wait until Kenny was at school, when she would have more time, but that we all hoped she would keep coming to the family group, where we needed her help. This she accepted, but kept reminding me whenever I saw her, that one day she would be a 'proper volunteer'.

One January, I went to see her at home, to ask whether she would like to come on the next course of preparation, beginning at the end of the month? Well! Her face lit up and she responded immediately that this had been the best week of her life. The Council had just decorated her front room and I had invited her to become a Home-Start volunteer.

Jane was rather quieter than many of the other new volunteers on the course, but she attended regularly and even took pleasure in borrowing books from the college library.

When the course ended, I told the group of volunteers as I always did, that if they were the last to be matched with a family, it wasn't because they were "bottom of the class", but rather that it was more dependent on where a family lived, or what their needs were. But I did have some concerns about Jane.

However, as I found throughout my eight years with Home-Start in Leicester, somehow miraculously, there was always just the right volunteer for each family. This time, it was a health visitor who phoned me to talk about Angela, a young mother who also happened to have severe learning difficulties. She lived on the same estate as Jane and was finding it hard to cope alone with her baby son. *"She bathes him with his nappy on"*, the health visitor told me.

Jane proved to be a wonderful volunteer – kind, thoughtful and always willing to pop round to Angela and the baby whenever needed.

Three weeks after introducing them to each other, I went round to see how they were getting on together. *"Oh, I really love her,"* Angela told me. *"She comes round every day and helps me out. When my health visitor told me to give him halibut, I said to Jane, what's halibut and she told me it is a sort of fish."*

I left them to it, but heard many anecdotes from Jane, during her support sessions.

After I left Home-Start in Leicester, Jane still sent me a birthday and Christmas card every year. So when I retired, she came with some of the original families and volunteers for lunch at home. She had turned grey in the intervening years, but otherwise looked as winsome as ever. She sat quite quietly, until one of the other mothers, who lives near Jane, started to tell me about her. *"D'you know Margaret, our Jane isn't a Home-Start volunteer anymore, but she does all sorts of other volunteering around our area. She goes shopping for an old man in a wheelchair, and helps with his cleaning. She helps mothers with young children. She helps keep doctors' appointments with people who are ill. She'll help anyone."*

Jane smiled at me sweetly as always, and then nearly bowled me over. *"Our Sheena's a Home-Start volunteer now Margaret,"* she announced. Well! And before I could close my mouth to respond, she added *"and she's doing an Open University degree."*

Soon afterwards, the Midland scheme where Sheena is a volunteer happened to 'phone me, so I enquired about her. *"Oh, Sheena,"* said the secretary. *"She's one of our most popular volunteers. The mums all love her . . . . .and right now I'm helping her to type up her OU work."*

★★★

The stories about Joan and Jane are just two of the many thousands of families visited by Home-Start schemes all over the UK and in other countries too.

I chose these two mothers particularly, because they are still in touch with me. Several other original children who are now parents themselves, let me know regularly where and how they are. Last Christmas, we opened our front door to find Mark, who I had known since he was a year old, standing there, holding his new baby and wanting to introduce me to his delightful partner.

When responsibilities are shared, when help becomes mutual, then a community can really begin to act as an extended family, with the ability to re-form, trans-form and re-create itself. This metamorphosis must happen naturally and laterally though. It cannot be imposed. It might happen spontaneously in certain circumstances, but in my experience, it is more likely to last and be genuine, if it develops from a culture of individual support, kindness and generosity of spirit.

Chapter 5

GROWTH AND DEVELOPMENT
Home-Start - the National Voluntary Organisation
1981 - 1998

"Symbolically the concept that is embodied in the word 'bridge' is surely the most powerful and evocative in the vocabulary of our experience . . . to make connections where none exist, lies at the very heart of our imagination."

Peter Behrens, Architect.

My remit was to "go national". But how?

We would mirror the Home-Start approach to families and volunteers, by providing personal support, friendship and practical help too, in new areas wishing to establish schemes of their own. We would not be there to dictate exactly how each scheme should be run. Rather, it would be vital for us to learn from each of them, about existing needs and services for their local families, whilst sharing with them, the Home-Start approach.

New Year's Day (not then a public holiday) in 1981, saw me all alone in two small rented rooms on the top floor of a terraced house. I had left behind all the familiar work with Home-Start during the past eight years, the families, friends, volunteers and local colleagues from other agencies.

As small compensation, I did have a room full of cards sent to me, overflowing with love and best wishes for my new job/way of life. I was starting with a total grant of £19,000 annually from the London Law Trust for two years.

My first thought was of the Tomi Ungerer painting, "Wir Bauen Ihnen Kreative Brücken" – We build creative bridges for you. I could identify with the boatman, punting a traditional bridge from shore to shore, ensuring links were made possible between the two.

But first I needed to establish our office and appoint a part-time secretary.

Shirley Smith, an interior designer friend, popped in to talk about furnishings.

It was a privilege to be able to create an office, which felt serene and uncluttered, with soft colours – very different from the usual voluntary organisation, which in those days tended to be tatty and heaving with 'work'. Somehow this had become the accepted image in the not-for-profit sector. Together, we decided on cream, pink and brown as our colour theme, reflecting calm, femininity and earth. We bought domestic rather than office furniture, as this was far less costly, and I headed for MFI and County Hall, where voluntary organisations could benefit from a 30% discount on all soft furnishings. I spent the next two weekends making curtains.

From then, until I retired 17 years later, I always had either individual blooms or flowers, from our garden, in my office. Putting them into water, would be the first thing I did on a Monday morning, much to the irritation of some of my colleagues. I found this simple gesture lifted my spirits, linked me with home, and ensured that my personal priorities were in perspective.

There were already eight established or embryonic Home-Start schemes - in Leicester, Nottingham, Ripley, Hinckley, Charnwood, Melton Mowbray, Huntingdon and Bristol. The latter had received funding from the Joseph Rowntree Memorial Trust.

> ***"We had a nice airy room on the first floor of the Quaker Meeting House in Bristol. The afternoon sun seemed to pour in to match our bright ideas and plans. Having Margaret as a member of our committee and being able to use her experience of Home-Start in Leicester helped greatly. Volunteers flocked to join preparation courses fifteen to twenty at a time and expansion was rapid."***
>
> **Libby Lee, Home-Start Bristol.**

I had brought with me 20 letters of enquiry, each wanting to know how to set about establishing the Home-Start approach to supporting families in their area. So I had some ready-made contacts and could begin.

Philip Ray, the previous General Secretary of the Council for Voluntary Service in Leicester, was now working in the same job in Sheffield, hoping to launch Home-Start there too. He was very clear that it was important for the new national organisation to be set up as a separate, independent entity, rather than as an extension of the Leicester scheme. This would give us credibility, he suggested. So perhaps my lonely state was justified after all.

The new Steering Group, with four of my original colleagues from the Leicester Home-Start Support Group, plus an observer from the Department of Health and Social Security, met for the first time towards the end of January. It was gratifying to learn that the DHSS considered that the formation of a national family support organisation was well-timed, since there was a strong political movement towards community care, as opposed to statutory service and institutional care.

It was suggested that I should keep a 'Diary of Development', to record the formation of new schemes, as well as of our own daily work. This proved to be not only fascinating at the time, but a real bonus now, when remembering just how Home-Start grew up.

I met Albert Clark, head of Law at Leicester Polytechnic several times, to discuss in detail the form, which our new national Home-Start organisation should take. Models we considered included a National Federation, National Council, Standing Conference, or National Association. All were membership bodies, in which local branches elected a representative to one of the regional councils, who in turn elected representatives to the national committee.

I had already learned a great deal from my previous involvement with other national organisations, such as the National Marriage Guidance Council, the Pre-School Playgroups Association, OPUS (a phone-in Organisation for Parents Under Stress) and others. Their experience helped my resolve that we should never play the game of being a membership organisation, where the majority of people had to be represented by someone else.

I was also adamant from the start, that Home-Start's central office should not impose development on any area of the country. We would be re-active, rather than pro-active. We would respond to people seeking information about Home-Start, by helping them to establish it themselves in their own locality. Each new scheme would be responsible for its own formation, funding, staffing, and development, managed by and for its local people.

Reflecting the voluntary ethic of choice, our national organisation would be alongside each locally based Home-Start scheme, offering guidance, information and learning opportunities.

HOME-START CONSULTANCY IS BORN.

After much discussion, it became obvious that our new national organisation, should become Home-Start Consultancy. According to the dictionary, the very word to 'consult' involves a two-way process: You consult me about the nature of Home-Start, and I consult you about the gaps for parents and children in your area of the country. Together then, we could establish a local Home-Start scheme as effectively, inexpensively, and simply as possible. That felt like the right way forward.

We would be partners. Neither the national nor the local organisation would be more or less important than the other. We would of necessity, be interdependent. New schemes would be like spokes on a wheel, with Home-Start Consultancy at the hub.

Together we would build a national family support organisation based on trust, good communication, respect and understanding. We would share with each other the successes as well as the difficulties, so that new Home-Start schemes could build on the experience, in the most positive way.

The consultancy model was fully accepted at our next Steering Group meeting, when it was acknowledged that responsibility held locally can mean more freedom to respond immediately to local needs.

> ***"The inter-relationship between Home-Start Consultancy and the local scheme provides the vital ingredients of mutual trust and empowerment. Autonomy and even idiosyncrasy are encouraged to suit the personalities and the framework of the scheme."***
>
> **Ruth Dale, organiser Harrow Home-Start.**

Anthony Mellowes, professor of law at King's College London, and founder of the London Law Trust, produced our Trust Deed. This allowed for a separate Management Committee to support me with issues arising from the day-to-day running of the Consultancy, leaving the trustees with the responsibility for overall policy, finance, senior staffing and general development.

Several possible logos for the new organisation were considered, but the Ancient Symbol of Friendship, was unanimously agreed. It epitomised partnership between everyone in Home-Start, - families, volunteers, staff and management committee members, as well as with outside people and agencies with whom we worked.

The first general leaflet for Home-Start nationally was produced within the first three months too, with an excerpt from the Guardian newspaper article about us, on the front. This stated that Home-Start provides "breathing space for parents and elbow room for the professionals". Those first 4,000 copies went very quickly.

The following year-by-year account of the development of Home-Start as a national organisation, highlights how we sailed, lurched and survived its inexorable growth, during the first 18 years. Some of the issues, difficulties and ideas, which arose at the time, are detailed in **Appendix I**.

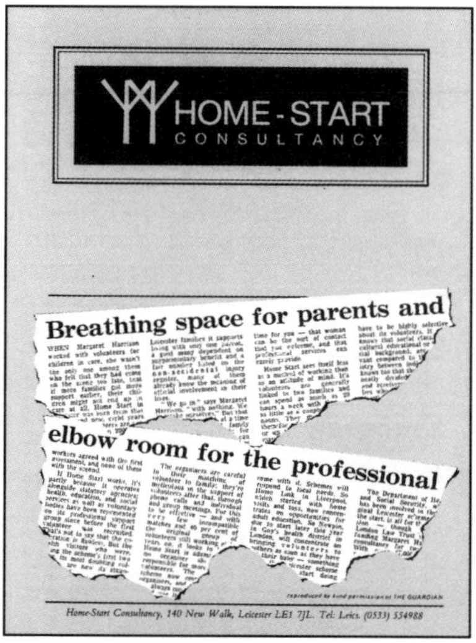

April 1981 – March 1982

During the year, our first four Trustees were appointed for Home-Start Consultancy, which was registered as a Charitable Trust. They were:-

Major-General John H. Page, Director of the London Law Trust (sole funder).
Penny Nairne, - wife of Sir Patrick Nairne, former Permanent Secretary at the Department of Health and Social Services.

> ***"I was always warmed by the welcome I received in Leicester, by the brightness and comfort of the premises – and by a delicious lunch. It felt worth the journey from Oxford for that alone! But these were expressions of important parts of the Home-Start ethos: that EVERY aspect of its particular activities should be carried out to a high standard and that, whatever role, we should get pleasure and fun from belonging to this great and growing family".***
>
> **Lady Nairne, Trustee.**

Joan Cooper, former Chief Inspector in the Home Office Children's Department.
Her Honour Judge Jean Graham Hall, – a High Court Judge with particular experience of working with children and families.

They too agreed unanimously that the new national organisation should be a Consultancy, responding to expressed needs around the country, rather than actively promoting the Home-Start model. Local schemes should be independent, rather than centrally managed. They would work to the standards and methods of practice which, in collaboration with experienced colleagues, we teased out at the time.

THE HOME-START APPROACH.

What was the Home-Start approach? Was it as we had developed it in Leicester, or now that there were other schemes too, what were our shared values? What were the essential concepts, which should be adopted in future by all new schemes wishing to call themselves Home-Start?

A group of 10 of us, with practical Home-Start experience either as an organiser, or statutory management committee member met on three separate days to discuss and debate our special approach to supporting families. We knew we could not take on the world, so resolved that our focus should continue to be on parents with at least one child under the age of five. We agreed that

- Visiting families at home is essential, providing parent-to-parent support, friendship and practical help.
- We work with and through the parents to meet their needs, as well as those of their children, through volunteers with no financial reward and no statutory authority.

- There is no time constraint. The volunteer visits a family as often and for as long as it suits them both. This really removes all pressure for parents to change or perform within a given contract.
- The voluntary ethic pervades Home-Start. We choose to exist as a voluntary organisation. Volunteers choose to spend their time with us, and above all, because our support, friendship and practical help are *offered* to families, it is their choice to accept or reject us as they wish.
- There would be no single way to prepare or to train people in Home-Start. There would be no single approach or manual, which could be considered to be the only way. We all felt it important for people to share their own experience, personality, strengths and weaknesses, in a non-didactic way, always remaining open to new learning opportunities.
- We would build on the families' strengths, emphasising the pleasures of family life.
- Everyone involved in Home-Start would benefit - families, volunteers (including management committee members), organisers, referrers and their agencies, and also staff involved in the national organisation.
- In Home-Start we celebrate what *is* and what *can* be achieved, often against all the odds. By having fun together, by lightening up, many of the seemingly intractable problems either miraculously evaporate, or take on a different perspective.

  I always remember Freda, a mother who lived with her two children in abject poverty. She had asked the Council to re-house her, but each time she was offered other accommodation, she insisted that she really wanted a red bathroom suite. When the social worker was with her, she moaned and sobbed about her problems. When the Home-Start volunteer was with her, she became transformed, enjoying the fun and games and new opportunities with her children. Eventually she even trusted her volunteer enough to accept a house with a white bathroom.

- Home-Start enables people to regain control over their own lives, with responsibility back in their own hands.

All in all, the Home-Start approach is about process as well as results. We agreed too, that it is more about people's attitudes and practical approach, than about fixed methods.

But we all also agreed that there are specific features and boundaries, which each new scheme would have to include in its structure, in order to be called Home-Start.

With virtually every word debated, together we came up with our 'Standards and Methods of Practice', for anyone wishing to establish a local Home-Start scheme.

Our diligence proved well worthwhile, as the10 vital points survived virtually unchanged, for the first 25 years! **(See Appendix III)**

> ***"I just loved those early days, when we all sat round the table together and hammered out those original guidelines. Do you remember how hard Chris Beddoe from social services made us work! We all brought food – gorgeous food - to share at lunch-time. We were inventing it together and we learned so much from it too. Looking back now, I realise we were pioneering a unique voluntary organisation. It was all such fun at the time!"***
> **Christine Tracey, Organiser Home-Start Melton Mowbray.**

That first year of Home-Start Consultancy was really exciting. We were ploughing a new furrow, with very many people keen to join in, helping with publicity, giving us contacts, suggesting ways of doing things.

To my amazement, at the end of our first year, the DHSS actually approached us to offer funding. In retrospect, I realise just how unique this gesture was. They wholeheartedly endorsed our approach of offering support to families at home, preventing breakdown. The Department would contribute up to 49% of our total funding - never more, we were told. The trustees considered this to be an ideal arrangement; neither too intrusive nor too demanding.

April 1982 – March 1983

A shock start to the year came when the AA (Automobile Association not Alcoholics Anonymous) launched their own 'Home-Start' for members' cars, which had broken down at home. John Page, as Chairman of the Trustees, expressed our concern at their choice of title, but due to a recent change in patenting law, we unfortunately had no recourse, since they were offering a completely different service. To this day the name is a source of confusion.

The Remit of Home-Start Consultancy was to:

a) Provide information and personal guidance for existing schemes;

b) Ensure high standards of practice through induction and on-going training to newly appointed organisers and management committee members;

c) Offer information and guidance to all enquirers;

d) Organise seminars, workshops and conferences as appropriate.

With enormous outside interest in the Home-Start approach, several important questions were voiced.

- If the right attitude is so vital, how are people trained to have this?
- What percentage of the course of preparation for volunteers focuses on the needs of children, when Home-Start purports to be about supporting parents?
- Shouldn't money invested in training volunteers be invested in the families themselves?
- Are all the volunteers women?
- Is Home-Start directed towards the mother and the home? What about the father?
- With current awareness of physical and sexual abuse of children, how much of Home-Start is related to these issues? Isn't it very dangerous for the people involved?

We were always mindful of these and other issues raised, in our on-going work, and in the course of the year, they were discussed with other organisers, volunteers, families, trustees, management committee members and our legal adviser.

When considering the role of our trustees, Joan Cooper, ever wise, insisted that the trustees were there to guard, not to initiate.

Some Highlights from the Diaries of Development 1982/3

The Home-Start constitution was accepted and registered with the Charity Commission, so that each independent scheme could have charitable status in its own right. Attached to it were the agreed Standards and Methods of Practice, ensuring that all who registered in the name of Home-Start were legally bound in a common approach to supporting families.

Home-Start was given wide-ranging publicity in professional journals, magazines and newspapers. It was included in TV programmes, such as When the Bough Breaks, Brass Tacks and Coping. Radio broadcasts included You and Yours, various Radio Leicester and Radio Nottingham interviews, as well as programmes on social responsibility.

A Special Donations Fund, established through the London Law Trust, proved invaluable to areas such as Coalville and Harrow, which basically needed £200 to convene meetings and apply for funding to set up Home-Start.

The NSPCC, both from their headquarters as well as their Midlands region, were in touch with Home-Start, stating that they were

> ***"keen to do something more concrete and your organisation seems to be fulfilling this need".***

Leicester Home-Start obtained charitable status, based on the constitution which by then, we had devised for all new schemes. At its inaugural meeting, the first ever Home-Start scheme finally severed its umbilical cord from the Council for Voluntary Service, after nearly 10 years of essential nurture, support and friendship. In retrospect, I still believe that this would also have been a more appropriate time for the Home-Start national organisation to have separated both from Home-Start Leicester and from the CVS, making the whole transition from local to national smoother. They always say that child development itself is smoother when it is allowed to develop naturally from stage to stage, rather than lurching forward and changing at times of transition.

Encouraged by Major-General John Page, the Ministry of Defence invited me to make the first presentation at their headquarters in London on how Home-Start might help Service families. The meeting was attended by representatives of the Army, Navy and Airforce. I vividly remember that Home-Start

Consultancy paid my fare and I took my own sandwiches. There were obviously defence cuts at the time!

Fiona Sibbick, who had been involved in the Pre-School Playgroups Association, spent New Year's Day 1983 with me, proposing to set up six Home-Start schemes in different areas of Shropshire. Her parting words were *"I'd really like to start where you are now!"*

We were delighted when Peter McLachlan and Sophie Bryson, from the Belfast Voluntary Welfare Society, worked hard to launch the first scheme in the Province, in Belfast. The first organiser was Valerie McGuffin, who was to play a significant leading role in Home-Start's development, until she retired in 2002.

Princess Diana, we were told, specifically requested copies of Home-Start leaflets when she visited the DHSS Children's Division.

International requests for information came from Australia, Austria, Bermuda, Canada, Germany, South Africa, Hawaii, Japan, USA and the United Nations International Consultation on Pre-school Education.

We appointed Marie Forsyth on an 18-month contract. She had recently won a Cosmopolitan magazine Journalist of the Year Award, and would help us to produce the first series of user-friendly guidelines on every aspect of establishing and maintaining a Home-Start scheme.

These included the nature of a voluntary organisation and vital legal requirements for employing staff. Such written procedures were important administrative tools, which meant that new schemes could be set up quickly and efficiently, without having to re-invent the wheel. It also absolved me from the huge responsibility of remembering to pass on verbally to all new schemes, everything that was important. New schemes were then free to focus on their main task of supporting families in their locality.

April 1983 – March 1984

At the beginning of the year, there were 24 established Home-Start schemes with 38 organisers. Over 30 other schemes were in the process of being launched and enquiries had been received from over 250 other areas of the country. Our staff still consisted only of Marie and me, with two part-time secretaries. By the end of the year (March 1984) there were yet another 12 new schemes.

I particularly remember some of them, including Bolsover in Nottinghamshire, where there was no previous history of voluntary work, and Dacorum and Uttlesford, for their unusual names.

> ***"I did not have any difficulty in getting top officials from the local Council of Voluntary Service, Education, the Police, Health Services, Doctors, Social Workers, the Churches and other interested parties to attend our family support meeting. They were bowled over when they heard that Home-Start would be based locally and managed autonomously but guided by the Consultancy."***
>
> **The Rev. Canon Basil Jones, Chairman Home-Start Dacorum.**

Market Harborough began when Leicestershire Social Services agreed to fund all Home-Start schemes in the county as part of its Child Care Strategy. This was a significant development, at a time when we were persuading other local authorities that our methods of providing family support in the short-term could have significant long-term effects, preventing family breakdown, and reducing social services workloads in future.

In Havant, the extremely enthusiastic chairman was John Derben, a local builder. On the day we interviewed for their first organiser, he paid for the panel, the interviewees and the members of the Steering Group to have a sit-down lunch together. "Well, I thought that was expected of the chairman", he said smiling generously. "Isn't it?"

We established a pattern for inducting all new organisers, which was to last for 13 years. They were invited to spend a full day with me in Leicester, so that we had time to get to know each other personally. It gave me the opportunity to learn from them – about their attitudes, expectations and particular needs for family support in their areas of the country. They in turn, enjoyed learning about Home-Start and its philosophy. We shared our mutual commitment to family life. There can be nothing so potent as individual one-to-one contact, for a really worthwhile and memorable mutual exchange.

We always linked each new organiser and, when requested, their management committee members, with an established Home-Start scheme in their area of the country. They met regularly without anyone from the central office present

– a wonderful way of sharing the load.

Fundraising through known Trusts began in earnest, as this was to be our last year of full funding from the London Law Trust. With our grant from the DHSS, we were determined to retain a combination of voluntary and statutory funding, for we valued our independence, which enabled us to respond immediately to needs and developments, and to adopt a flexible and spontaneous approach.

One great act of kindness to Home-Start Consultancy, occurred just before Christmas. We had been asked to move our offices with just two months' notice and no assured on-going funding. Colin Towell, a complete stranger from a local Housing Association, heard of our plight through an estate agent and within a month we had moved to rent the top floor of the Association's offices in the beautiful pedestrianised New Walk, close to Leicester station.

> ***"Offering someone a home just before Christmas is quite moving, but something Housing Associations do fairly frequently. It was a pleasure to negotiate with Margaret."***
>
> **Colin Towell, De Montfort Housing finance manager.**

Two Home-Start organisers from Nottingham and Sheffield were co-opted onto the Home-Start Consultancy management committee for a period of two years.

After a special meeting, our management committee agreed to recommend to the Trustees that an annual meeting should be held for organisers and members of local Home-Start management committees, to discuss issues of common interest, which were identified. Some organisers were already meeting on a regional basis, and the possibility of developing a more regional structure was mooted.

A wonderful accolade for Home-Start in Melton Mowbray came from the then Area Director of Social Services. He publicly acknowledged that Home-Start had really made a difference, by providing preventive work for families with young children, who had been referred by health visitors and other local agencies. The social workers' caseloads of families with problems had decreased markedly. It was only when it was recognised by the family and the volunteer, that the problems needed professional input, that the family and Home-Start volunteer together requested Social Services involvement.

It was certainly easier to demonstrate the effectiveness of Home-Start in a small town like Melton Mowbray, with a population of 22,000, than in a city the size of Leicester, where the population was 300,000.

Health visitors all over the UK were keen to see Home-Start established in their part of the country. They told us they valued our provision of parent-to-parent support at home, *"given in an informed, sympathetic, practical 'roll up the sleeves', companionable way."*

I was still largely on my own in Home-Start Consultancy, trying to find the best way to give adequate support to all the new steering committees and newly appointed organisers. So I was immensely grateful when most of the existing schemes offered their lateral support to new steering committees or newly appointed organisers, on the basis of 'each one reach one.'

> ***"I used to love going over to Sheffield to talk things through with their two new organisers and really felt cheated out of a task which extended and stimulated me too, once you appointed regional consultants."***
>
> **Beryl Riley, organiser Home-Start Ripley.**

In the autumn of 1983, the government made money available to areas of the country which were finding it difficult to attract funding for new and innovative voluntary projects, for the benefit of young children. The Under Fives Initiative was announced by Tony Newton, Under Secretary of State for Social Services. Home-Start was to receive funding for 10 new schemes, respresenting 10% of the total money allocated by the Department.

We set up an Advisory Panel to establish a selection and monitoring procedure for areas wanting to bid for funds to establish Home-Start. Budgets were modified so that UFI funds could be allocated to 11 rather than just 10 new schemes as originally planned. These were in counties such as Bedfordshire, Essex, Lincolnshire, Norfolk and Shropshire, where there was little previous experience of innovative, modern voluntary organisations.

The first conference, arranged for Home-Start management committee members from schemes all over the UK, attracted 70 people to Leicester. It was declared a great success. Morale was high. We all shared delight in our successes. This event later became known as the annual Management Committee Consultation days, which we eventually held in different regions of England, and in Scotland and Northern Ireland.

Derbyshire County Council expressed fears that they would be unable to support Joint Funding bids from four potential Home-Start schemes, as they would be organised outside the statutory sector and *"could be seen as privatisation"*.

In other areas of the country too, there was opposition to Home-Start from the NALGO trade union, wishing to protect employment opportunities for their members. As a result of our meeting with the General Secretary, they generously conceded that our approach to supporting families was complementary to the statutory services.

The first Home-Start scheme began in Wales, in Aberconwy, with a £1,000 start up grant. It was an act of faith until Urban Aid funding was secured the following year. Sylvia Chadwick, who was a Home-Start volunteer for the first 7 years, later became the organiser, still in post in 2003.

Marie Forsyth's 18 months work as our Information Officer ended. I was to miss her lively, critical mind and constant refreshing humour. After she left, she wisely wrote in our 1984 Annual Report:

> ***"If Home-Start is to survive I think it is essential to preserve its simplicity. Since its inception the movement has had to co-exist with the complex bureaucracies of the statutory authorities and in future it will be subjected to increasing scrutiny in the form of monitoring and evaluation projects. I do not doubt that there is a need for research and that the evidence may help in the future development. But before the whole idea is lost in a plethora of statistics I think it should be remembered that it is impossible to measure the help that any person can give another. If the idea of Home-Start is a good one, the main emphasis should be on keeping it going. Home-Start needs money and it needs organisation, but only to further one aim – to be able to offer help to the people who need it."***

Looking back, 20 years later, has anything changed?

In order to remain in close contact with organisers from around the country, I would often meet them half way between Leicester and their scheme, one at a time, for lunch. This encouraged our friendship, trust and cooperation in a fun and effective way, raising our morale and motivation for us both.

The DHSS invited us to display Home-Start information at their Day Conference on Supporting the Informal Carers. Our stand turned out to be right next to where the 600 delegates queued for coffee, so that a considerable number of our leaflets and the flyer for Willem van der Eyken's book Home-Start: a Four Year Evaluation were well distributed.

Other Home-Start organisers began to be asked to speak on various training courses throughout England, to trainee teachers, nursery nurses, pre-school playgroup leaders and to students on university extra-mural studies courses. The word was spreading.

During the year, future funding was agreed. We received a really motivating, substantial one-off grant from the Joseph Rowntree Memorial Trust. The Carnegie United Kingdom Trust gave us the first of what were to become life-giving grants over many years, towards training and development. Much smaller, but helpful amounts were received from Hambro Life Assurance, Tootal Limited, Barclays Bank Trust Company Ltd., and Dalgety PLC. These were a considerable encouragement to us all.

Speaking to new groups of Home-Start volunteers around the country, I was always so pleased that they included parents who had themselves been visited. The relationships forged with their volunteers were continuing to encourage others also to pass on their support, friendship and practical help to ever growing numbers of families.

There was a constant stream of approaches from other organisations wishing to run home-visiting family support schemes. These included Social Services departments, hospitals, maternity units, day nurseries, family centres and other voluntary organisations, including Save the Children Fund, the Children's Society, Barnardo's, MIND and various community development projects. We shared all we could for we considered it important for as many families as possible to benefit, even though other organisations were not working strictly to the Home-Start remit.

Discussions continued with the Army, the RAF and SSAFA (Soldiers', Sailors' and Airmen's Families Association). They valued the idea of Home-Start for service families, but this would be a very new venture for them, outside their control. Time and further discussions were needed.

Sir Alan Reay, an ex-military man and a consultant paediatrician, wrote us a letter of considerable endorsement:

> ***"Although Home-Start has enormous potential in many fields, I believe it could be the most promising development in primary prevention of child abuse that I have come across. The professionals will never have the resources to support all vulnerable mothers (even if this were the ideal) and I believe you have hit on an answer."***

Obtaining funding for new schemes in Scotland, Wales and Northern Ireland, presented a great problem. Often one year funding was offered through the Manpower Services Commission, which was tempting but unrealistic. We were determined only to start once three years' funding was committed. In Scotland this was often through the Unemployed Volunteers Action Fund (UVAF), which required us to train volunteers towards future employment. Not an ideal situation, but it meant that Home-Start could take off north of the border, and certainly we always endorsed the notion that volunteers too have the opportunity to develop.

April 1984 – March 1985

"History teaches that progress is a matter of inching forward," according to an Oxford University historian. In developing Home-Start nationally, we were doing just that - ensuring that at each stage we were able to retain our quality, effectiveness and enthusiasm.

Local authorities were then beginning to feel the full impact of cuts in the funds available to them to support voluntary organisations such as ours. The result was that, although in the previous year the number of schemes had doubled, this year there were only five new ones, taking the number to 48. There were also still 36 potential schemes waiting to be launched, delayed only by financial restrictions.

Remarkably, there were still no English schemes in the North West, the South East or in London itself. Were they resisting something that had been developed in the Midlands?

With a long awaited grant specifically for training and development, Linda

Hart, who had been a teacher and had worked since 1981 as an organiser with Home-Start Leicester, was appointed to join me in Home-Start Consultancy. She took on special responsibility for the Under Fives Initiative schemes, and launched relevant training for chairmen, treasurers and secretaries. She also produced a quarterly newsletter to facilitate up to date communication.

Linda's creative energy amused us all in so many ways. When given responsibility for decorating her own office in our beautiful art deco premises, she painted her antique fireplace bright red! A few weeks later though, mysteriously, one Monday morning it re-emerged matt black.

At our first conference in Scotland, we were unexpectedly faced with the same antipathy from health visitors, that we had originally experienced in Leicester. They saw the Home-Start volunteers as a potential threat to their profession. Of course we undertook to draw the distinction of our respective work, more clearly in future.

The first Home-Start scheme began in Perth, Scotland, growing quickly both numerically and geographically with its two most able co-ordinators, Judi Sutherland and Sue Gamwell. Both are still in post 19 years later.

We set up six bi-monthly groups around the UK for all organisers to meet one another for support and to share resources.

We were acutely aware that, with our staff of three, including a secretary, it was not always possible to give individual schemes around the UK the close and frequent support, which they needed and welcomed. But their lateral support to each other, their enthusiasm, creativity and dedicated work, were a great source of inspiration and motivation to me.

The trustees agreed that once money became available, Home-Start Consultancy should appoint new staff, to be based in the regions, rather than building up the office in Leicester. Each regional consultant could be more in touch with, and responsive to local needs and local resources. Travelling time and costs would also be kept to a minimum.

During the year, a new Controller of SSAFA, Major-General Charles Grey, was appointed. He was very keen to see Home-Start launched for Service families. I asked if the families themselves had been consulted, and whether the staff in the Divisions were in favour? Within a month I found myself with BFG

(British Forces Germany) introducing the idea of Home-Start in four army garrisons and two RAF stations. I listened and learned rapidly about their very different approaches to welfare and families with difficulties. There was some internal dissent, but generally Home-Start was considered to be a good idea.

> ***"A treasured memory is of a lunch with General Sir David Ramsbotham, then commanding the Third Armoured Division in Germany, who greeted me with his most exciting discovery of the week. Had I heard of this wonderful organisation Home-Start that was going to make all the difference to the many lonely women whose partners were serving under his command? My confirmation meant that Home-Start was the sole topic of conversation for the rest of the meal. My husband just quietly seethed – he had wanted to talk about Cold War strategy."***
>
> **Dr Elizabeth Bryan, Home-Start Consultancy Chairwoman.**

April 1985 – March 1986

This was a year in which only two new Home-Start schemes began, bringing the total number to 50. But there were also 50 steering groups in existence, just waiting for funding before they could begin. It was salutary to acknowledge that each of these locally grown and locally based embryonic Home-Start schemes was entirely dependent on the local knowledge, energy and enthusiasm of their Steering Group members, with just a little encouragement now and again from Linda or me.

There were three particular highlights during the year.

1. In October 1985 we held our first national conference, at the Friends' Meeting House in London. The focus was **Creative Partnerships in Family Support.** The most memorable outcome was that, in future when Home-Start was to be involved in case-conferences, they should be held in the family's own home. I'm not sure that this was ever fully implemented.
2. We negotiated the first **Home-Start staff pensions** in the voluntary sector, based on the Social Workers' Pension Fund.
3. The third and biggest development took place in February 1986, when

> Sue Pope, previously founder and organiser of Home-Start in Herefordshire, was appointed as the **first ever Home-Start Regional Consultant.** She would work from home, but be employed by Home-Start Consultancy in Leicester. Our overhead costs had to be kept to a minimum. It was agreed that initially England should be divided into three wedges, with Sue responsible for the West/South West of England. Then, when more funding became available, the next two Regional Consultants would cover the North and the South/South East. We would create regional circles of belonging.

I was sent on the first of several very different management courses, which I attended over the years. None was really appropriate for the structure or approach of Home-Start. They included one run by the National Council for Voluntary Organisations, based on an Army model by John Adair. The Association of Chief Executives of National Voluntary Organisations ran theirs on traditional voluntary membership organisation lines. Then there were various business models.

Charles Handy, whose work has always inspired me, had said at the National Marriage Guidance Council's annual general meeting that year,

> ***"Voluntary organisations are a little different from other kinds of organisation, and they need different kinds of management. I find myself saying particularly to business organisations, that if they want a key to the future they ought to take a look at the voluntary world. But I wonder if just as many voluntary organisations are trying to become what they see as more businesslike.***
> ***I have a great worry that voluntary organisations get too close to business and its current practices, and that they only start to read the books as they are going out of print. My message is that you have to find your own solutions, and they may be solutions that would benefit the rest of us."***

We did eventually do just that, but not knowingly at the time.

During this financial year, the DHSS increased our grant to £30,000 per annum, i.e. 40% of our annual costs. It felt good that this was to cover non-restricted revenue costs.

As a nascent national voluntary organisation in the 1980s, we had certainly not yet been accepted as an essential partner in the statutory/voluntary provision of family support in this country, despite the volume of work and evident positive results. Survival continued to be difficult for all but the 11 local schemes funded by the government's Under Fives Initiative.

> **I particularly remember a very creative AGM in the autumn of 1985, when local funders were threatening to pull the plug on Sheffield Home-Start. As people arrived, the tape of a crying baby was played at the back of the hall. As the meeting began, the volume was increased, making everyone wriggle, at this invasive noise. The Councillors in the front row, including David Blunkett, then Chairman of the Social Services Committee, turned to the top table, from where a speaker was already in full flow, and urged in a loud voice *"Give them the money!"***

It is surprising how quickly we all forget the anguish and helplessness engendered by a baby crying loudly, once we have passed on to the next stage.

The Home-Start Consultancy pack, comprising 44 leaflets on every aspect of establishing and maintaining a Home-Start scheme, was in constant demand, not only by existing and potential Home-Start schemes, but also by other voluntary and statutory agencies wishing to adapt them for their own purposes.

April 1986 – March 1987

To me, the organisation had begun to seem like a monster! I had begun to feel we had grown too big. There was just so much potential to provide ever more support to families throughout the UK and also abroad. Without more staff, the avalanche of work ahead seemed impossible to stop. The DHSS was telling us that in a period of financial constraint, we simply must *not* continue to develop further. But the Consultancy wasn't responsible for the growth. The impetus was coming from local communities, which were seeking our support and guidance to develop their own Home-Start schemes.

With two grants, one anonymous and another from the Tudor Trust, we were at last able to appoint two more regional consultants – Sue Everitt, founder and organiser of Royston Home-Start, and Maggie Rowlands, co-founder and organiser of Sheffield Home-Start. Both still hold senior positions in Home-Start in 2003. It was becoming important to appoint separate consultants for Scotland and Northern Ireland too, as soon as further funding could be secured.

I had spent a week at meetings in Montrose, Aberdeen, Dunfermline and at a Perth Home-Start Interest Day, which 50 delegates attended from all over Scotland. The time was ripe for development. But we could not contemplate it without a Scotland-based Consultant. The Carnegie Trust invited us to apply to them.

The first two pilot Home-Start schemes working with British Forces families in Germany, were established in Münster and Hohne. Sue Pope, new Regional Consultant, helped with interviewing the first organisers. I arranged their induction in the UK in our central office, but also via visits to individual schemes which already had involvement with the nearby RAF stations in this country - King's Lynn, Doncaster and Melton Mowbray.

Just as the train pulled out of Leicester station, taking Wendy and Carole from Germany to our colleagues in Doncaster, I realised I had not given them descriptions of organisers Glenys and Margaret who would be meeting them at the station. I need not have worried, they told me later, as they had "the Home-Start look", with smiley faces and twinkly eyes. They had bonded immediately.

One of the ironies of working with MOD funded schemes, was that when I visited them, I was met by a chauffeur driven car at Rheindahlen airport, stayed in an officers' mess (*"Do we really have to put up with these women here now"*, came one poorly disguised whisper over dinner one evening) or with the garrison commander and his wife.

On one such occasion in Münster, I felt I was being treated particularly like royalty. Brigadier Evans and his wife Ginny then confided that the Queen Mother was coming to stay the following week, and all the staff, including Sergeant Brown, who served me sherry from a silver salver, were rehearsing!

Conversely, when the organisers from Germany, and later Cyprus and Gibraltar, visited us in England, it was I who drove to pick them up at Luton airport, brought them to stay with us at home in Leicester, cooked their dinner, served their breakfast, changed their beds and ran their induction sessions at the office. Such was the reality of life in the voluntary sector, and I loved the contrasts.

I remain indebted to the garrison commanders' wives, Ginny Evans and Anne Wilkes, who were so encouraging of our work. They could so easily have insisted that it was the officers' wives who should continue to meet, greet and support newly arrived families. Instead, they spoke on Home-Start's behalf at various Services Study Days and were so persuasive, that by the end of the year the MOD was discussing setting up 15 more Home-Starts, including the first in Cyprus.

> ***"It was with a sense of relief and expectation that we heard in 1984 that there would be two Home-Start pilot schemes for British Forces families in Germany. The traditional role of the officer's wife visiting the soldier's wife was breaking down. The officer's wife didn't want to visit and the soldier's wife didn't want to be visited. Welfare problems within the regiment or unit, had been carried out in a hierarchical way."***
>
> **Ginny Evans, Garrison Commander's wife, Münster.**

With 20 new Home-Start schemes established in the UK during the year, bringing the total number to 70, and with three newly appointed regional consultants, the trustees, management committee members and I began to feel optimistic and buoyant once more.

Significant Issues at that Time included:

Vetting volunteers. For me, it seemed far more important to undertake rigorous recruiting, preparation, matching and support of all volunteers and staff in Home-Start, than to rely solely on personal references.

Insurance for volunteer home-visiting, including legal expenses insurance for the schemes, were negotiated and produced for the first time in the voluntary sector.

Child Care Law. We had considerable input, both in writing and in meetings with the government's Department of Health and Social Security.

Equal Opportunities Policy. We produced this for Home-Start in writing for the first time.

Research was being undertaken on different aspects of Home-Start, nationally and locally.

Umbrella organisations were encouraged to let their own Home-Start schemes grow and become independent within three years, so that they could be autonomous entities in the community, as were all other schemes.

Partnership between voluntary and statutory provision, between Home-Start volunteer and family being visited, between Home-Start Consultancy and each local scheme, enabled all to complement each other, rather than emulating each other, making a more complete whole in each situation.

> ***"Home-Start is a reminder that professionals do not have a monopoly on care in the community. Volunteers, qualified by virtue of their life experience and personalities, prepared and supervised by the Home-Start staff, have important resources to offer both the professionals and families."***
>
> **Gillian Corsellis, Chairwoman of the Under Fives Initiative Home-Start Advisory Group.**

Publicity. It was hard to juggle the balance between too much publicity, which raised false hopes of Home-Start support for families in areas of the country with no available scheme, (there were 70 out of a potential 750 at the time), and too little for successful fundraising.

The first six years of Home-Start Consultancy had proved that it really was possible to develop a UK-wide organisation, consisting of a central hub, regional/national consultants and each local scheme enjoying independence, whilst being interdependent.

Open communication and excellent co-operation between schemes and the Consultancy were strongly maintained via regular study days, focus days and seminars held centrally and regionally for organisers, secretaries and management committee members. We all felt we were in it together, pioneering a different, informal approach to supporting families, as well as to developing the organisation nationally, which was even beginning to spread internationally.

A Bulletin was distributed monthly, with news, views and reviews, as well as a newsletter three times a year.

DHSS Under-Fives Initiative

During the previous three years, Home-Start Consultancy had administered just over half a million pounds on behalf of the Government's Under Fives

Initiative. In his final report for the DHSS, Willem van der Eyken suggested a number of characteristics which had made Home-Start schemes so attractive to local authorities in such a relatively short time:

- Networking closely with professionals and other voluntary agencies.
- Striking a sympathetic chord with all those who have had children themselves, in an easy-to-grasp concept.
- Highly cost-effective.
- Close support for schemes.
- Negotiations at local and national level.
- Relevant information and guidance materials.
- Prevention and hence investment for local authorities and a wide range of other referrers, who consider Home-Start to be a valuable adjunct to their own provision.

The Under-Fives Initiative was rounded off in December 1986 with a conference organised by the DHSS for all participating schemes, with the theme Practical Action for the Under-Fives.

Some of the comments received about Home-Start during the year

> ***"A social worker nowadays is a juggler in keeping in the air a galaxy of demands, responsibilities, expectations, many of them with legal overtones . . .how can I find time to work at the depth and involvement which families with young children demand and need? I cannot; Home-Start can, and does. Thank God for Home-Start!"***

Social Worker.

"As a health visitor, I used Home-Start for a number of my families. I found their practical help and support was extremely useful, and eased tensions in many situations. Now, as a mother of twins – one of them with a breathing problem – my own health visitor and I made arrangements for a Home-Start volunteer to visit me . . . .So I can really see the benefits the organisation can offer, from both sides of the fence."

Ex Health Visitor.

"From the medical point of view, the value of Home-Start and its place within the Primary Health Care Team is unquestionable."

A General Practitioner.

"P.S. Thank you for looking after our Mummy. Love and kisses."

Paul, Lisa and Craig.

April 1987 – March 1988

During the year there were 85 established schemes around Great Britain. Their average cost was £22,000 per annum. The average cost of Home-Start was £360 for each family visited during the year, the equivalent of keeping one child in care for two weeks, or one parent in a psychiatric hospital for three days.

The average team for one full-time organiser and secretary, was 35 Home-Start volunteers, visiting 60 families for approximately 14 months each.

In Leicestershire, where the first Home-Start scheme began, the social services department was funding six Home-Start schemes within the county, directly out of their main programme budget. Many other local authorities were considering Home-Start as part of their overall child-care strategy.

My own role had changed. There were now other members of Home-Start Consultancy staff linked with existing and potential schemes all over the UK. But it came as a shock to me when, out of the blue, at one of our management committee meetings, everyone present, except me, decided that my title should be changed from Senior Consultant to Director, in line with the language of other voluntary organisations at the time.

Being the Director felt as if a more didactic role was expected of me, whereas I felt I was more of a conductor, orchestrating the different players, to create a harmonious, productive whole. So why could I not simply be called by my own name – Margaret Harrison, a Senior Consultant?

I wished my new title could have reflected the mutuality, which I felt existed throughout Home-Start at the time, and which my chairwoman Elizabeth Bryan expressed so well in the year's annual report:

> ***"Just as the volunteers both give and receive from the families that they help, so do the organisers, management committee members, regional consultants and our director, Margaret Harrison, give and receive from each other. They radiate this same mutual respect, support, energy and enthusiasm".***

During 1987/88, there were several reviews of the work of Home-Start, both at local and national levels.

1. **Arthur Young Management Consultants** very generously undertook a voluntary review of Home-Start Consultancy. They endorsed our simple approach and structure. The two identified weaknesses were our lack of a national profile *("indeed its very name has been taken over by the AA")* and the continuing difficulties in securing funding at both national and local levels.

2. **The National Institute of Social Work** compared the work of Home-Start alongside social work provision in an area in the south of England. Researcher Jane Gibbons concluded that:

   'Home-Start through its volunteers, is well able to work with a wide range of families, including those with severe difficulties. The organisation offers a qualitatively different kind of service, which is truly complementary to that of the statutory body'.

3. In order to review the work of Home-Start nationally ourselves, **Home-Start Consultancy** sent a **questionnaire** to all schemes which had been running during 1987. This was then followed up by a personal visit by a member of Home-Start Consultancy staff. Most revealing from this exercise was that:

- On average, nearly 2,000 volunteers each worked four hours a week directly with families.

- Almost 50% of referrals were made by health visitors, 25% by social workers and 10% were self-referrals from parents themselves.
- Much of the work had been preventive, we assumed, because families were coping again and children had been removed from the At Risk Register.
- Much of what the volunteers did, had also been remedial. Many families had been prevented from breaking down.
- Perhaps best of all, many parents who had been visited, had chosen to become Home Start volunteers themselves.
- The growing numbers of schemes developing in Scotland and Northern Ireland, highlighted the urgent need to appoint Home-Start Consultants in each of those countries too.

April 1988 – March 1989

Home-Start, now 15 years old, was not just a 'flash in the pan'.

There were 115 schemes in total established throughout the UK, and with British Forces families in Germany, Cyprus and Gibraltar. In other countries, there were two schemes in Israel, serving both Jewish and Arab communities, as well as others in Australia, Canada and the Republic of Ireland.

Home-Start Consultancy had a rewarding year, with the appointment at last, of three additional consultants to work with new and existing schemes in Scotland, Northern Ireland and, funded by the Ministry of Defence, with British Forces families. By basing Home-Start Consultancy staff in regions of England and the other three nations of the UK, we were avoiding developing a monolithic, highly centralised organisation.

At this time too, more schemes developed in Wales, when the Welsh Office funded a development worker in the valleys of South Wales. She was another Sue!

The average cost per family visited, was less than the previous year, highlighting that, with more schemes, efficiency can actually reduce costs.

Coatbridge in Scotland and Milton Keynes in England, were the only Home-Start schemes ever to close because of lack of local funding. Remarkably,

Naomi Eisenstadt, who now heads the government's Sure Start programme, was a community worker in Milton Keynes at the time. Then, nine months later (good gestation period!), a new active Steering Group was formed there, to negotiate once more for local funding, which was soon obtained.

In John Bowlby's latest book A Secure Base, Home-Start was suggested as a "prospect for prevention" in the chapter on Violence in the Family.

Essex County Council provided the first generous and creative triple funding for Home-Start schemes in the county – 50% social service, 40% health and 10% education. The proportions were just and right. In addition of course schemes raised money themselves for outings, parties, social events for families and fun days for all.

Home-Start appeared in booklets accompanying various BBC programmes, including The Baby's Fine – But How Are You?, Baby Blues, and When to Worry.

In the tabloid press, Agony Aunts Claire Rayner and Deirdre Sanders began to advise anxious parents to contact Home-Start. They did, and we were swamped.

Out of 85 Home-Start schemes, which existed throughout the year in the UK, 77 received all or a substantial part of their grant from Social Services departments.

During the year, 55 Home-Start volunteers supported parents with 40 sets of triplets.

It was said that voluntary organisations were the new 'Colleges of Society'. Certainly the educational value to everyone in Home-Start was abundantly clear. Individual people can both contribute to their community and learn from it.

"Being part of Home-Start has been a five year course for living".
Sandra, volunteer.

Many of the parents – one in 10 at the time - chose to become volunteers, giving back much of what they themselves had gained from Home-Start's support to their own families.

Some of the 2,284 volunteers who worked with Home-Start during the year, also chaired their local Home-Start management committees.

Almost 12,000 children plus their parents, were supported in 1988/9, by Home-Start volunteers in 85 schemes in the UK, during the whole year.

Many schemes had started to provide additional resources for families, including post-natal support groups, exercises in public relations, family groups, and toy libraries, and had developed imaginative methods of fund-raising. There was always scope for innovation and initiative, without compromising the Home-Start ethos.

In August, the government announced a new initiative for children and their families living in deprived city areas. This was the Inner Cities Initiative, and Home-Start received funding to begin new schemes in the London boroughs of Hackney, Newham and South Westminster, as well as in Birmingham and Central Manchester. The funding allowed us to appoint an extra member of staff, Pam Cooke, to assist me and take special responsibility for these schemes.

These new city schemes made us focus in a new way on Home-Start provision in multi-ethnic communities. We appointed organisers from different cultural backgrounds, who spoke several different languages. In some of the London Boroughs which have Home-Start, 26 different languages are spoken. In Hackney some of their courses of preparation for volunteers were held in Turkish.

The three long-established Home-Start schemes in Sheffield, Nottingham and Bristol, also benefited from Inner City funding to extend their work into black communities. Significantly, in an area of Bristol, there had to be a greater focus on encouraging families to come to a Home-Start family group first, before the offer of support at home was an acceptable, trusted option. Interestingly, this varied approach was mirrored some years later in Um el Fahm, a muslim Arab town south of the Galilee.

"Those early days were so exciting, weren't they Margaret?"
Libby Lee, organiser Home-Start Bristol.

At the end of the financial year, in March '89, with an increasing number of organisers, the first annual national study days were held in Swanwick, which could easily accommodate up to 300 people. The theme was **Taking Home-Start into the 1990s Together.** Representatives from 96% of schemes throughout the UK, Germany and Cyprus were present. We all agreed that the Home-Start ethos and Standards and Methods of Practice, with only very minor changes, were as appropriate then, as they had been for the previous 16 years.

One memorable debate with experienced organisers, at those study days, remains vivid in my memory, probably because it was an emotive subject. Should Home-Start volunteers be paid? Those arguing for, were as eloquent and convincing as those against. As the assembled organisers were invited to vote, I held my breath. Would this change the nature of volunteering in the 90s and constitute a significant change in our whole philosophy and approach? Surely it is a feature of a civilized society, that people should contribute to each other without financial reward?

To my relief and amazement, when the votes were counted at the end, only three organisers voted *for*, including the two involved in opening the debate, because as they said afterwards, *they had to!* Thank goodness we were still united in our voluntary ethic and voluntary approach!

> ***"The Study days really are so valuable, even though they must be exhausting for you. It is wonderful to be part of such a warm, caring and enthusiastic team. I'm only sorry that you don't see the 'knock-on' effect that the recharging has on our families – we've even just booked Father Christmas!"***
>
> **Fiona Sibbick, Shrewsbury Home-Start.**

Yet another review was undertaken, this time on the Future of Home-Start, by my chairman, Clive Bate, and deputy chairman Herbert (now Lord) Laming. We analysed the development of Home-Start under three main headings: Services, Resources (other than finance) and Finance.

It is interesting, I think, to compare the 1988 estimated costings for Home-Start Consultancy, the central organisation, with actual costs 10 years later and beyond. Their budget forecast indicated the need to provide annually:

★**£55,000 for Central Office** (unless either the accommodation or management structure changed significantly), plus

★**£20,000 per region,** plus

★**£500 per scheme.**

Assuming there would be roughly 25 schemes per region, we worked out the implications of two different levels of growth:

***180 schemes, in 7 regions:** £55,000 + £140,000 + £90,000 = **£285,000**

***280 schemes, in11 regions:** £55,000 + £220,000 + £140,000 = **£415,000**

I am amazed to note that the figure for Central Office was for salaries for the Director, Assistant to the Director, full-time secretary, part-time secretary and part-time legal adviser, as well as for accommodation and administrative costs. The organisation was highly cost effective, with every pound raised, having a high-gearing effect.

With hindsight, I believe that, had we been more confident in our modest, lean approach to supporting the ever-increasing numbers of schemes throughout the UK, we could have avoided the seemingly inescapable slide into a more bureaucratic, hierarchical structure at that point.

We should have continued to find creative ways of sustaining our ever-growing organisation by building on the enormous wealth of talent and willingness to help each other, which existed at the time, throughout Home-Start.

Instead of which, ten years later by 1998, the cost of Home-Start Consultancy, was around £1 million, providing training, information, guidance and support to 250 schemes in all four nations of the UK as well as with British Forces schemes in Germany and Cyprus. The schemes themselves raised and ran on £11 million during the year.

Assuring quality is indeed a pivotal function for a central national body. The paradoxes for the organisation as a whole, were succinctly recorded by Charles Handy some years later, in The Empty Raincoat (Hutchinson, 1994). We had become:

Global yet local;
Small yet large;
Centralised yet de-centralised;
Autonomous yet part of a team;
Delegating yet controlling;
Planned yet flexible;
Differentiated yet integrated at the same time;

Mass marketers yet catering for the individual;
Hard and soft.

Charles Handy suggested that an organisation needs both hard and soft features - the structured, controlled, more masculine side, yet the flexible, more responsive feminine side. Significantly, he stated *"Both are needed for success!"* We had both, and were only too aware of the paradoxes.

In Home-Start, the structured framework we had created, was intended to free the Home-Start volunteers to be flexible and sensitive to the needs of the individual families they supported. It worked.

It is said that parents who are tough and strict, yet tender and relaxed, are the ideal combination.

April 1989 – March 1990

This was a significant year, as we were forced to request a financial contribution to Home-Start Consultancy from each Home-Start scheme. This was initiated by the DHSS, who were insisting that their grant to us would have to cease unless the schemes contributed towards the costs of our services to them. We were told that all other voluntary organisations and universities charged between 10% and 25% for their administrative costs.

After much discussion with all relevant people within Home-Start, we finally decided to charge just 1% of schemes' statutory core grants. This, we agreed, would affect each in equal measure, whether they received £10,000 or £50,000 each year. We were immensely grateful that every single scheme, understood our plight, and responded positively to our request. I still think this showed a considerable level of trust, and an acknowledgement of the mutuality of our respective roles throughout Home-Start.

Virginia Bottomley, Secretary of State for Health, increased our funding from £45,000 to £70,000.

One of innumerable acts of kindness to me, came in May when my father died. At the end of the day shortly afterwards, I arrived home, tired and sad, to find a small oak tree in a pot on the doorstep. With it was a loving note from Fiona Sibbick, organiser of Home-Start in Shrewsbury. Wonderful, kind, thoughtful and generous Fee! She ran her scheme with the same human qualities for everyone and now she had come all the way from Shrewsbury to Leicester for me!

Sadly, in 1990 we had to say good-bye to three people who had been particularly significant in the original (in every sense of the word) life cycle of Home-Start Consultancy. John Page, whose vision and unstinting support had led originally to us taking the leap to 'go national', retired after 10 years. It was a source of amazement to me, that someone who had been a very successful Major-General in the army, also had the sensitivity to head a voluntary, family support organisation. But this should not have been a surprise, as he so deeply valued his own close family.

Joan Cooper, one of our first trustees, who was a constant source of encouragement, enlightenment and kindness, chose also to retire at this time.

Eva Gibson, our senior secretary, left when she reached retirement age, but then promptly returned as a volunteer!

When he left, John Page introduced Chris King, a relative who had built up his own business extremely successfully. On his first visit to our office, Chris and I went out for lunch and all he wanted was spinach soup. When we returned to the office, he put a cheque on the coffee table, face down "for the lunch". I demurred, knowing what a frugal lunch it had been. But when he left and I checked the cheque, it was memorably LARGE!

April 1990 – March 1991

At the time of reaching our majority – 18 years old – with 141 schemes in the UK and abroad, our sense of optimism was high; the opportunity to be altruistic as important as living and breathing.

We held a national conference in London, with the theme Preventing Families Breaking Up or Breaking Down: Our Shared Responsibility. I remember panicking that no one would attend, but in the end, our Friends' Meeting House venue again was filled with over 300 of our colleagues from government departments, Home-Start schemes and related statutory and voluntary agencies. The Anna Scher Theatre group gave a memorably stimulating performance on the needs and relationships of children and young people.

In the early '90s, new legislation affecting our work with parents and children, and other key issues, had to be addressed. Our very able consultants produced some really straightforward papers, winning for Home-Start a reputation for high quality policy analysis, and well-documented practical advice for the voluntary sector. Even more importantly though, they formed the basis for our own training and road shows throughout the UK.

These included

- **Service Agreements,** between social services departments or health authorities, which were now becoming purchasers of services, rather than as before, the sole providers. These Agreements specified the quantity, quality and price they would contribute towards the work of Home-Start with parents and children, but clearly involved some very sensitive, yet formal negotiations.
- The newly implemented **Children Act 1989,** much of which was immensely encouraging of our work in preventing family crisis or breakdown.
- Over 2,000 Home-Start staff, volunteers and management committee members took part in Home-Start training, in connection with **HIV infection and AIDS.** This was recognised in the voluntary child-care field as being a very important contribution to education and prevention.
- Our Practice Paper **Home-Start and Child Protection,** led to 13 workshops throughout the United Kingdom, attended by 98% of the organisers.
- Other papers on the **NHS and Care in the Community Act, Quality Assurance and Equal Opportunities,** were equally successful.

Towards the end of the year, Lord Joseph had encouraged two of his influential colleagues, to help with fundraising. Michael Green, Chairman of Carlton Communications Plc., and Bernard Taylor, Chairman of Medeva Plc., respectively set up an Appeals Committee and provided free accommodation for a fundraiser in St. James's Street, London.

Without doubt, the new systematic approach to fundraising through such generous and influential supporters, was to be a turning point in the history of Home-Start.

April 1991 – March 1992

This was a remarkable year for many reasons.

Her Royal Highness, **The Princess of Wales** accepted our invitation to become Patron of Home-Start. Patrick Jephson, her private secretary, told me at the time that they had made inquiries about our status and function, from government, businesses, the voluntary and statutory sectors, as well as a wide range of individual people. *"And your organisation came up with a whole row of cherries"*. What a delightful accolade!

Patronage, we were told, lasted initially for five years, but could be renewed after a review. Home-Start schemes had to channel their requests for Princess Diana's involvement in their events through me. These were then considered by Her Royal Highness, twice a year. We were advised to inform the Palace immediately, if we had any very good or very bad news, which might potentially appear in the press, such as "Di charity in fraud probe" or "Newark Home-Start is a winner!"

Appropriately, Princess Diana's first engagement, was a visit to Leicester Home-Start on 1st November 1991, to celebrate the 18th anniversary. Some of the original parents, who by then were grandparents, were present, as well as a hall full of young families and volunteers involved in the scheme. The Princess dropped the silver knife as she was about to cut the cake, giggled, wiped it on her skirt and proceeded with the festivities.

A new focus on training in Home-Start began with the appointment of Maggie Rowlands as our Training Consultant.

A new staffing structure was implemented, with Sue Everitt and Sue Pope, each taking responsibility for half the UK, East (with Scotland) and West with Wales and Northern Ireland. Two new regional consultants were appointed to replace them, to listen to and meet the needs of the schemes, reporting back then to the two newly appointed senior staff. We were determined though, to keep our developing structure as flat as possible.

The annual meeting at the Department of Health (formerly the DHSS) became increasingly difficult. The civil servant who met my chairman and me each year, said once, after a particularly long there-is-nothing-more-to-be-said silence, *"But you will let us know, Margaret, if Home-Start is going to the wall!"*

Not so long afterwards, a new Government Initiative was announced to support families. This was to be an action research project, with us receiving funding to flood the Metropolitan District of Wakefield, with Home-Start provision. The population of 310,000 was in small towns, rural and mining communities and inner city areas. The new project was to be called Wakefield CHIPS (Comprehensive Home-Start Initiative for Parental Support). The impact on families was to be evaluated in a research programme by Leeds University's Department of Continuing Adult Education.

The results were to be published in 1996.

April 1992 – March 1993

Three new grants early in the year, proved an enormous encouragement to Home-Start Consultancy.

1. **The Baring Foundation** really helped our cash flow, by repaying the outstanding mortgage on our offices at 2 Salisbury Road, Leicester.
2. **Next Plc** donated a fully equipped office for a new London-based Consultant, in their head offices in Edgeware Road. This came about through an introduction by Lord Joseph, to Lord Wolfson, chairman of Next.
3. **The Welsh Office** released funding for a Consultant/Development worker for Wales, working four days a week. Christine Wilkinson was appointed, and each country in the United Kingdom now had a responsible member of staff based there.

The UK senior Consultants had their titles changed to Assistant Directors.

Celebrations are important in the lives, not only of individuals, but also of organisations. It was a particular pleasure to celebrate 10 years of Home-Start in Northern Ireland, with many of the original families, volunteers and supporters present. Lady Mayhew, the wife of the Secretary of State for Northern Ireland, was present, lending her deep understanding of the need for Home-Start.

Mary, the first parent ever supported by Home-Start in Belfast, spoke very movingly about her own experience.

Mary's Story

I first heard of Home-Start in 1983 from my social worker. I had two daughters aged 8 and 6 and a baby boy. My husband gambled a lot and we moved house frequently to avoid debts. I had been through a nervous breakdown and overdosed on four occasions. Life was very stressful.

As far back as I can remember, we always had a social worker attached to the family, not by any means a bad thing. My father drank heavily and often beat us for no reason. By the age of 12 I had been in five or six children's homes, either when my parents split up, or when my mother went to hospital to have another baby. One day when I came home from school, my sister was in the social worker's car outside and the Police were inside. They arrested my father and my sister went away to have a baby. My father went to prison. During the next year my mother's boyfriend raped me, but I told no-one. I was too frightened of being taken away. At the end of the year my mother had a nervous breakdown and we all went into a home. I was too old to stay with my brothers and sisters and was moved to an all girls' home. About a year later my father got out of prison and returned to my mother. They tried to get us back, but the judge refused, saying that I should remain in care until the age of 18. It seemed like a life sentence, but looking back they were the best years of my childhood.

Things got worse after I left the home. When I got depressed I found it easier to go along to the doctor and get some tablets, they would blot everything out and I did not have to cope with life. Through my social worker I was introduced to my volunteer from Home-Start, a new friend, someone I could confide in. I slowly became more confident and learnt to trust her. She was not judging me and was not someone who would take my children into care. Over the next few years I don't know how I would have coped without the Home-Start volunteer, through my husband's assaults on the children, his attempted suicide, my own depression and major surgery. Home-Start was always there, giving support and friendship and helping me to gain confidence in myself through trusting me. Four years ago we lost our house through my husband's gambling and decided to try a new start in a new town.

Unfortunately he went from bad to worse and drank more than usual. One evening he started to wreck our home. I could not take anymore. He returned to the town we had left and we divorced. Since then my life has changed for the better. I remarried two years ago and am now happy and secure. The one thing missing from my life was Home-Start. I contacted the local group and went on the training course. I then joined the committee as the representative volunteer and was asked to become a fund-raising co-ordinator.
I would like to say thank you to everyone in Home-Start. Because of them I am confident and enjoy life. I still get depressed, but I now know how to cope. Also, for the first time, I do not have a social worker in my life, but I do know where they are if I ever need them.

April 1993 – March 1994

It was salutary to realise that, 21 years after the tentative beginning of the first scheme in Leicester, Home-Start was considered to be centre-stage within the tapestry of social and economic change in the UK.

Policymakers, government departments and the Audit Commission, quoted the Home-Start ethos and approach in their focus on:

- **the health of the nation;**
- **crime prevention;**
- **education for parenthood;**
- **caring for people;**
- **safer cities, and even**
- **military drawdown.**

Clearly, the simple offer of support, friendship and practical help in their own home, to a young family at risk of breakdown, or exhausted from the daily struggles of life, was considered to be a step towards preventing longer term problems developing.

Some comments about Home-Start at the time included:

> ***'Having a Home-Start volunteer – a female confidante – is a significant health benefit for parents.'***
>
> **Dr Margaret Oates, Honorary Consultant Psychiatrist, Queens Medical Centre, Nottingham.**

> ***'I agree that voluntary organisations play an important role, for example Home-Start. The Government support Home-Start with a £115,000 grant. That money is well spent as a contribution towards preventing later problems.'***
>
> **Viscount Astor – Parliamentary Under-Secretary of State, Department of Social Security.**

> ***'We recognise the very important part played by voluntary organisations like Home-Start in providing support in the vital task of bringing up their children to respect the law.'***
>
> **Michael Howard – Home Secretary.** This was news to us!

It was at this time, that Jane Kaufman Associates, invited by and paid for by Richard Macaire, one of our very supportive and generous trustees, made three significant recommendations:

1) We should change the name of Home-Start Consultancy, to Home-Start UK. The business world had changed since our early deliberations of developing nationally. Now everyone was setting up consultancies for which they charged large fees. No wonder then, that Home-Start Consultancy, a not-for-profit organisation, was finding it increasingly difficult to attract funding.

2) Our partnership logo of the Ancient Symbol of Friendship should be re-presented in white, set in a red circle. This would be a fresh image, which would link the past with the future.

3) We should form a separate trading company, which would be VAT exempt.

All the above were accepted, though the office in Northern Ireland had some reservations about the 'UK' and agreed to use the name 'Home-Start Northern Ireland' when suitable to do so. Schemes themselves agreed that by our Silver Jubilee Year, all would be using the round red friendship logo for a united image.

Four major events were held during the year, in celebration of our 21st Anniversary, generously sponsored by Barclays. These were:

- **A major conference,** in Kensington Town Hall, London, with the focus on The Family – A Cycle of Courage. Larry Brendtro, from his experience of working with native Americans, told us that without a word for "child", everyone up to the age of 11 is known as a "sacred being". This seriously influences the way children are revered by the adults in their lives.

- **Family Album** – snapshots of Home-Start in Words and Pictures, with statistics and quotations, was produced by Dr. Sheila Shinman, supported by Sue Everitt and Sue Pope.
  The text was based on work with 500 families during the preceding year, covering parts of the UK, Australia, Canada, Israel and with British Forces families in Germany. It showed just how much ordinary families and ordinary volunteers could do for each other in a very natural, remarkable way. Sue Townsend, the Leicestershire author of the Adrian Mole books, officially launched the Album, at Leicester University.

  In it, the volunteer/parent relationship is movingly described by Virginia Satir, who is known as the earth mother of family therapy:

  "I want to love you without clutching,
  Appreciate you without judging,
  Join you without invading,
  Invite you without demanding,
  Love you without guilt,
  Criticise you without blaming,
  Help you without insulting.
  If I can have the same from you
  Then we can truly meet and
  Enrich each other".

- **International Study Days** in Swanwick, where nearly 200 organisers from Home-Start in the UK and other countries met. We learnt from each other about the many different issues and difficulties confronting family life in other parts of the world.

  When Satish Kumar, visionary, author and philosopher, began his talk to us, he began by saying ***"I came to speak to a Voluntary Organisation. I have found a Family."***

- **Family Fun Day celebrations,** when over 10,000 families throughout the UK celebrated Home-Start's 21st anniversary wherever they were, on Midsummer's day.

It was also at about this time, that Scotland and Northern Ireland, followed closely by Home-Start in Germany and the Training office, each set up their own Support and Advisory Groups. In no way were they substitutes for the central management committee of Home-Start UK. Rather, they each comprised around eight people who, because of their varied backgrounds, could support and advise the paid staff on issues such as funding, development, publicity, recruiting and interviewing staff. A similar group for Wales was set up two years later.

Shortly before I retired, the two Assistant Directors in England also established their own Support and Advisory Group, so that there was by then, one in each of the UK nations.

April 1994 – March 1995

This was still Home-Start's 21st anniversary year, which coincided with the International Year of the Family. Throughout the UK, schemes encouraged their local councils to incorporate the Home-Start logo of friendship in their plantings in city centres and parks. This led many people to find out more about Home-Start.

Our annual meeting was held on the HQS Wellington on the Thames sponsored for our special anniversary again, by Richard Macaire. Home-Start schemes, and colleagues from statutory and voluntary organisations enjoyed the event with us. Sue Pope led an amusing, but salutary presentation about family life at the beginning of the century, compared with 1994.

Virginia Bottomley, Secretary of State for Health, visited Home-Start UK in Leicester. She expressed surprise at the small number of staff based at central office.

Clive Bate, in a session with senior staff to help us guide Home-Start schemes in their negotiations for funding, explained the **SPIN** model. It consists of

1. Hearing from the *other* person, about the **S**ituation as they see it.
2. Asking them about the perceived **P**roblems
3. Then questioning the **I**mplications, which would then lead to the
4. **N**eed, or pay-off, for Home-Start. i.e. Statements of clear wants and desires, which Home-Start could meet, given adequate funding.

The late Paul Eddington spoke on behalf of Home-Start on the radio's Week's Good Cause. He raised almost £15,000 on our behalf.

Sponsored by Chris King, another of our generous trustees, a new Newsletter was launched, with literally thousands of copies sent free to all Home-Start schemes in the UK. It was for them to distribute locally, within and outside Home-Start, to help to raise our profile. Whether or not they did the trick we shall never know.

The Royal Mail in Kent, an unexpected source, provided generous and helpful leadership training for Home-Start UK staff, to honour our anniversary year.

Because of problems that had arisen in other agencies, the implications of volunteers taking families to their own homes was to be reviewed, insurance taken out and our guidelines re-written. I find it difficult to equate such caution with the boost to families by the spontaneous, affectionate actions of a Home-Start volunteer, who has contributed unstintingly, within the safe boundaries of our working practice.

The voluntary sector so often straddles the division between statutory provision and spontaneous acts of kindness to each other by ordinary people every day. If, for example, two people meet on a bus, one needs help and the other offers it, it is surely their responsibility to decide whether to accept. Volunteers in Home-Start on the other hand, can act spontaneously, but within the framework of an accepted charity.

Our new fundraiser, Glyn Berwick, armed with a Master of Business Administration degree, produced a fund-raising paper, based on the policies and ethical code of the ICFM (Institute of Charity Fundraising Managers). It was distributed to schemes for comment and use. This was sent out to over 200 schemes one Friday afternoon. Unfortunately, an overzealous new secretary, deciding that the heading of the paper was neither sufficiently descriptive nor prescriptive, added that it had to be used by all in Home-Start. In an organisation, which never believed in telling schemes what to do, this caused quite a rumpus!.

The Quality Assurance paper, distributed to schemes with the annual invoice for their 1% TIG (Training Information and Guidance) fee, was fine-tuned once again. We agreed that this was our best form of insurance against a "rotten apple in the basket" syndrome.

With the proliferation of ever more new Home-Start schemes, we were advised by our trustees to maintain a balance between a maximum and an optimum level of service. We would never be able to provide all the support sought by nearly 200 very busy local schemes. But neither should they be deflected from their core work with families, by an overload of training and consultation meetings arranged by Home-Start UK. There was so much that schemes could do to support one another laterally, with practical everyday issues too.

April 1995 – March 1996

To share the load within Home-Start UK as it developed, each member of staff was invited to bid for involvement in a long list of specific core responsibilities. They each responded with characteristic enthusiasm and responsiveness. We were fortunate to have staff with so many talents.

The list included human resources, external and internal communications, policy, interpersonal skills, disability and special needs, adopted children, family breakdown and access, prisoners' families, crime prevention, counselling, legislation, multi-cultural issues, marketing, all schemes to work within the Standards and Methods of Practice, forward planning, structure and progress, IT, fundraising and links with government.

At the same time, we also carried out an audit of who had links with other organisations or individuals supportive of our work.

Looking to the future, with my retirement three years away, it was decided to invite a complete outsider to make recommendations about **the future structure and role of Home-Start UK. Rosemary Jackson,** a forward thinking management consultant from Coverdale Consultants, was appointed.

A meeting was held with senior staff and national consultants in January 1996 to discuss the findings from questionnaires, which Rosemary had sent out to all schemes and to the consultants. The responses had been very positive, showing remarkable commitment to the ethos of Home-Start. Some schemes were suggesting greater control by Home-Start UK, but others just as clearly valued their autonomy very highly.

Funding, a higher national profile, Home-Start UK as a resource centre, more government lobbying and advocacy for Home-Start, setting quality standards, clarification on 'mutual accountability', were all issues raised. There was high praise for the training provided. We were made aware that the Services schemes working in a completely different environment to the UK schemes, often felt left out.

Rosemary Jackson indicated clearly that:

- The structure of Home-Start was a two-way flow, rather than line-managed. The senior staff team of seven, would carry out Rosemary's recommendations for the future.
- Schemes should not expect support from a regional consultant after the first year, but more lateral support between schemes would be facilitated by the regional staff.
- All members of the senior staff team should be based in the central office, to facilitate better communication, and this should happen gradually with natural fall-out and retirement.

Sir Peter Barclay, chairman of the trustees at the time, commented that simplicity was fundamental to Home-Start's success.

> ***"Simplicity must continue to be reflected throughout the organisation, or there will be a discontinuity, which will get out of hand."***

The management committee wrote to all schemes conveying their thanks for the thought, care, wisdom and strength that they had contributed to the review.

> ***"I really must highlight your interest in creating a structure where decision-making REALLY happened at local level and ensured the centre was there to add VISIBLE value to that local process. Therefore the effort put in by all to create a national structure which had a VERY light touch and really served the needs of local work, was most unusual in my experience."***
>
> **Rosemary Jackson, management consultant.**

April 1996 – March 1997

In the Labour Party's policies for partnership between government and the voluntary sector, which appeared in Building the Future Together, in 1997, it was stated:

> **"Having sought the views of the Voluntary Sector and responded to those views, we now invite voluntary organisations to join us in the continuing process of building a partnership through which Government and the Voluntary Sector can tackle the task of making Britain a caring, efficient pleasant and creative place to live."**

I was invited to meet Alun Michael, the senior Cabinet Minister, who had chaired the ministerial working party. He told me that I should imagine the shape of a banana, held upright. The top could see the bottom, but not what exists in between. The analogy was that the government and the community were in direct sight of each other, but that it was the voluntary and statutory sectors in between, which would be responsible for implementing changes, needing to listen to and communicate closely with both the top and the bottom.

In many unitary authorities, Home-Start had become a valued local resource for young families, outlined in their Children's Services plans. As there was a move towards a more integrated approach between social services and education, there was an important contribution by local Home-Start schemes on the Early Years Forums, where it was recognised that our volunteers' work encouraged more healthy, stable, happy families, with supported parents and protected children.

During 1996, the results of the three year CHIPS (Comprehensive Home-Start Initiative for Parental Support) study was published under the title Negotiated Friendship – Home-Start and the Delivery of Family Support, by Nick Frost and his team in Leeds University. This stated:

> **"The majority of those supported could be defined as 'socially excluded'. In our sample 61% were economically inactive, 54% were lone parent families and 70% lived in rented accommodation. Certainly Home-Start seems to reach those excluded groups. Importantly, however, Home-Start reaches all sections of the population – our sample included couples from professional backgrounds, who were owner occupiers, for example. Our interviews suggested that there was little stigma attached to being linked to Home-Start – likely because of its ability to work with all sections of the community."**

April 1997 – March 1998

This was the last working year before my retirement. What a year it was!!

Individual schemes and regional groups throughout the UK invited me to their AGMs and for special celebrations. There were sketches, debates and of course, food.

To mark the beginning of our Silver Jubilee year, we took a roadshow of seminars to 14 destinations throughout the UK, focussing together on Strong Families: Strong Communities. We learned from a wide range of professions about the services and gaps in supporting families in their areas of the country. A vivid memory was hearing that, in one London Borough, the cost of just eight children in the "high risk category", cost the local council £1.3million per annum, which represented 52% of their children and families budget. i.e. each child cost them £160,000 per annum in 1998.

A most memorable experience was a night-sit I offered to a family with new-born triplets when I was en route to a meeting in the south of England. The family already had three other children, including an autistic son and another who had just started school. During my 12 hour stint 7 pm – 7 am I had still given only 12 bottles with accompanying burping and settling, out of the daily 24 and done only nine nappy changes out of 18. The parents were well organised and caring, but exhausted. They had several Home-Start volunteers to help them during the daytime. But the relentlessness of their situation touched me deeply. I still rarely go to bed without thinking about all the other families with multiple-birth children around the country.

The Labour Party led by Tony Blair was elected in June. At the Labour Party conference he urged that we

> **"draw deep into the richness of the British character. We cannot be a beacon to the world, unless the talents of all the people shine through."**

He emphasised duties rather than rights, and actually used words like cherishing, creative and compassion.

In Northern Ireland, Home-Start received considerable funding through the European Union towards work for 'Peace and Reconciliation'. This enabled the capacity of Home-Start to be almost doubled in the Province, some schemes developing satellites, which eventually became independent themselves.

As I retired, there were 240 Home-Start schemes in the UK and with service families in Germany and Cyprus. There were 78 steering committees and areas of interest, actively seeking funding. The Home-Start approach had been adopted and adapted in over 100 schemes in seven other countries, as diverse as Australia and Israel, with people or organisations in over 30 other countries asking for guidance to establish their own informal family support service, based on our experience.

The costs of our national central organisation, were nearly £1 million pounds. We had four Assistant Directors with responsibilities in Scotland, Northern Ireland, Wales and the west of England, British Forces Germany and Cyprus and the East of England. We had an Assistant Director responsible for Training, a full-time fund-raiser, eleven regional consultants with their own administrative assistants based in the four nations of the UK. In the central office in Leicester, in addition to the Director, we had a financial administrator, legal adviser and three administrative staff.

At the outset of our Silver Jubilee Year, and following the tragic death of

Princess Diana, we had a new Patron, Her Royal Highness Princess Alexandra, the Hon. Lady Ogilvy, GCVO. She was totally in tune with our work and immediately attended our Carol Concert and other events.

London-based charity consultants, together with selected trustees, recruited and appointed my successor. Brian Waller, who had been Director of Social Services in Leicester before early retirement the previous year, had been on the Home-Start UK management committee since 1992 and even before that had been appreciative of Home-Start since his social worker days in Yorkshire in the 70s. He was thoroughly in tune with our ethos and approach and brought with him experience of the statutory sector. His appointment was for three years.

During my last year, I attended many crucial meetings, with the Social Exclusion Unit, civil servants and government ministers. Particularly important to Home-Start's future, was a meeting with the Under Secretary of State for Health, Paul Boateng, whose mother was herself an active Home-Start volunteer.

In the presence of my chairman, Chris King, and Kay Bews, Assistant Director, the Minister emphasised that the Home-Start approach, which the government valued, should not be changed in order to receive substantial government funding in future. He was clear that Home-Start should remain focussed on the under fives and their parents, should not be obliged to teach parenting skills, but should continue to offer support, friendship and practical help.

At meetings with Tessa Jowell, Public Health Minister, and David Blunkett, Under Secretary of State for Education, we discussed our plans for the expansion to 760 schemes, which we had originally predicted would be in place by 2001, if adequate funding had been available.

I was also invited to attend a ministerial seminar on parenting, chaired by Jack Straw, the Home Secretary, which emphasised the urgent need for increased support for families. Two meetings with Norman Glass at the Treasury focussed on the Comprehensive Spending Review of all children's services. Home-Start's provision for families was acknowledged as crucial, at a key stage of family life.

So here we were, a quarter of a century since beginning the first Home-Start in Leicester, having our approach wholeheartedly endorsed.

Shortly before I retired, my chairman asked me to write down some ideas and challenges about Home-Start in the future.

Some Ideas and Challenges for Home-Start in the Future.

- Home-Start's development should continue organically, responsively and as simply as possible, with emphasis on ease and efficiency, rather than on power, hierarchy or money.
- Home-Start should never become led by theories or outcomes, but rather remain based on our practical approach, responding to what **families** themselves say they need. "Here I am. What shall we do together today?"
- Any emphasis on quality and value for money, should not negate the flexibility and spontaneity of Home-Start.
- Home-Start continues to exist to protect the best interests of the families, rather than to cover its own back.
- Our practice continues to be sound and fair.
- Home-Start should not be looking for quick results, but have the flexibility to offer time and human resources, regardless of whether it takes three months or three years to help a family to cope again.
- Home-Start remains based on human qualities for which one can neither legislate nor train – the sharing of compassion, kindness, optimism, respect, trust and humour.
- It does not become the puppet of the funders.
- Accreditation will distort motivation.
- Lines of communication should continue to be two-way, spontaneous, flexible and open, with known authority, but otherwise with a light, warm touch.

After 25 years in the organisation, I was leaving on a high. The month before I left, the Department of Health committed £1.03million to Home-Start UK and local schemes for 1998/99. We had a stable, experienced senior staff team. There was continuing development of schemes throughout the UK and in other countries too. The Policy and Practice Guide had been fully up-dated. A Staff Handbook for employment practice, rights and responsibilities had been completed. And with the appointment of the new Director, Brian Waller, who also lived in Leicester, the central office would remain here for the time being, providing stability and continuity for the existing small staff team. What a perfect send off!

March was a month of overlap and induction. Together Brian and I focussed on every aspect of the organisation. We had meetings, both internal and external, including my final meetings with the management committee and trustees.

With amazing coincidental timing, the Charity Commission sent an officer, Tony Vail, to discuss with us the structure of Home-Start, with the central organisation supporting locally based schemes, each of which was separately registered with its own charity number.

What would Tony Vail make of it all? What would he be recommending? This had been really the biggest, most controversial issue, during the previous ten years.

To my intense relief, almost as a gift on my retirement, he completely endorsed our structure and approach. He even teased us that the Commission was overloaded each year with a whole shelf full of individual Home-Start annual reports. But then he added with a broad grin that, to our huge credit, they all spoke with one voice, indicating the unity of the organisation, and that each one was of the highest standard.

The Charity Commission was impressed by the relatively low costs involved in running our national voluntary organisation independently of the local branches, which are locally funded and locally managed.

He took away copies of the Policy and Practice Guide including the Home-Start Agreement Among All in Home-Start, indicating that it was a blueprint for the charity sector.

This was the greatest accolade to our staff, trustees and management committee members, who had worked so well together to develop Home-Start nationally over 18 years.

RETIREMENT CELEBRATIONS

Retirement celebrations began, with my husband Basil involved too, at the most memorable party of my life held in Hillsborough Castle, Northern Ireland. It was also to mark the beginning of our Silver Jubilee Year. *"What is Home-Start?"* asked a group of the castle staff as we left, *"because usually there are hushed tones and much formality at our parties, but this evening there was such a lot of chatter, laughter and obvious friendships".*

My wonderful Trustees, treated Basil and me to a superb sit-down dinner for 25, at the Savoy Hotel, London, overlooking the illuminated Thames. I was honoured to be named 'Founder and Life President of Home-Start'. They presented me with a beautiful garden seat, with a plaque commemorating my quarter century with Home-Start – '1973 – 1988'. Ooops! It had to be removed, and another decade added!

Next, the Home-Start UK staff organised two-day celebrations at Launde Abbey in Leicestershire. All the usual ingredients of food, fun, thoughtfulness, love, laughter and immense generosity were present. When, at the very end, I asked that Glyn should play Auld Lang Syne on the piano while we all linked hands, he burst into the song from the film 'The Full Monty' instead, playing "I believe in miracles, you sexy thing!" We all cried with laughter.

Because my retirement was something I had planned for and anticipated with delight, this was the only time I cried. With two grandchildren and two more on the way, I would be a Home-Start volunteer once more.

Finally, at the 1998 Study Days, with over 300 organisers present, we had the biggest party I am ever likely to attend. The sketches, the teasing (*"she must have 360 white blouses and has never changed her hairstyle in 25 years!"*), the laughter, the memories were at once structured yet spontaneous, once again vividly reflecting the Home-Start approach. Our colleagues from Home-Start in other countries were there too.

I was presented with the largest ever album, containing separate pages of memories from each Home-Start scheme. The piano accordion, with vouchers for 20 lessons is one of the loves of my life. The secretaries from all over the UK gave me an exquisite white Royal Doulton 'Gift of Freedom' figurine. A china bus, carrying replica Home-Start UK staff, announces on the side "World-Wide Home-Start Tours 1973 – 1998." And thanks to all the generous and treasured gifts, Basil and I now have enough garden tables and chairs to entertain our family and friends in comfort, particularly those with Home-Start connections.

The evening ended with over 300 of us, each holding a candle and passing the flame from one to another around the hall. The light of our mutual Home-Start friendship was so very memorably bright.

Chapter 6

A SISTER ORGANISATION IS BORN
Home-Start International

"Our joining this international Home-Start organization encourages my hope that this project will be a model of possibilities of dialogue between very different populations. We can make a small contribution towards a better world, where there is more love, friendship, belonging and caring. An old proverb says, 'a small candle can split the darkness'. If we can join many candles, there is a possibility of a much stronger light and finding a way to improve the welfare of people."

Sarah Zacharia, Jerusalem co-ordinator.

"You will never understand child development in your own country, unless you have experienced it in another culture".

Larry Brendtro, Reclaiming Youth At Risk, USA.

By the late 1980s we began to realise that people in other countries were seriously beginning to be drawn to the natural Home-Start approach to supporting families. They were attracted by

- the voluntary ethos of choice,
- the not-for-profit motive, and
- the contribution of ordinary people to their local communities.

The concepts of voluntary work and of informal, yet organised family support are new to most. In other European countries there is no word for 'volunteer' and the voluntary sector itself is still different from so-called Non Government Organisations – NGOs. We have learned that all around the world, political systems, and the statutory and private sectors alone, can never meet all the needs of parents and children. Nor should they be expected to.

Ina Bakker from the Netherlands Institute of Care – Zorg – and Well-being (NIZW) once graphically described the spread of Home-Start. She pictured it beginning as a small nursery garden in Leicester, becoming bigger and busier, so that it had quite naturally evolved into a 'wholesale and export centre'. Seeds, flowers and trees had been sown and grown throughout the UK, but then had also been planted in Canada, Hungary, Australia, Israel, the Netherlands, Norway and the Republic of Ireland.

Knowing that the seed had come from good stock, trialled and tested in the UK, she said the host country must ensure that their own soil is well prepared and fertilized, to make these seeds grow into strong plants, nurtured by a good local gardener.

What an exceptional opportunity had begun to open up for us all to learn together about family life around the world!

★★★

So how did Home-Start begin to develop internationally – into other countries and within other cultures?

I now realise that, even during the 1970s, while supporting local families in Leicester, I had met many people who came to the highly regarded Voluntary Workers' Bureau, to experience for themselves some of the innovatory projects for volunteers in the city. Others I had met at international conferences in this country, or through Leicester University Departments of Psychology, Sociology and Law.

The first visitors to Leicester Home-Start, were from India (arranged by an Indian psychiatrist at the Leicester Child Guidance Clinic); from Cologne University in Germany; from Dublin and Lisburn in the Republic of Ireland, through the Family Psychiatric Service and the Eastern Health and Social Services Board respectively; from Australia where Margaret Henry was pioneering parent-to-parent support for aboriginal mothers in Brisbane, and from the Netherlands. Professor Henry Kemp, pioneer in child abuse work in America, was planning a conference in the Netherlands, and had invited me to submit a paper on Home-Start's approach to preventing family breakdown.

And so the ball started rolling. The Amsterdam conference led to visits to Leicester by people from Christchurch New Zealand, Oslo Norway, Monash University Melbourne Australia, and Capetown South Africa,

> ***"I cannot wait to get a Home-Start project going in Cape Town – we really need it!"***
> **Helen Starke, Child Welfare Society (Kindersorgvereniging).**

The idea of working through volunteer parents, to support the entire family at home, began to be adopted by hospitals, community projects and pilot studies through universities. None was called Home-Start, but the seeds had been sown.

Then, once Home-Start Consultancy, the national organisation in the UK, was established in the early 1980s, I was invited to discussions with the World Health Organisation and with UNICEF in Geneva. I also spent three weeks in Vienna, Linz and Graz in Austria, through a Council of Europe Fellowship. The people I met there envied the British history of volunteering and of community self-help, because they had had a socialist welfare state for the previous 18 years. The only voluntary work was carried out through the Church.

A group of Caritas volunteers tried to initiate a Home-Start type scheme on the outskirts ofVienna, on a very large estate of high-rise flats, which housed hundreds of young families. "Hoffen heisst den nächsten Schritt nehmen" (to hope is to take the next step), they told me.

Other international contacts began in those early days, through Home-Start articles in journals, Willem van der Eyken's descriptive study of Home-Start: A Four Year Evaluation, and via individuals passing on the idea.

The development of Home-Start in countries other than the UK or with British Forces families in Germany, Cyprus and Gibraltar, began with Israel, the Republic of Ireland and Australia, all in 1988, Canada in 1989, Hungary in 1992, the Netherlands in 1993 and Norway in 1995.

(The following memories are of different lengths, which in no way reflect the places these countries or their people hold in my heart. Rather, it is a reflection of the material I had available at the time of writing.)

ISRAEL

In the summer of 1986, we had the first opportunity to present Home-Start in another country, when the Organisation Mondiale pour l'Éducation Préscolaire (OMEP) invited Dr. Sheila Shinman and me to speak about Home-Start practice and research at a conference in Jerusalem. We were promptly taken out to lunch by Aliya Kedem, the Co-ordinator of Early Childhood Services in the Ministry of Labour and Social Affairs. She told us that our approach was exactly what was needed to support families in all the varied communities in Israel.

When we returned to England, all went silent.

Then, at the end of the year, a letter appeared on my desk, on yellow lined paper hand-written in red biro. Assuming it was from a Home-Start family in this country, I put it aside to deal with that afternoon. I used to receive many such letters, usually telling me how they had appreciated the help of their Home-Start volunteer.

However, this one turned out to be drastically different. It was from the Ministry of Labour and Social Affairs in Israel, saying how impressed they had been by our presentation and the work we were doing to support families. If they provided accommodation in Israel, would we pay our fares to go and begin discussions on how Home-Start might be set up in their country?

I promptly replied that we had no extra funding for travel, but that we would be quite prepared to camp when we got there.

And so it was that, in September 1987, Sheila and I spent 10 days meeting community workers, educationists and families in nine very different communities all over Israel. We talked with representatives of other voluntary agencies, learning how they were set up and run. We had meetings at the Ministry, but were not allowed to shake hands with the Orthodox Jewish Minister. We met colleagues from the Hebrew University of Jerusalem.

In Tel Aviv we spent a morning talking with social workers in the district known as 'Central Bus Station', where people arrived from other parts of the country, with no accommodation, no money, no work and no family or friends.

The heat was almost unbearable. The small first floor room where we met was filled to overflowing with social workers exhausted and stressed out with impossible caseloads. Many of them moved on to other work after two years, realising the impossibility of their duties. Suddenly there was a huge commotion as an irate father, cursing the social workers as he ran up the stairs, stood in the doorway, threatening to hurl a wooden chair at us. Fortunately, the tension was deflated by a calm and sympathetic senior team leader.

Sheila and I were then taken to visit families living in abject poverty, sometimes simply in spaces covered with sheets of corrugated iron. Their dignity and spirit were amazing. Home-Start, we were told, would be their only hope to settle down with their young children, in their new environment, to make a fresh start, supported by another caring parent. They wanted the scheme to begin "tomorrow".

In Ashkelon, an essentially Jewish community, we met with leaders to learn about the needs of young families moving into the town. They were keen to find ways of motivating local women to help and support some of the Jews from other countries who were given free housing, education and health services for five years before being expected to work and to contribute to the community themselves. The population had increased from 60,000 to 100,000 in just three years.

Most memorable of all, was a visit to Um el Fahm, a small hilltop town near the Galilee. It was an Arab Muslim community. We had bumped our way there, in a small car, over unmade roads, through the dust and relentless heat. Chickens, children and gaggles of women were everywhere. The smell of sewage was strong, and I noticed that much of the effluent ran in small channels down the middle of the narrow streets.

We spent the morning with a male community worker who, in excellent English, told us about his work and outlined some of the problems. The only voluntary work in the town, we were told, was undertaken by men. When eventually he paused, I asked him about single parents who might need support. *"No!"* he replied instantly. *"We do not have single parents. It is not allowed. If a girl who is not married becomes pregnant, then she quickly disappears."*

The enormity of what he was telling us was chilling.

That afternoon, Sheila and I sat in the Mayor's parlour - a small room full of men, smoking and drinking strong black coffee. We were warmly greeted by the new Mayor, who began to tell us about his community and his responsibilities. After about an hour of listening, I ventured to ask him what were his priorities during his next three years in office?

He hesitated for a brief moment, but then spoke fluently.

"A road", he said. Yes, that would be good, because at the time none was made up. ***"Sewage"***, he added. Yes, to have a proper sewage system would certainly be an important priority. Then he paused, leaned forward and almost shouted out ***"HOME-START"!*** ...... What!? Was this man really indicating that having Home-Start in Um el Fahm would be a priority? But before I could close my mouth again to speak, he added ***"and a football pitch!"***

Well, then I knew he really was speaking sincerely! And true to his word, he agreed that Mohammed, the community worker, should come to learn more about Home-Start from practising schemes in England.

So in April 1987, we had three visitors from Israel, sponsored by the British Council, wishing to establish the first pilot schemes there in Jewish and Arab communities. Chana Greenberg, an orthodox Jewish grandmother with reverential humanity, arrived at Heathrow airport with Mohammed, who brought Adibe, his new wife of two weeks. Basil, my husband, and I noticed as they came through the barrier, that the new bride walked deferentially several steps behind.

"Does your wife speak English?" I asked.

"My wife does not speak," replied Muhammed. *"That is what we expect in our culture."* So I was surprised to notice Adibe smiling as we spoke together in the car driving up to Leicester. It transpired that she was a graduate of Haifa University, who taught Arab Studies. In due course, she participated fully in our discussions and even Mohammed expressed his surprise at her aptitude and insight, when we discussed the Home-Start ethos and approach.

The three pioneers returned to Israel and established 'Ha Ken' (The Nest) Home-Start, in three very different communities, with full government funding. These were in Tel Aviv (Central Bus Station district), in Um el Fahm, and in Ashkelon.

In Um el Fahm, the Home-Start approach was adapted because it was unacceptable for women outside the immediate family, to visit in the home, "risking their own reputations". They had to establish a family group for parents and children, where they could meet volunteers informally. Then, as friendships gradually developed, a volunteer would be allowed to offer support, friendship and practical help to young mothers and their children at home.

> ***"Ha Ken Project has introduced new norms of family and social behaviour into the Um el Fahm community. Women who have become volunteers have become involved not only with "their" family, but have developed a social awareness and sense of communal responsibility to all mothers whom they see struggling under difficult conditions. This act of reaching out to each other in the community, would have been unthinkable before the project".***
>
> **Hula Schlesinger with Jona Rosenfeld in Out From Under – Lessons from projects for inaptly served children and families. Jerusalem 1995.**

In Tel Aviv, Ha Ken was an arm of the social work department. Volunteers were recruited and supported by Betty Cohen, a social worker, who was allowed 10 hours each week to select, prepare, match and support a team of volunteers working directly with young families at home.

In Ashkelon, the scheme was most like the UK model. Though established as part of the Department of Welfare Services, it was registered as a charity, with its own Managing Board. This met monthly to support the two part time organisers, and comprised representatives from welfare, health, a care centre clinic for mothers and children, education and Ha Ken volunteers. By 1995, there were 60 volunteers working with 100 families each year.

Rachel Larea, their first organiser wrote to me,

> ***"Margaret, when you suggested to me to adopt the logo, I confess I was too stupid and arrogant to do so. It was important for me to be independent and to create my own scheme. Now, after quite a time, I feel different; more and more I find that the ancient symbol of friendship expresses all I feel and think about Ha Ken. That symbol is something above gender, faith, or nationality. It means we are equal human beings. And this equality enables us to share, to feel empathy and to help each other".***

When Basil and I visited Rachel and Zafrira's scheme in 1996, we met all the relevant referrers and supporters of Ha Ken. In the evening, 68 volunteers gave us the best party we had ever experienced. We were given an Ulele (tongue chanting) welcome. Traditional food, as for a wedding feast, was provided by volunteers from Ethiopia, Georgia, Morocco, Russia, and Israel. They danced, they acted out sketches of arranged marriages and family life, and we were then presented with a collage of photographs which had been taken of our visit to various locations in Ashkelon *during that day*. It had already been framed! The Deputy Mayor generously offered Home-Start participants from other countries, free hotel accommodation and facilities, should we ever wish to hold one of our conferences in Ashkelon, his town.

> ***"Everybody can be a volunteer. You do not have to be a respected member of the community, just be yourself and respect others for being too."***
>
> **Rachel Larea, Ha Ken organiser.**

I was privileged to visit Israel almost annually until I retired, as I had been invited to join and then to chair for three years, the International Initiative for Children, Youth and Families. This was a new enterprise, established and funded by the Dutch government, to work with policy makers, practitioners, researchers and managers to promote new and sensitive ways of working with people within their own communities. Israel was a leader in this respect and hosted our meetings at least once a year. I was always inspired by the people and their philosophies.

Even as early on as 1991, the government had offered to sponsor the development of Ha Ken wherever it was requested throughout Israel. Within a few years, there were 29 schemes, including one in an essentially Druze community, plus others working with the Arab or Jewish communities.

The first National Co-ordinator, Chaya Leibman, was appointed, followed some years later by Hula Schlesinger.

Study days for all Ha Ken co-ordinators, or for coach loads of volunteers, were held regularly in different parts of Israel. They too believed that for trust, respect and good communication to spread effectively, it was important for people to meet one another face to face. I was impressed by how their Ha Ken schemes reflected so well the ethos of Home-Start. These were wise, experienced, caring women.

At the end of one course of preparation for volunteers, the participants had been asked to think of the course as a shopping basket, and to say what they would keep and what they would throw away. They all agreed that they would keep everything except their prejudices. These they were learning to recognise, and would jettison.

A story for volunteers, which I remember for its poignancy, was about the difference between the Galilee and the Dead Sea, both of which are fed by the river Jordan. The Galilee is alive, because it both receives and gives water. The Dead Sea is dead, because it only receives and doesn't give! There is much to be learned from water – its fluidity, flexibility, dependability and the fact that it soothes and sustains all life.

On another occasion, I had arrived from England in the very early hours of the morning, to speak at a conference. Still half asleep, I crossed a road on the outskirts of Jerusalem, about to step onto a pedestrian crossing, when a car hooted loudly several times. What was I doing wrong? I stepped back. And only then peered into the car, to find it driven by the only other person I knew there at the time, Mili Maas – a researcher of international renown, involved in Ha Ken. She took me home for breakfast!

***

Isifya is a Druze community, south of the Carmel hills. Druze is a restricted sect, developed from Islam, whose members believe that the soul does not die but goes through another body and has another life. The Druze never accept others into their community; both parents have to be Druze for the child to be spiritually accepted. Women do not go out to work outside the home, although the attitudes of young women were changing in the 90s.

The Home-Start approach began in Isifya, when a young single Christian Arab woman, Hoda Rouhana, undertook to co-ordinate it. At first there was suspicion, but then, when the men realised that Ha Ken was by women for women in the home, they gave their approval. By the end of the first course of preparation for volunteers, word had spread, and, as with many of the other schemes in Israel, women were already queuing up to attend the next course. Quickly it had become known that, through Home-Start, women were allowed out, to attend training, to do voluntary work, to listen to talks (including birth control and violence in the family), and to be in touch with professional institutions in the village.

When we met in Leicester in 1995, Hoda told the international group that she had the highest regard for the Druze women with whom she worked. They were immensely brave. They were beginning to challenge traditional attitudes, and had already established a shelter for women who needed to escape violence.

Yet again, the Druze experience convinced me that each Home-Start scheme, wherever it is based, must remain autonomous and develop from locally expressed need, with local choice. It must not be imposed on any neighbourhood, but if a particular community is informed and chooses to adopt and adapt the approach for families, then it is given every encouragement, all resources and back-up by the national coordinator. So much can be learned from each other.

Just as with individual families we support, the unique identity of each community can be respected and protected.

In 1997, shortly before his assassination, Yitzhak Rabin presented Ha Ken in Tel Aviv with his Prime Minister's Peace Prize. Arab, Jewish, ultra orthodox and secular women, rich and poor Ha Ken volunteers and families were working so very naturally together.

Family life and family needs genuinely transcend different religions, politics and cultures.

AUSTRALIA

In 1988, I was invited to speak about Home-Start at another OMEP conference. This time it was in Canberra, Australia. Three lively women who had spent their working years with families and pre-school children in caravan parks in Newcastle, New South Wales, joined me in a vivid sketch about family life, as part of my presentation.

These three, who have remained friends to this day, took the idea of working with parents and children through volunteers, back to their own project, and then established the first Home-Start scheme in Australia in 1989, funded by the Van Leer Foundation and with lovely Gus Eddy as the first coordinator.

This scheme was in East Lake Macquarie, under the umbrella of the Family Action

Centre of the University of Newcastle, about 100 miles north of Sydney. They adopted in their entirety the original Home-Start ethos, principles and practice.

Just one year later, Gus came to the study days in Swanwick and showed us a video of their first year. We were astounded at the similarities between volunteers, families, energies and commitment in Home-Start, two opposite ends of the world.

> ***"Families can't believe people are willing to help them for nothing,"* said Gus.**

After the first few years, an audit of home visiting was undertaken by a National Child Protection Committee set up by the Commonwealth Government to identify best practice and identify gaps in providing support to families. They focussed on prevention rather than crisis, and concluded that Home-Start was truly valued by referrers and families alike.

In 1994, under Commonwealth funding, the Family Action Centre gained a three-year grant to disseminate the Home-Start model throughout Australia. Marilyn Barnes became the National Co-ordinator and spread the news nationally. Home-Start was becoming well known in the country, and Dr. John Irvine, a child psychologist, agreed to be Patron. He is a renowned media personality in Australia, as well as a popular author. He has been a wonderful supporter of Home-Start, and truly believes in the preventive approach to family support.

A second scheme began in Nyngan NSW in 1995, funded by a Rural Health Support, Education and Training grant. The population was 3,600, making confidentiality a problem. Two neighbouring towns, Cobar and Warren, each about 135 miles away in opposite directions, were also expressing interest in adopting the Home-Start approach. One volunteer made a round trip of 60 miles each time she visited her family in the outback.

I vividly remember giving my first talk in Sydney and mentioning how Home-Start works in rural isolated communities in the UK. Gently a woman told me that she had travelled 400 miles that day, from *her* rurally isolated community, to hear about Home-Start.

In Sydney, the first scheme developed under the umbrella of the Benevolent Society, reinforcing its role in preventing child abuse.

By 1996, Home-Start also existed in Corowa, Copelan, Tuggeranong, Coffs Harbour, and Wellington - i.e. there were eight Home-Start schemes altogether in New South Wales, and many enquirers from other states.

Another evaluation undertaken at the time, by Community Solutions declared that "the preventive and early interventionist approach taken by Home-Start was of particular interest to government." It also stated "The greatest challenge confronting existing Home-Start schemes and Home-Start Australia's endeavours to help the establishment of new schemes, is lack of funding".

Too true! The intrepid Debbie in Nyngan, whose funding was withdrawn, continued to run the organisation as a volunteer herself. Her tenacity paid off two years later when her scheme was fully funded once more.

Marilyn Barnes, who had worked with Home-Start in Newcastle NSW before establishing Home-Start Australia with vision and optimism, must be commended for her commitment to developing Home-Start, through all its ups and downs.

In 1997 she invited me to speak at a Home Visiting Conference in Canberra. One member of the organising committee was a representative of Good Beginnings, a brand new family support initiative, based entirely on Home-Start (they had been to visit Home-Start UK and schemes here). But as they said *"Good Beginnings will be founded and developed in Australia, to be exported to other countries in due course."*

There was no competition. There are more than enough families who need support. Our only concern was that their organisation should be effective and sensitive for families. They changed the structure, widened the scope, and Good Beginnings began.

On several of my visits, Home-Start Australia arranged for colleagues and me to meet for discussions with government officials at local, regional and national levels, including the NSW Minister of Community Services, Roy Draper, and the Federal Minister for Health and Welfare in Canberra, Judi Moylen.

Administrators in the Department of Community Services, Child and Family Services stated:

> ***"The need to re-examine the range of child protection services and to move from a Departmental service delivery system which emphasises the role of statutory intervention to the detriment of preventive and supportive services has been identified in our Strategic Directions in Child Protection report."***

It was also being recognised that the Home-Start volunteers themselves were gaining a boost for their own self-confidence. When Loretta aged 50, in Kotara answered a Home-Start advertisement, she had just sold a business, was out of a job and was upset about being separated from her own three children who had moved away.

> ***"The walls of the house were closing in. I felt lost. But then Home-Start gave me a new lease of life, by helping others, I found a new direction for myself."***

In 1999, with the development of the Families First Initiative, very akin to Sure Start in this country, I was invited to speak at a parenting conference in Melbourne, sowing the seeds for the first Home-Start scheme in Victoria. The timing was perfect, as it allowed me to join in the lively 10th anniversary celebrations of Australia's first Home-Start scheme in NSW.

It was that initial scheme which had set the tone, with fun, flexibility and freedom of spirit. They had it and they spread it – to other schemes in their country and also internationally. They wrote Home-Start songs and sketches, and took every opportunity to travel to other countries. Their energy and enthusiasm still know no bounds.

THE REPUBLIC OF IRELAND

Anna Lynch, was a social worker in Dublin in the 1980s,when there was 75% unemployment, too much child abuse, and a need to focus on prevention rather than on crisis. Anna had heard that in parts of the UK, Home-Start, a voluntary organisation, was offering support to families at home through volunteers – other parents. She attended several of the meetings in Northern Ireland, where Valerie McGuffin had launched the first scheme in Belfast, and declared herself hooked on the Home-Start approach.

Anna's tenacity in seeking funding to begin the first scheme in the Republic was quite remarkable. She eventually succeeded through the National Lottery, and set up the first scheme in Blanchardstown, just outside Dublin. The Lottery funding sounded frivolous and insecure at the time, but 10 years later, schemes in England followed Anna's lead.

My memory is of a group of lively women, whose motivation to volunteer, had been inspired by Anna. At their weekly family group I met parents and children. Their sense of humour was infectious and so was their level of compassion for each other. Their Home-Start was in full swing when I visited.

> ***"Being a volunteer is a bit like boiling an egg. You start off raw and thin-skinned. A while after plunging in, you begin to get into shape and become more firm. Then hopefully, if you get the timing right, you become nice and solid, but with a sunny soft centre, and definitely not hard-boiled."***
>
> **A volunteer in Blanchardstown Home-Start.**

For support and encouragement, Anna related to other co-ordinators north of the border. She also joined in study days and other Home-Start events in England, contributing her real insight into the needs of parents, as well as her delightful sense of fun and her memorable Irish dancing.

In the 1980s, the voluntary sector in the Republic had been small and poorly supported generally, but slowly Anna and her team gained respect through their steady, high quality work with families. Eventually the Health Board contributed funding and a second scheme also began in Cork. For many years the intrepid Anna worked towards the expansion of Home-Start in other communities too, but had to do this alongside her work in Blanchardstown.

More recently, Anna told us that often she had felt rather like a foster child attached to the family of Home-Start in the UK, but that once she began to meet representatives from other countries, and attended our international meetings, she had become enthusiastic about belonging to the international Home-Start community.

HUNGARY

When I ran a workshop at the Mental Health in European Families conference in Prague in 1991, one participant was particularly enthusiastic. He was Dr Csaba Rátay, a family therapist from Hungary, who simply asked whether I would be prepared to support him in promoting Home-Start in his country.

Six months later, I spent a week visiting Budapest, Kécskemét, Eger, Miskolc and Satoraljaujhély, - quite a tongue twister - in the famous Tokai wine-growing area, and we also went to Kosice, over the border in Slovakia, where there was a neglected, disaffected Hungarian-speaking community.

Around 70 people attended that first meeting, at the Ministry of Welfare in Budapest. People shared their experiences and views openly, some keen, others more doubtful. Ágota Benkö was there, on 9th March 1992. Almost a decade later, she was to become significantly active in the development of Home-Start in Hungary.

I spoke either through an interpreter or Csaba at all the venues. It was very disconcerting that sometimes when I spoke two sentences, it took a very long time to translate, but by contrast, when I said quite a lot, it was interpreted in three words! *"I am interfering, not interpreting,"* Csaba told me brazenly.

At each meeting, there was general apathy at first. Volunteering and voluntary organisations were simply not part of the Hungarian culture. Indeed, they had been banned since World War 2. Most women worked and had time only for their own families. There was little sense of neighbourliness or of caring for people outside the immediate extended family.

Wherever I went, I listened intently, wanting to absorb and to learn as much as I could about this former communist country. There was simply no history of people helping each other. Csaba told me:

> ***"People don't interact; families don't interact. They communicate through notes. The only gold medals are for the highest debt rate, the highest suicide rate, the highest rate of alcoholism. 50% of men die before they retire at 60 years. The divorce rate is 35%."***

Gypsies were viewed as criminals in society, and the children's homes I visited often had the second generation of gypsy children, who had been taken from their parents at birth.

So it was not surprising that families expected the very best professional help they could get. Certainly then, Home-Start seemed like a non-starter.

But towards the very end of nearly every meeting, I found that one person would suddenly declare that they really hoped that the Home-Start approach would take off in their country. They genuinely liked the idea of parents helping each other. This always caused the rest of the audience to turn to face the loner and between them, in their own language, at their own pace, they would agree that this English voluntary family support scheme was, after all, just what they needed.

Keen at least to establish the first scheme in Budapest, Csaba undertook to work every Saturday for 18 months, simply to earn enough money to pay the salary of Zsuzsa, (Sue), the first Home-Start organiser in Hungary. He also found a derelict building in Zone 1, which together with family and friends, he decorated and equipped, to establish a Family Therapy unit, from which the first Home-Start scheme would also be run.

The name would be Add Tovább, a famous phrase in a children's nursery rhyme, which means "pass it on". It automatically elicited smiles. Csaba was convinced not only that a smile begets a smile, but that a mother who had been helped herself, would pass it on to another family experiencing difficulties. So Home-Start – Add Tovább - was born in Hungary.

A second scheme in Kécskemét followed, but for much of the time the organiser there, another Zsuzsa, worked voluntarily, unable to attract any funding for such a new and unheard-of project. Defining and limiting Home-Start to young families proved difficult, when there were so many old people needing practical help, and older children committing suicide.

With grants from the British Council and Know How Fund, reciprocal visits were arranged between Hungary and the UK, with Csaba and the Hungarian organisers coming to England each year, to visit practising schemes, to learn more about Home-Start training and to participate in our meetings with representatives of embryonic schemes in other countries too.

Despite their energy and creativity, Add Tovább constantly found it difficult to attract enough volunteers, and to find families who would accept unpaid, informal support at home. Finding funding to develop and sustain new schemes was virtually impossible during those early years.

In 1995, President Göncz himself offered his support, but at the time, there was not even money available for health services, social work, or pensions.

Some years later, at the beginning of the new century, Ágota Benkö, the Founder of the Large Families Association in Hungary and then in other European countries, undertook to support the development of Home-Start. I have the greatest respect and humility for all that she is undertaking to ensure that families receive the effective and affective voluntary support they so desperately need.

CANADA

In 1984 I was invited to make a presentation on Home-Start at an International Child Abuse conference in Canada. Afterwards, Margaret Haslam-Jones, a determined social worker, who had emigrated from England, was keen to establish Home-Start in Montreal. It would be the first bi-lingual scheme, French/English, based in Brossard.

It was three years before Sue Everitt, our UK Consultant, was invited to meet Margaret and husband Tom (treasurer), and their committee in Montreal, to give encouragement. Funding was really proving impossible to obtain. Margaret Haslam-Jones attended several of our courses and visited schemes in England almost annually it seemed, to keep up her motivation. But it was to be another two years before a grant was obtained. The first Home-Start scheme in Canada would begin at last proving that tenacity can win in the end.

When in 1989, Première Pas/Home-Start was launched in Brossard, just outside Montreal, the co-ordinator Alicia Zlatar, invited me to spend a few days with them. I was able to talk about the Home-Start history and approach with volunteers, management committee members and also actual and potential funders. I also learned from the scheme about their situation and needs. It was such a warm and happy time together.

Slowly, over the years, four more schemes began around Montreal, and by the time I retired, there were requests for guidance on establishing Home-Start in other parts of Canada, including Winnipeg, Vancouver and Edmonton.

One dilemma which arose was whether the first experienced organiser of an initial scheme in a new country would be the appropriate person to become the national co-ordinator for new and developing schemes. It was agreed that this might not follow automatically, just as the initial organiser of a scheme does not necessarily become senior, when other staff are appointed.

THE NETHERLANDS

Continuing her 'market garden analogy', Ina Bakker from NIZW in Holland, described how the Home-Start seed had first been transplanted to her country.

In the early '90s, the Dutch Ministry of Health, Welfare and Sport had decided to consider importing successful 'plants' from other countries, rather than trying to propagate new ones themselves. An international conference had been held in Scheveningen for selected people working with children and their families "from the ground up" in other countries. I was privileged to run a Home-Start workshop on that occasion.

Together we analysed the common principles which had proved vital to each of our projects. They were, quite simply:

- Work with the whole family within the community, not just with the child;
- Work in a positive, productive way, step by step, achieving realistic goals;
- Build on strengths rather than emphasising problems, focussing on the possibilities and resources of everyone involved.

The Dutch government had adopted these for their new community 'gardens' and had begun to grow new initiatives for families, which included Home-Start.

In 1993, two of their 'gardeners', NIZW and LIOSE, an organisation which promoted social-educational work in the Province of Limburg, together undertook to establish three pilot Home-Start schemes in the Province. They would be researched, videoed and written up in a book, all after the first year. If successful, Home-Start would then be replicated throughout the country. Just like that!

There was however, an important difference. The three pilot schemes were not funded as independent organisations, but rather as "independent parts of an existing organisation." Salaried, established community workers were required to spend eight hours each week on Home-Start work – supporting families with one child under six (school age), at home, through trained and supported parent volunteers. They hoped to appoint a local parent co-ordinator in due course.

Accordingly, during 1993/94, the pilot schemes began in Maastricht, Venray and Heerlen.

It was agreed that Home-Start UK would participate in the training of the first group of Dutch organisers, with costs paid by the NIZW. Sue Everitt assisted with this.

An Agreement was drawn up between NIZW and Home-Start UK, which stated:

> **"Home-Start UK and Home-Start in the Netherlands will retain close links with each other and avail themselves of training and information-sharing opportunities.....The relationship between Home-Start UK and Home-Start in the Netherlands is founded on trust and co-operation. Success is dependent on good communication......The relationship between Home-Start UK and Home-Start in the Netherlands cannot be enforced. Like all other relationships within Home-Start, it is entered by choice and similarly it can be ended by choice. We believe that this freedom epitomises the ethos of every aspect of Home-Start."**

We were off to an excellent start, as was to be expected where there was such a will to succeed, backed by generous resources, imagination and flair.

The results of the research in Limburg province "Home-Start Evaluated", emphasised that:

- The families reached by Home-Start were not an average group. 30% had only one parent, only 12% worked outside the home, and 44% had low educational attainment.
- Families lived through "five times as much negative and radical happenings, (decrease of income, problems with health, contract with

police, justice or violence.)"

- Next to the afore mentioned families, there were also those with highly educated, married and working women.
- The motivation of the volunteers was to do something of value for other people, which was also challenging and interesting.
- Remarkable is the fact that when the level of a volunteer is more or less the same as, or comparable to the families they visit, the outcome is more successful.
- The problems the mothers wanted to work on with the volunteers were mainly emotional support and educational themes.

In 1997, Humanitas , the Dutch charity which focuses on often marginalised groups of people in society, celebrated its Golden Jubilee. To mark this significant occasion, I was invited to be there when they launched a new (for them) initiative to support family life - Home-Start - which they would sponsor around the country. With a combination of the generosity of Humanitas, the experience of SIMBIOSE, and a government willing to promote voluntary family support relatively quickly, there were already over 50 Home-Start schemes throughout the Netherlands.

Marijke Galama was appointed as the first National Co-ordinator.

The Dutch too, we have discovered, enjoy excuses for celebrating. With their renowned creativity, they held a memorable day of fun and learning for volunteers and coordinators in Amsterdam Zoo in 1997. I was privileged to be with them. One unique touch was each of us being given a picnic lunch in a cotton bag, printed with the Home-Start logo of friendship. It meant that as we walked around the zoo at midday, members of the general public constantly stopped to ask about our organisation. The Home-Start profile was certainly raised on that occasion.

In 2001, Home-Start Rotterdam, working mainly with Islamic immigrant families, invited me to be guest speaker at their conference. Fadma Bouchatiou, their senior co-ordinator, emphasised how Home-Start for families and communities fits well within the teachings of the Koran.

The numbers of volunteers from cultural minority groups in the Netherlands was growing, as was the practice of volunteering, in all age groups. Experience showed though, that Home-Start volunteers were committing themselves for longer than any other volunteer group.

Eight years after the first pilot schemes began in the Netherlands, Home-Start was established in all 11 Provinces.

> ***"Start where they are and build with what they have" is an ancient Chinese wisdom brought into daily practice by Home-Start. The Home-Start formula – providing voluntary support to families – is a great success in many countries and the Netherlands is privileged to be among these countries now."***
> **Drs. Fokko P.C. Kool, Netherlands Ministry of Social Affairs.**

NORWAY

> ***"In England, people are born with the voluntary ethic. In Norway, people are born with skis on!"***
> **Bente Brostrom, Founder of Home-Start in Norway.**

Through the International Initiative for Children, Youth and Families in 1995, I was invited by Rigmor Grete Moe, from the Nik Waals Institute, to give a formal talk on Home-Start in Oslo. At the time, the government had set a target for establishing Volunteer Bureaux throughout the country, to encourage more citizen participation. Perfect timing to establish Home-Start there. The other attraction for Norway, was that Home-Start had a values system, which was based on equality and co-operation.

The Blue Cross were keen to support Home-Start and sent representatives from Frederikstad, Baerum, Aske, Oslo and Trondheim to learn from Home-Start in the UK. We quickly established that they all had the Home-Start laugh, so were guaranteed success.

The first scheme in Norway began in Trondheim with Anne Berit Lund as the first co-ordinator. Sadly we only knew Anne for two years, as she died of cancer. But her contribution to launching a new approach to family support in her country will long be appreciated.

A national committee was set up. Kay Bews from Home-Start UK visited for a week in 1997, and gradually more schemes began. Our colleagues from

Norway reported that it felt as if the road was being built as they walked! With over 200 volunteer bureaux throughout the country, the search for volunteers was generally successful.

"For us, Home-Start is like a fairy story . . .and in Norway we like fairy stories."
Bente Brostrom, Founder and Chairman of Home-Start Norway.

WORKING TOGETHER TO ESTABLISH HOME-START INTERNATIONAL

For the ethos of good communication, openness and trust to develop between all countries which had started Home-Start, we considered it important for us all to begin to meet regularly. Together we would create a bond of understanding. The United Nations International Year of the Family in 1994 provided us with the ideal opportunity to do so for the first time.

First International Meeting in England, May 1994

Generous funding was obtained through the British Council and the Know How Fund for travel costs to invite our colleagues from all the other countries, (except Norway, which had not yet begun), to join us at the first ever Home-Start International Study Days, held in Swanwick in Derbyshire.

There were over 200 organisers from the UK schemes, as well as those who worked with British Forces in Germany and Cyprus.

"I remember the wonderful, entertaining evening of international culture (not to mention consumption of many bottles of wine from a variety of countries) which included a rendition of Tulips from Amsterdam, when 300 bulbs were thrown out into the hall for everyone to catch. There was Hungarian and Irish dancing and who could ever forget the deadpan delivery of Snow White by the girls from Germany? Henk from Holland even got you in his grip on stage, for a Latin American tango, Margaret! Those study days were without doubt the most enjoyable I have ever attended. It was terrific to feel a part of an extended international family."
Mandy Lindley, organiser Home-Start Portsmouth.

There was much to share and much to be learned from the international experience, so 20 of us, including Home-Start UK staff and I, returned to Leicester for two more days together. Accommodation was provided by family and friends. We worked hard, played hard, and thoroughly enjoyed the stimulus of each other's company.

Together we considered the Home-Start aims, our focus, the methods, structure (for funding, management, volunteers, families) and of course, the Home-Start ethos.

We acknowledged the importance of all schemes in other countries being independent, as they are in the UK. Each would be rooted within its own culture and community, with local funding and a local support structure.

As each country's national organisation developed, we agreed that it too should be funded independently. Already at this stage, there were the beginnings of national structures, in Israel and the Netherlands, with staff based centrally and regionally within each country. Each central organisation would be committed to promoting the welfare of parents and children by providing effective training, information, guidance and support (TIGS) to each existing and potential Home-Start scheme within their country.

The amount of contact or control Home-Start UK should have in relation to schemes which developed abroad, before they had their own national structure, was raised. It was decided that this should be a topic for a separate meeting.

But it was agreed that Home-Start UK should be the lead organisation for promoting and supporting effective development internationally. Other countries, which already had Home-Start, would also offer support, friendship and practical assistance to enquirers, where appropriate (e.g. the Netherlands would help with Surinam, Hungary with other central and eastern European countries, and Australia with New Zealand and the Antipodes.)

Whenever it became appropriate and possible in future, each country might pay a fee to Home-Start UK, for the franchising expertise, training, guidance and support provided.

The joint Standards and Methods of Practice and Principle could be adopted and adapted, in different communities, but consultation and contact with Home-Start UK were strongly recommended.

We all agreed that young families all over the world deserved the very best personal support, their local community could provide. Wherever Home-Start was involved, volunteers would ensure that the needs of the families were paramount.

We were aware that our international dialogue had only just begun, and funding permitting, resolved to meet again one year later.

Home-Start UK Meeting about international developments June 1995

The significance of Home-Start's international development had really begun to dawn on us, not only for families in other countries, but also for the organisation as a whole in the UK.

Before the next meeting with our international colleagues, therefore, I invited an organiser (Paula Spencer, South Shropshire), a chairperson (Judith Colegate, Reading), an external research adviser (Dr Sheila Shinman), a consultant (Sue Belcher, north region), and the consultant for Northern Ireland (Valerie McGuffin), to meet with me to consider the implications of international development, of which they all had some experience.

Together we considered differing cultures, statutory provision, value placed on human life, political change, financial constraints and the vacuum of social care networks.

We were concerned to establish whether interest from another country was rooted in the needs of families or in fulfilling the self-interest of the enquirer - like two Gambian Pastors, whose motive appeared to be to escape from their country.

We recognised the need to distil the core principles which underpin Home-Start, while allowing each country to adopt and adapt our approach within its own culture.

For UK schemes at that time, an Agreement Among All in Home-Start, for quality assurance was envisaged. Maybe this could form the basis for a similar agreement with each other country, to maintain the ethos, whilst recognising that a lead-in period of up to three years might be needed.

At the next meeting with our international colleagues, we decided to establish a Steering Group for an International Home-Start Consultancy, so that the next steps forward would be taken together.

Second Home-Start International Meeting 15/16 November 1995 Leicester England

Background to the Meeting

There had been amazing parallels between the development of Home-Start nationally in the UK, and Home-Start internationally.

In the UK, by 1980, there had been eight local schemes. There had been over 20 other areas seeking support to establish Home-Start in their communities when, in 1981, it had been decided that we should go national. Then, 14 years later, with Home-Start already established in eight different countries and with 21 others requesting information, the scope to develop internationally became apparent.

So in November 1995, funded mostly by the British Council, 29 people from the eight countries (which now included Norway), met in Leicester to discuss the future.

We agreed which elements of Home-Start should be adopted, and which could be adapted in other countries. From those present, it was clear that the approach could work in diverse cultures and countries. But we were equally clear that it should not be imposed, but rather that it should develop through individuals, organisations or communities requesting it.

Because of the significance of this meeting, I list below the names of the people who attended. Those who formed the eventual Steering Group to establish a sister organisation, Home-Start International, are indicated with an asterisk*.

- **Netherlands** –
  ***Ina Bakker** (NIZW – National Institute of Health and Welfare)
  Annemarie van Wijmen (Coordinator Maastricht, Limburg)
  Matt Wierts (Coordinator Heerlen, Limburg)
- **Australia**
  Sheilah Bartlett (Home-Start co-ordinator, Sydney, New South Wales)
  ***Marilyn Barnes** (Home-Start Australia consultant)

Debbie Roach (Home-Start co-ordinator, Nyngan, NSW)

- **Norway**
  ***Bente Brostrom** (Norwegian Institute of Child Welfare Research)
  Margareth Bergmann (potential Home-Start Frederikstad)
  Anne Berit Lund (Home-Start organiser Trondheim)
- **Republic of Ireland**
  ***Anna Lynch** (Home-Start co-ordinator Blanchardstown, Dublin)
- **United Kingdom**
  Sue Belcher (Home-Start consultant Northern Region)
  Chris King (Home-Start UK trustee and Chairman of the management committee)
  Sue Everitt (Home-Start assistant director, UK East)
  ***Margaret Harrison** (Home-Start UK director)
  Dr Sheila Shinman (External Research Adviser)
  Berwyn Peet (Home-Start consultant London)
  ***Judith Colegate** (Chairman Home-Start Reading)
  Paula Spencer (Home-Start organiser South Shropshire)
  Angela Plowman, my Personal Assistant, taking notes.
  Edit Bodis (Hungarian interpreter)
- **Israel**
  Rachel Larea (co-ordinator Ha Ken,Ashkelon)
  ***Hula Schlesinger** (national co-ordinator, Haifa)
  Houda Rouhana (Co-ordinator, Isifya)
  Rawda (Co-ordinator, Isifya)
- **Hungary**
  ***Zsuzsa Dobos** (Co-ordinator, Budapest)
  Maria Pater (Co-Ordinator, Budapest)
  Dr Csaba Ratay (Founder and Chairman, Budapest)
  Zsuzsa Farkas (Co-ordinator, Kécskemét)
- **Canada**
  ***Alicia Zlatar** (co-ordinator, Première Pas/Home-Start, Brossard, Quebec)

Together we considered and re-wrote drafted papers on the process of Launching Home-Start in other Countries, the International Standards and Methods of Practice, (the most significant changes were to call Home-Start an "independent organisation" rather than a voluntary one; and to call the management structure a "support structure/committee"). We debated the ethos of Home-Start, and were delighted at our base of common values. We incorporated future plans for international development in the Home-Start UK Five-Year Framework for Development, 1995 – 2000.

Our colleagues had brought with them samples of their leaflets, posters, newsletters, videos and research materials. Between us, we already had a rich source of guidance and information.

We agreed to meet annually, to take shared responsibility for the development of Home-Start internationally and, to this end, to form an International Steering Group.

Visits had been arranged for participants to spend time with the following schemes:-Kingston (Surrey), Corby (Northamptonshire), Goole (Yorkshire), Mansfield (Nottinghamshire), Ely/Cardiff (Wales), Brentwood (Essex), Herefordshire, South Shropshire, Torbay (South Devon), Leeds (Yorkshire), South Cumbria (Lake District), Stockland Green (Birmingham – Midlands), Portsmouth (Hampshire), Dublin (Republic of Ireland) and at the Marble Arch office of the London Regional Consultant.

Accommodation was generously provided in private homes or small local hotels, according to choice.

Rachel Larea from Ha Ken, Ashkelon, Israel wrote afterwards:

> ***"The most important thing to the development of Home-Start is to have established an international steering committee, as we have just discussed in November. I think the unity is vital. Sitting and listening to all those wonderful people that are Home-Start all over the world, I could feel those qualities of friendship, empathy, sharing and kindness which make Home-Start come through.***
> ***I am also very satisfied with the decisions and the ideas we discussed at the meeting. It is a very good feeling to be a part of a big movement, to contribute and to learn from others."***

Major-General John Page makes his point.

Kathleen Marshall and Angus Skinner at A Good Start in Life Conference, Scotland.

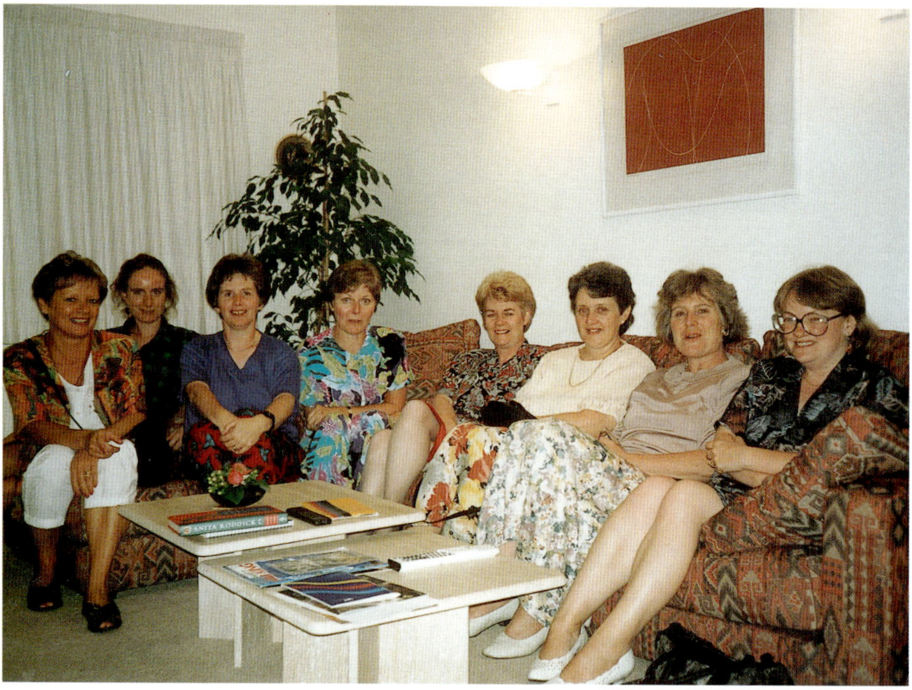

Home-Start UK staff Sue, Fiona, Sue, Sue, Maggie, Valerie, Sue and Kay.

Albert Clark legal advisor at work.

Family Album book launch with Sue Townsend and Sheila Shinman.

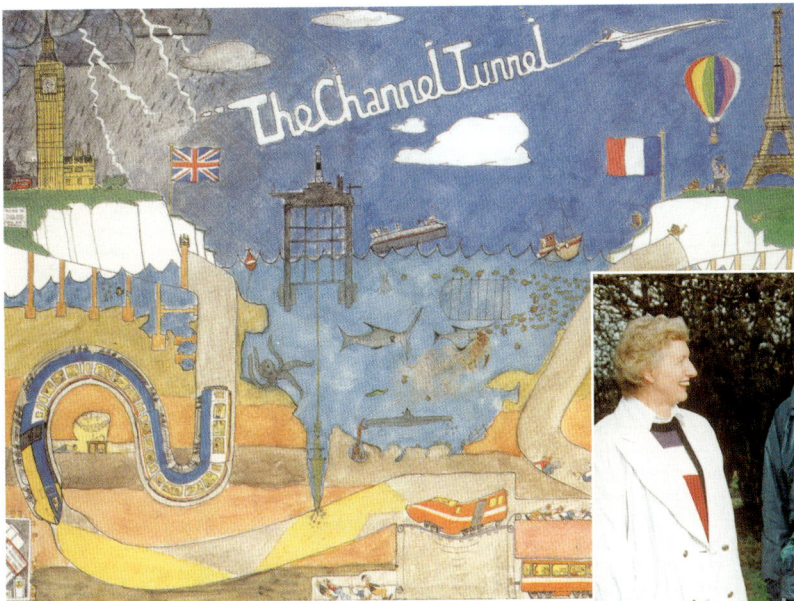

Chis King, intrepid Channel Tunnel walker.

Fun and Laughter.

Parlimentary presentation with Lady Plowden and Virginia Bottomley.

Our Royal Patron helps to celebrate Home-Start Leicester's 18th Anniversary.

Pioneers from the Netherlands singing Tulips from Amsterdam at Swanwick International Study Days.

Csaba Ratay and colleagues launch Add Tovabb Home-Start in Hungary.

L. Chana Greenberg, mother of Ha Ken Home-Start
Centre. Betty and Tel Aviv colleagues with the Prime Minister's Peace Prize
R. Ashkelon celebrations

Home-Start is launched in Australia.

Our Norwegian colleagues had the Home-Start laugh.

Home-Start UK trustees at Margarets retirement party.

Hoda and Chaya with volunteers in Isifya.

Anna and performers from N. Ireland lead the dancing at Margarets farewell party.

The Third International Meeting in Leicester 1996.

The International Steering Group met for the first time on 31st May/1st June 1996. First, it was good to catch up with news and ideas from the countries attending.

The Netherlands reported that the three main lessons they had learned in the past year from Home-Start, were:

- Learn to sit on your hands;
- Let the family set the agenda, and
- Listen to the mother.

Israel was working towards extricating the Ha Ken schemes from under the welfare department. Norway had established a National Reference Group. In Quebec, Canada there was no well-established voluntary sector to support Home-Start. This also applied to the Republic of Ireland, where the Health Board was becoming more powerful, and considered Home-Start to be "lightweight". In Hungary most of the organisers of schemes in Budapest, Kécskemét, Monor, Dunaujváros and Káposvár were not being paid for their work. Funding remained a significant issue.

Australia, unable to attend, had reported to me on the phone, that a new organisation to be called "Good Beginnings" based on Home-Start, was being launched. They had told Marilyn *"If you were a company, we'd buy you out"*. Also, sadly, although Ministers from Western Australia had already visited us in Leicester, they had decided to launch Parent Link, not Home-Start there.

For me, it felt immensely supportive that during the two days working together, we made seven significant decisions for future effective international development:

- **Logo/name** – the name Home-Start is registered as a trademark in the UK, the logo is copyrighted to Home-Start UK. Other countries would need to register the name Home-Start in their own country and find out if the same logo is being used elsewhere. However, a new EEC Trade Marks Office for Harmonisation of the Internal Market (Trade Marks and Design) had recently opened on 1st April 1996, whereby registration could be covered in EEC countries.
- **Quality Assurance** – would be a shared responsibility, *"through*

support and equality" said the participants, *"with shared information and good communication"*. In due course there should be internationally agreed standards.

- **Training** – It was agreed that Maggie Rowlands, responsible for training in the UK, could offer five days a year to facilitate/advise/initiate training opportunities in an international context, adapting the UK training materials.
- **Structure** – Ina from the Netherlands provided diagrams of two potential models - a sunshine and an atomium, - to illustrate the future relationships between each country and with the UK. The sunshine model was unanimously agreed. She said, *"It is not a coincidence that Home-Start UK takes the lead as it has 23 years of experience."*
- **Future funding** for an international organisation. - The Steering Group delegated to me the responsibility for raising money for a "three year pioneer phase, based in England."
- **Umbrella organisations** – After some discussion it was agreed *"the nature of the umbrella does not matter, but the ethos, attitude and approach of Home-Start do!"* But we all agreed that whenever possible, Home-Start locally and nationally in each country should remain independent and autonomous.
- **Support of national consultants** (or pioneer schemes). – In addition to support from Home-Start UK central office, nine of our own staff members had offered to provide training, guidance, information and support for up to five days a year each, to the existing seven other countries, as well as to India and developing countries. Their time would be donated by Home-Start UK, and their expenses paid by the host country, if at all possible.

There was a general sense of achievement over our two-day meeting. We acknowledged that we shared the responsibility for developing Home-Start internationallly. We had established a firm base for the future.

My next task was to make a bid to the international grants committee of the National Lottery for funding.

I did so. . . . . . . and it failed!

Our 1997 planned meeting was cancelled, postponed until we could all come together again during my retirement celebrations the following year.

11th May 1998 Extra-Ordinary Meeting of Home-Start UK Trustees to discuss the development of Home-Start International

Home-Start UK Trustees considered it vital to hold an extraordinary meeting to consider the international development from the UK perspective, now that I had officially retired. They acknowledged the considerable amount of work which had already been carried out with the International Steering Group and endorsed their paper on Core Elements of Home-Start in Other Countries. The international work, like that in the UK, had already begun without creating dependency.

The Trustees noted with amusement and some concern, that the relationship of Home-Start UK to Home-Start International, was one of a child giving birth to a parent!

My role in establishing Home-Start International was agreed, in line with the paper, which had been drawn up after the International Steering Group meeting 18 months previously. Four Trustees – the chairman, Chris King, Ginny Evans, Wendy Rose and Bernard Taylor volunteered to become involved in supporting the development of a sister organisation, with its own director, trainer and administrator. Ultimately outreach workers for different countries might be employed.

19th May 1998 Fourth International (Steering Group) Meeting in Swanwick Derbyshire England.

The sun shone. We sat outside in the grounds. There were 15 of us from all countries except, unfortunately, Hula from Israel.

Mindful of our exciting international potential, and because there are great variations in national systems, we agreed it is essential that the voluntary sector cooperates when working internationally. We therefore discussed models of other charities, which had been successfully transposed to other nations. These included the Bernard Van Leer Foundation, World-Wide Fund for Nature, Alzheimers International, and Befrienders International, which had developed from The Samaritans.

We also focussed on the future relationship between national Home-Start organisations in each country and the central international organisation once it was set up. To this end, we also considered adapting the Home-Start UK Agreement Among All in Home-Start, with something similar at international level.

Clearly there was an urgent need to raise money, to appoint staff for a sister organisation, which we agreed would be called 'Home-Start International', before the current impetus was lost. There were two filing cabinet drawers full of contacts and enquiries from well over 30 other countries.

My role in international Home-Start development in future was again endorsed by those present. Sample job descriptions for future international staff were discussed. Fundraising approaches to ignite the Home-Start International Plan 1998 – 2001 (which I had had to produce for the National Lottery application) were agreed.

In acknowledgment of my retirement, I received enormous generosity and personal kindnesses from all my international colleagues, with whom I had worked so closely over the years. With their sense of purpose, humour and spirit, the future for families internationally was bound to be successful.

Judith Colegate who had contributed to all our meetings, from her many roles within Home-Start Reading in the UK, wrote the following thoughts about the international development of Home-Start.

> ***"Having lived abroad for many years, I realised that the British notion of volunteering was quite unknown in most other cultures. I knew you were keen to get as much as possible done without any finance in place Margaret, and I was cautiously delighted to be invited to the series of meetings in Leicester with delegates from schemes already extant in Ireland, Israel, Hungary, Holland, Norway, Canada and Australia. I was intrigued that everyone seemed to do things in their own way in their own country, but everyone subscribed to the basic tenets – and it worked! . The winning combination of simple but basic working principles married to a flexible approach to individual circumstances could not fail.***
>
> ***Each of our meetings had a theme and a purpose, so that when eventually we had a funder we would have prepared a draft of standards and methods of practice ready for consideration by***

Home-Start International.
It was an exciting time, but also frustrating. We were ready – all that was lacking was the money. At one stage I looked at all my files labelled "H-SI" and honestly wondered if it would ever come to fruition.
A 'champagne moment' for me was when, at an early meeting with our colleagues from other countries, Hula described the effect of Home-Start on the various communities in Israel. It was so moving and unaffected, that it reduced me to tears."

Funding Success at Last for the Birth of Home-Start International

With time to spare and a trip to America paid for by Reclaiming Youth International, which I had been invited to join after I retired, I set about fundraising in earnest.

The second application for National Lottery funding failed again, despite predictions to the contrary.

I approached banks – ING, Swiss, and the World Bank, as well as Commercial Union Plc. An exploratory meeting with the Charities Aid Foundation led me to the Peabody Trust, the Soros Foundation and the Commonwealth Fund in New York. Lloyds TSB Foundation for England and Wales, Kelloggs UK and British Telecom, had all stated that their UK funding could not be used for the benefit of people in other countries.

Eventually though, through the Baroness Brigstocke, a Vice President of Home-Start UK, I had a lead to the JP Morgan Bank in New York. The Managing Director of the Morgan Guaranty Trust Company of New York informed me that there was a family trust, which might be interested in international family support.

Shortly afterwards, I found myself in Claridges, in London, describing the Home-Start approach to two members of the Niarchos family.

Then, in October 1998, THE letter arrived! The Stavros S. Niarchos Foundation had approved a grant of £360,000 payable over 3 years to Home-Start International.

Without delay, we quickly opened a separate bank account!

What a pleasure it was to inform all members of the International Steering Group and all our colleagues in other countries of our funding coup. In the UK, Brian Waller, my successor and I sent out a joint letter to all schemes, stating that in future there would be many and varied opportunities for Home-Start schemes and individuals involved in them, to link with/or host people from other countries. Almost by return, we received 239 replies!

ESTABLISHING HOME-START INTERNATIONAL

My Trustee colleagues who had supported and trusted me so implicitly during the years with Home-Start UK, were thrilled too, at our opportunity to work trans-nationally and trans-culturally. Together we met monthly, between December 1998 and February 1999, to share the responsibility for establishing Home-Start International.

Everything was planned together - investment opportunities, registering as a UK based international charity and discussing the charitable trust deed, staff appointments and conditions of service, premises, on-going links with Home-Start UK, the induction of the new director and the appointment of trustees, including a treasurer for Home-Start International. We also planned and then held a meeting of the International Steering Group and colleagues in London in the summer of 1999.

A whole new and exciting era of opportunities was just beginning for families, volunteers, organisers and all of us now committed to international family support. We could learn about family life in other cultures and countries. Friendship would extend beyond our national boundaries. What valuable opportunities were just beginning for everyone involved in Home-Start, wherever in the world.

We appointed the new Director of Home-Start International, Tanya Barron, to begin work on May 1st 1999. She had come from the European Children's Trust and chaired the UNICEF Non Government Organisations Committee in Geneva. She was very committed to the need to support families as a whole, at home.

During her six-month induction period, I handed over to Tanya, the two filing cabinet drawers full of contacts from, by then, nearly 40 other countries, wishing to find out more about Home-Start and how it might work in their situation.

How could they adopt it and adapt it to support families in their countries?

OTHER COUNTRIES WISHING TO ESTABLISH HOME-START MAY 1999

African Countries

Botswana – information requested.
The Gambia – two Pastors had tried to arrange to come to the UK, where we had set up introductions to Marlborough Home-Start, which is twinned with the Gambia. They were prevented from coming by the authorities, who refused to grant them visas.
Ghana – information requested.
Kenya – The sister of someone involved in Home-Start in the UK, was working with children abandoned due to AIDS, many of whom were being looked after by five and six-year-olds. Sometimes two mothers would be left looking after 30 children while the other parents went to market. In Mombasa, where the population is mainly Muslim, *"programmes like Home-Start are needed for mothers"* we were told.
We had also had several contacts over the previous few years, from a minister of the church in Nairobi.
Liberia – information requested.
Namibia – information requested.
South Africa - Several people had read about Home-Start in Good Housekeeping magazine in South Africa, - our organisation had been adopted by the women's magazine for our 25th Silver Jubilee Year. But more importantly, Basil Pillay a visiting Professor of clinical psychology at Leicester University, determined to establish Home-Start in Durban, as he considered it to be *"an essential service in post-apartheid society."* We were advised to begin within a black community in Zululand or Transkei, regenerating "ubuntu", which means " a person is a person because of other people who care".

North and South America

Canada – More schemes developing in the Montreal area. Individual people in Edmonton, Vancouver and Winnipeg were seeking information and guidance.
USA – Serious interest expressed in New York (Red Hook Community in

Brooklyn), Connecticut (Yale University) and Los Angeles (including Hispanic communities).

Chile – Serious interest from several sources, including my close International Initiative friend Maria Elena Orrego, who was innovating family support systems in Chile through the Annie Casey Foundation. Home-Start Course of Preparation Manual and Guidance materials had already been sent to other groups, at the request of StefanVanistendael from the Roman Catholic Children's Society in Geneva. The Chilean family support workers, I was told, were confused about whether they should be encouraging women to volunteer or rather to work for money.

Ecuador – A colleague to visit Home-Start Bridgend Valleys in the summer.

Venezuela – requested information about Home-Start research. Particular interest expressed in Home-Start by the Centre for Family and Children Research at the Metropolitan University of Caracas.

Asia

Hong Kong – Valerie McGuffin, Assistant Director Northern Ireland, had hosted visitors through Queens University, Belfast.

India – Jenny Hurkett, UK consultant, had spent her sabbatical in Kerala and on subsequent visits met the minister responsible for families. Much interest has been generated, but ideally they would like to have someone from the UK based in the southern state. A jeweller in Kovalam produced silver Home-Start logo brooches for Jenny and for me, and to Jenny's delight, has kept the Symbol of Friendship on his wall.

A Home-Start volunteer in Leith, Scotland, offered free office accommodation in New Delhi through her family there. We also had a possible source of funding through a Home-Start UK trustee.

Sir Rod Hackney, community architect, offered support and contacts linked with his creative housing projects in India.

Japan – Contacts through wives of Japanese workers in Wales and Telford, England. Some had been Home-Start volunteers, or had had a volunteer themselves, before returning to their country of birth. In 1996, the Department of Social Welfare in Japan's Women's University, informed us that child abuse was only just beginning to be identified and that family support like Home-Start would be needed.

Myanmar (Burma) – Keen interest from a minister, who was never granted a

visa to visit England.
Surinam – Contact through Dutch colleagues, as this was a former Dutch colony.

Australasia

Australia - There was an urgent need for funding to establish Home-Start in other States, with particular interest having been shown in Victoria, Queensland and Western Australia.
New Zealand – The Director of Barnardos in Wellington, Ian Calder, had visited Home-Start in England in the mid-1980s, and was keen to initiate something similar for families there. In 1987, I had been invited to talk with his staff at their head office in the windy city. The seed for voluntary support to parents and their children at home was sown. Several institutions launched the approach, including Barnardos themselves, though none called themselves Home-Start.

Europe

Albania – a keen social worker I met at the International Year of the Family conference in Vienna in 1994, really wanted to find ways of introducing voluntary support for families.
Austria – previous interest had also been rekindled at the Vienna conference.
Belgium – contact had been established through the International Initiative for Children, Youth and Families.
Bosnia/Croatia – The Red Cross International Department in London had requested our cooperation in both countries, as had the University of Zagreb's Faculty of Defectology.
Channel Islands – Guernsey and Jersey. Interest had been expressed through the Children's Departments and a visit had already been paid.
Czech Republic – Anne Pemberton from Home-Start in Leeds had established interested contacts in the Czech Republic.
There were also social workers, clinical psychologists and paediatricians, whom I had met in 1991, when, sponsored by the British Council, I had been invited to speak at Palacky University in Olomouc. They had been keen for more support to adapt Home-Start for families, which they considered was desperately needed in their country. *"We have a big State sector working with old methods from the Communist era. We are very child focussed, but now thirsty for new*

systems and new ideas", the civil servant in charge of family services told me, over yet another glass of slivovice.

Denmark- For three years running, a Danish Early Childhood worker had brought 20 nursery staff to Leicester, to rethink ways of working with children by including their parents in partnership. Sue Belcher, a UK consultant, ran a Home-Start session for them at a summer school in Denmark.

Finland – I had established good contacts with Finnish people I had met while in Hungary and Israel.

France – A group of policy makers and practitioners who were visiting the social work department and Home-Start in Tel Aviv in 1998 at the same time as me, were keen to consider the application of Home-Start in their country.

Germany – Several academics in Frankfurt and Berlin were in touch, concerned that all welfare services in their country were becoming increasingly statutory and bureaucratic.

Greece – The Niarchos family, who had donated money to establish Home-Start International, were keen to see it working in Greece. A volunteer from Charnwood Home-Start had emigrated there, taking her knowledge and enthusiasm for family support with her. *"We must find ways to help people feel valued again."* Maria Niarchos.

Italy – requests for information.

Latvia – Continuing interest in this country, from the Union of Large Families Associations, through Agota Benko in Hungary. "We'll do what we can, with what we have, where we are."

Poland – requested information.

Portugal – Considerable interest expressed by policy makers, managers, researchers and practitioners at our International Initiative for Children Youth and Families conference held in Sintra in 1998.

Rumania – was seeking guidance from Home-Start in Hungary.

Russia – I had applied for Charity Know-How funding for a Home-Start scheme in St. Petersburg in 1998, which had been requested by Professor Marina Galina following a visit and showing of the Home-Start video by Alice Sluckin from Leicester the previous year. She said on her return, *"This was an invaluable introduction to Western-style democracy for the women of Russia."*

I found, on visiting the city myself 18 months later, that the ethos of volunteering, of neighbourliness, of kindness to others outside the immediate family, were alien concepts. There was a genuine fear of volunteers placing themselves in danger of injury or theft in Russian households. But the people I met were filled with pride, helpfulness and keen anticipation. *"We want to*

dismantle the wall between government and families" I was told.
There is, however, little incentive to establish a voluntary organisation in Russia, since the government takes 40% in tax from Non-Government Organisations. It was salutary to learn from staff I met in children's homes in St. Petersburg, that with Home-Start support, most children need not have been there.
Slovakia – Much interest in the Home-Start approach had been expressed by individuals during a conference at which I spoke in Bratislava in 1996. People there from post communist societies were keen to harness the ability of individuals within their communities to do things for each other freely, with love and with trust. Only in that way, they believed, could a person or a whole community grow in integrity and maturity. By 1998 they were seeking information from Add Tovabb Home-Start in Hungary.
Slovenia – A delightful young community worker from Ljubljana who came several times to the International Initiative meetings, was keen to establish Home-Start in his country.
Sweden – contacts through our colleagues in Norway. 80% of women worked. *"In Sweden, the State is seen as a mother/father figure, which provides everything."* They wished to encourage more community self-help.
Turkey – A group of Turkish social workers had visited the Home-Start UK London office and UK schemes in 1997, wishing to adopt and adapt the Home-Start approach in their country.
The Ukraine – Linna Kuts has annually expressed enthusiasm in her Christmas cards for establishing Home-Start ever since we met at a conference at which I spoke in Gödöllö University, Hungary, in 1996. Initially my letters to her were (probably) monitored and not received.

In the UK there are increasing numbers of families from other countries - Turkish families in Hackney, people from Estonia in Brent. In Croydon, 120 other languages are spoken. Leicester has a 45% Asian culture. In Leith in Scotland, 45% of the families visited by Home-Start were originally from Asian countries. The variety, the opportunities to learn from each other and to share, are endless, in the United Kingdom alone.

We are families, we are neighbours around the world, linked more importantly by our mutual interests and concerns, than separated by conflicting ideologies. We have found so far, in a small way, that it is possible to build on diversity, to share practical solutions and to take responsibility together for families nationally and internationally.

Parents, wherever they are, need someone to praise them and recognise what they have to cope with. They sometimes need the love and security of a friend – a Home-Start volunteer - who cares about them. They need new experiences and ideas, plus someone to acknowledge and support their responsibility as parents. All this, irrespective of culture, location, religion, politics or money.

The human spirit transcends them all.

Chapter 7

LOOKING BACK, LOOKING FORWARD
The Community of Home-Start

"Life must be lived forwards, but can only be understood backwards."
Soren Kierkegaard, Danish Philosopher.

"We are all made for community, for caring and for love. If I value you, I hope you will value me and that sets up all sorts of repercussions".
Archbishop Desmond Tutu.

Looking back over the first 25 years of Home-Start's natural development from supporting families locally, then nationally and internationally, it is possible to see clearly now, what together we have created.

Home-Start is a community, rather than a bureaucracy. Home-Start is an organism rather than a hierarchy.

Its magic is rooted firmly in the unique relationship between each volunteer and each family wherever they live. It is to sustain these pure and simple relationships, that all others have developed - between organisers and volunteers, management committee members and organisers, between volunteers themselves, between individual members of staff and schemes, between secretaries and organisers, between the central national organisation and each locally grown scheme.

I am struck by how often the word 'kindness' occurs. Everywhere there is a touch of kindness, both tangibly and emotionally. This is why friendship and support are such fundamental ingredients throughout the Home-Start community.

There is also a great sense of belonging to Home-Start - whether in Nyngan

(Australia), in Oslo (Norway), or in the Orkneys (Scotland), or whether to the national Home-Start centre in the United Kingdom, in the Netherlands or in Israel.

When everyone enjoys the opportunity to belong, interdependence is strengthened. Each person has a part to play. Each has a place. Each is valued. There is a mutuality of giving and taking, of providing and of accepting, in a non-competitive way. The community spirit pervades the whole organisation. When a scheme has an annual meeting or a celebration, invariably staff and volunteers from neighbouring schemes turn up too, like members of a family.

By becoming a part of Home-Start, in whatever capacity, everyone can experience the real sense of bonding. People feel committed to each other, as part of a community of people who are making a difference. For many, working in Home-Start is not so much a job, as a way of life.

When a community is rich in relationships, when taking responsibility for each other is a manifestation of caring, then costs and prescriptive measures can be low, while motivation and outcomes are high. Home-Start has found a way of igniting local talents, and of caring for each other, which, we are told, is the essence of human survival.

I am convinced now, that what has grown from our non-prescriptive approach to everyone, has been an organism, which is constantly evolving. We have found our own solutions just as Charles Handy suggested would be necessary in the voluntary sector.

> ***"It came as a shock when I started on my own professional path, to discover (unfortunately) how unique Home-Start is, and just how complicated other people can make such a natural process as caring and doing. Home-Start is obvious, so natural, so simple, not only for families, but also as a national organisation. If only people will let it be!"***
>
> **David Harrison, Family Service Unit social worker.**

When relationships are open and honest and trusting and fun, there is a great surge of hope. Hope for recruiting volunteers, hope for genuinely meeting the needs of the families we serve, hope for adequate funding.

Home-Start is immensely rich, in its human resources - the people who choose to contribute their humanity to its success.

> ***"Home-Start is an elixir; everyone wants to be a part of it."***
> **Alastair Stewart, TV presenter and a Vice President.**

Choice is very real, throughout the Home-Start community. People can choose how long they stay. Just as in a neighbourhood, they can stay or they might move elsewhere, sometimes taking the idea with them, and establishing a new scheme. Or they might become involved in an existing scheme – in another county, or another country.

To call themselves 'Home-Start' though, they choose to maintain the value system, which is implied, with its informality and real humanity. If they prefer a more formal role, within a different type of organisation, there are now a myriad of other opportunities and ways of supporting families from which to choose.

There are times when a person may wish simply to get on with their task locally, or to take more responsibility for neighbouring schemes, or even to move on to other duties within Home-Start.

The spread of Home-Start has nearly always happened naturally and organically – a community of plants, each locally grown scheme blooming first from its own roots. Then its seeds have spread on the breeze of success, to other communities at home and abroad. I believe that we should do more to ensure that the parent plant is left to nurture its own progeny tenderly itself, rather than expecting a central store to do it all for them.

Of course, the national Home-Start centre in each country is itself independently grounded, with a vital role to play. Its own freedom ensures that it is flexible enough to face both the inside and the outside worlds - inwardly providing a funnel for communication, funding opportunities, policy, profile, current legislation and trends. Outwardly it can ensure that the voices heard from its practice with local families and volunteers can, in a small way, inform future family policy.

Success

> ***"Over a quarter of a century, I have written countless articles about Home-Start, and have seen it grow and flourish not just locally, but nationally and internationally. It is so much more than just a success story: it is a concept which has given incalculable invaluable help and support to so many families in so many circumstances and in so many places, that it has become impossible to imagine a world without Home-Start. In a mere 25 years, that is a remarkable achievement."***
>
> **Joan Stephens, Leicester Mercury.**

Success does indeed breed success, and we all need the experience of succeeding, just as we need food and water.

We aim for this experience to be shared throughout Home-Start , with everyone gaining from their involvement – the families, who tell us what their relationship with a volunteer has meant to them; the volunteers who say that they have learned far more than they have contributed; the organisers who share with each other the triumphs as well as the difficulties, so that through shared learning they can move forward together; the secretaries who are our diplomats, to be valued on the inside as well as by the outside world; the professional referrers on the periphery, who value the informal, personal support for families which they themselves cannot usually provide. The staff of the national Home-Start centres, gain themselves from the schemes, through mutually expressed needs and services.

Maybe all this is why voluntary organisations have been called the new Colleges of Society. What a foundation on which to build!

Now though, into the new millenium, with the compensation culture gaining momentum, and too many important decisions being made for defensive reasons, can the free voluntary spirit survive? I believe it can and will, but only while those people who have chosen to be with Home-Start, continue to give themselves wholeheartedly to the task and to others, without fear. Where a relationship of trust and respect has been created, the litigation culture naturally subsides.

Home-Start is an art, not a business, and the art is to find ways of remaining uncomplicated and buoyant. It is a universal service, proving that it can support a wide variety of families in a wide variety of communities and countries. There will inevitably be challenges along the way. As author James Baldwin has written,

> ***"So long as the water is troubled it cannot become stagnant."***

But for those who stay with Home-Start, the rewards will remain great.

Home-Start's success seems to lie in the balance between stability and change. We stumbled on the formula by chance. The stability is based on our values, focus, methods and structure. The focus is firmly on the families we serve; the standards and methods of practice are enshrined with the constitution, which has remained stable for 25 years. The organic, independent structure is accepted wherever Home-Start exists.

These are balanced by the inevitable changes which occur within all of us who are involved, as well as in the turnover of parents, volunteers and members of staff, as each comes and goes.

I believe that during Home-Start's first quarter century, we have managed to avoid serious pitfalls. We learned from the wobbles and we have built on the strengths together. I am convinced that each of us has gained from the experience.

The Structure

No one wants to be a part of someone else's empire.

Home-Start is owned by each local community in which it exists, in each country. It can infuse local people with the desire to participate and to contribute, taking responsibility for themselves and for each other. Of necessity in some situations, we bring in a volunteer from outside a family's immediate neighbourhood, when it is important to begin without preconceived ideas. Too often gossip and labelling have made it nearly impossible for a stigmatized family to emerge from chrysalis state to butterfly.

Each scheme can be the hub of its own learning network. Locally based Home-Start schemes always take responsibility for their own successes and difficulties. The value of responsibility held locally is that it can be more immediate, more flexible, more practical and more responsive than anything which is (heaven forbid!) nationally managed.

Community solutions, which have grown organically to meet local needs, are much more likely to remain until their work is done, unlike those which have been politically motivated and imposed because of current thinking. Increasingly, it is expected that the public services - health, probation, education and social work – should support the more informal voluntary networks, with professional back-up when needed.

Growing within an organisation, which is based on a chain of reciprocal relationships, has not always been easy, particularly for those members of staff who have had formal training and believe in hierarchical line-management and accountability. For them, trusting, open lines of communication based on serving and service to each other, can be unsettling, until they begin to feel the real sense of being valued as a person, rather than simply for their output.

In my mind, I have always held onto the concept of the Mathematical Bridge, outside Queen's College, Cambridge. Inspired by Sir Isaac Newton, it was constructed originally, in the 18th century, with each wooden member perfectly balanced to support the others, without coach screws or nails. In recent years, because of the increased numbers of students, and no doubt also the compensation culture, it has been screwed and bolted.

Recently, when our daughter Clare was in Japan on a Taiko drumming course, one of the students asked Kurumaya Sensei, their teacher, if he could advise her how to prevent the bachi (drumsticks) from slipping out of her hands. His advice to the group was to relax their hands and hold them more lightly: once they stopped gripping them, they would actually no longer want to stray, but would stay in their hands more easily. A laugh circled the room, because, as Clare said, they all knew that the lesson had wider relevance, than simply holding onto their bachi.

Evolution

As Home-Start develops and the relevance of our approach is considered in other countries and cultures, I believe that if it is to survive, its future must be rooted firmly in the ethos and practice of the past.

> ***"When I took over from Margaret, I thought it might be helpful to try to look into the 'black box' – at the particular way in which volunteers worked with families. In doing this, I was following the scientific/analytical route that is so familiar to the research community and nowadays to funders. I thought that we might be able to unpick the elements within the black box and then provide extra training if we wanted to give emphasis to particular issues for families.***
> ***I now believe that this would be not just unproductive, but actually counterproductive. What works for families is the genuine and spontaneous friendship offered by volunteers which if too closely analysed could, rather like the roots of a plant taken from the soil, wither and die."***
>
> **Professor Brian Waller, Chief Executive Home-Start.**

Families must remain central to all that happens throughout the Home-Start community. It is the parents and only the parents, who can say what they need. The whole of the Home-Start culture is built around those needs. It is my hope that in years ahead, when there are celebrations, as in any extended family, it will be the parents and children of Home-Start, past and present, who will be invited.

I also consider it vital that each member of staff keeps in touch personally, with all aspects of the scheme. Everyone – whether a secretary, management committee member, organiser, consultant or director - could support a family, spending perhaps a couple of hours with them each week at home, to listen, to care and to help in a variety of practical ways. Not only would it rapidly increase the numbers of families being supported by Home-Start, but I believe it is the only way for everyone involved, to keep in touch with the central plot – to understand, to know, to see, to experience.

Similarly, I hope that all organisers/co-ordinators in a Home-Start scheme would continue to carry direct responsibility for a small group of volunteers and families themselves, rather than just managing and administering the scheme.

The relationships between all paid members of staff, and each of their committee members, need to be built on a true partnership, where each is valued by- and each values- the other, be they organiser, secretary, director or consultant. Each needs to be nurtured at times and, I believe, many of the administrative tasks can be shared.

Home-Start schemes and the national Home-Start centres, all need basic funding, just as we ourselves need daily water – nothing too exotic, but enough to be active and creative.

While Home-Start remains a truly voluntary community, without prescribed targets or didactic approaches, while each scheme is locally grown and locally based, it will remain fresh and free, able to focus wholeheartedly on specific needs of parents with their young children.

My journey

I am often asked whether I had any idea at the beginning that Home-Start would grow as it has. The answer is an unequivocal No! There was never any sense of missionary zeal. Together with all those who have made it work, we have simply built on what has been obvious, practical, easy and enjoyable. The wide variety of people, places, opportunities, experiences, and situations, have surpassed all my dreams.

Each next step in the development of Home-Start has been natural and sequential, like the development of a child. We crawled (locally) before we stood (nationally), before we walked (internationally).

Personally I'd like to be remembered for never having used a flip-chart, overhead projector, or made a powerpoint presentation about Home-Start. Just as volunteers go into families with nothing but themselves as the resource, apart from the occasional toy, book or food, so I have always believed that it is important to share the Home-Start experience with humanity and humility, person to persons, with no more than an occasional hand-out. Joyce Grenfell was right when she pointed out, at my Churchill Fellowship interview, the importance of simply sharing oneself.

Others will, of course, see the task differently, and I would never judge them for performing it their way. After all, that is fundamental to the Home-Start ethos. I remain humbled, excited and grateful that others should wish to share and join in the journey.

Building, together with my many colleagues, a new kind of voluntary community has been a secondary challenge, after first finding new ways to support families. It too has proved to be immensely fulfilling. We have learned to draw out of each other what **can** be done, whilst helping each other through the difficult patches.

I am filled with gratitude to the people who are continuing the promise of Home-Start for parents with their children, for their local communities and for their own societies. I remain in awe of the goodwill of the thousands of volunteers, without whom none of this could exist. Now that I am a volunteer again myself, since retiring, I can understand the pressures, but I also reap the rewards.

There must be so many parents and grandparents like me who still have the urge to reach out, spending time with other parents and their young children at the start of family life. I recently met a grey-haired elderly man, unobtrusively helping at a Home-Start Christmas party. The hall was filled to overflowing with parents and young children. *"Why have you chosen to volunteer for Home-Start?"* I asked gently. *"Because I have such a happy family life myself,"* he replied simply. Ah! I can identify with that. After all, Home-Start itself grew out of happy family life. When later he told me his name, I realised he was Dr. Shah, a much loved former general practitioner.

My own sap is still rising, my feet are still firmly on the ground, and family life – my own and others' – still foremost in my heart and on my mind.

Conclusion

As a community, as an organism, with the emphasis on relationships and good communication throughout the organisation, it is essential that people have the opportunity to meet each other face to face, as often and as easily as possible. Only then can they see the glint - fear or friendship - in each other's eyes. This is why, as Home-Start grows ever larger, it is essential to keep it in small enough circles, for people to keep in touch, both literally and laterally.

We also need to allow time for each other, time to listen, time to care and time to be together, when and wherever we can. This is a reflection of the support and encouragement we share with families and applies throughout the Home-Start community.

Vaclav Havel has said: *"Out of happiness, all good affections grow."*

This is a challenging thought in a world where violence, drugs, depression and crime are so prevalent. Yet we know that happy healthy relationships can lead not only to happy healthy parents and children, but also to happy healthy communities. Clearly, our future is largely dependent on the well-being of the mothers and fathers of today.

So why is it taking us so long to realise how essential it is to ensure that every parent in the land has the individual personal support they need – either from friends, relatives or neighbours of their own, or from a Home-Start volunteer at their side?

Could every government policy be examined and tested for support of family life? Could Home-Start, along with other family friendly provision, be written into every Social Services' Strategic Plan, or into every Health Trust's Primary Health Care Plan?

As a co-operative partner in the array of services now provided for families, I hope we shall never become consumed ourselves, with ever more training, management and accountability, but that we build on our flexibility, spontaneity and simple approach. Nor should Home-Start is subsumed by various government initiatives. We need to continue to do what we do uniquely well, valued by parents and professionals alike, but in partnership with each other.

Volunteers can continue to be with families in whatever ways they are needed – giving friendship, time, understanding, respect, hope and practical help. Together they can access other vital resources within their community, or they can help cook a meal, listen to each others' stories, play games, send a card, make music, and walk out to a wider world, with confidence, together. The possibilities are endless, the pleasures immeasurable.

A touch of human kindness and a sense of hope, can lead irrevocably to greater personal well-being. It can rekindle that twinkle in the eye, the spring in the step and the sound of laughter. A Home-Start volunteer, backed up by the Home-Start community, can lead to a cycle of people helping each other again, with ever-widening circles of friendship.

Together, let's continue to share the magic and our humanity with families.

APPENDIX I

LESSONS FROM HOME-START LIFE

A more detailed look at some of the issues and some of the concepts

After a speech in Edinburgh, in the early days of Home-Start, someone told me that I talk in lists, rather than paragraphs. Just as I was busy digesting this pronouncement, she added "but it is much easier to remember your way!"

So, this section of the book will address, of necessity superficially, some of the issues, concepts and topics which have pervaded Home-Start during the first 25 years. Hopefully they will provoke discussion, disagreement and the glaring realisation of all that I have omitted to include. More formal papers exist, which we have devised together over the years, on many of them.

For ease of identification, not in order of priority, they appear in alphabetical order. (Shame that some of the more boring topics are at the beginning.)

ACCOUNTABILITY

One of my concerns about accountability is that, in the interests of the scheme, there can be a certain loss of spontaneity and freedom for the family. Approaching parents with an open heart and helping hands feels very different from meeting them with a form in the hand when what we genuinely offer is support and friendship. Whose needs are we meeting – the funder's, the parent's or Home-Start's?

AGREEMENT AMONG ALL IN HOME-START

In the early days, the quality assurance of Home-Start was communicated to all schemes in a paper, with our annual request for their TIG (Training, Information and Guidance) Fee. We spelled out what services they could expect from Home-Start Consultancy/UK, regionally and nationally, in return for their feedback. We learned about their experiences, their needs and their ideas. We all understood that the relationship between Home-Start Consultancy and each independent scheme could not be enforced. Like all other relationships within Home-Start, it was entered by choice. Similarly, we stated it could be ended from choice. We believed that this freedom epitomised the voluntary ethos, based on mutual trust and co-operation. Success depended on good communication. It ensured that we all worked as effectively as possible to the ultimate benefit of the families.

Then, as the development of Home-Start accelerated, it was suggested by insiders and outsiders alike, that we all needed a more formal way of ensuring quality standards and methods of practice. But can one quantify quality, when it is dependent on people and relationships?

A group of staff and management committee members met to develop ways of ensuring that the excellent practice developed within the first 200+ schemes, would be replicated and upheld, by all others in future. An 'Agreement Among All in Home-Start' was produced, and although I had not been a member of the group, it fell to me as Director to "sell" it to 300 organisers at our 1996 Study Days. All credit to those who developed it, and because it was based on the already accepted Standards and Methods of our working Practice, every scheme signed up to it.

ANNUAL GENERAL MEETINGS AND THE ANNUAL FORUM.

Our Trustees wished to keep the structure as simple, and the formalities of Home-Start Consultancy/UK, as few as possible. They met two or three times each year, to consider policy, finances, senior staff and development in detail. The AGMs, to agree the annual Home-Start UK report and accounts, the auditors, the appointment of officers and any other business, were dealt with in half an hour before their September meeting.

Once a year, Home-Start Consultancy/UK staff, management committee members and trustees spent a day in the summer, ALL together at an Annual Meeting, drawing on combined experience and skills, to focus in depth on particular issues of significance to everyone. These included the effects of current legislation, the changing needs of families, up-dating and involving the funders, or focusing on the future.

The schemes themselves had many other opportunities in the course of each year to meet Home-Start UK staff and other representatives for in-depth discussions about any aspect of the organisation. (See Management Committee Consultation Days, and Study Days, Focus Groups and Roadshows.)

ANNUAL PLANS

Not everything of value starts with a strategic plan. Martin Luther King had a dream!

For the first 20 years, we never planned ahead, because we worked re-actively rather than pro-actively, locally with families and professionals and then nationally with Home-Start schemes. It was always so important that local families, and later different areas of the UK, should decide for themselves that they wanted Home-Start. We would then provide them with the guidance and support of another organiser, of a regional consultant or me, backed up with the written Policy and Practice Guide, on every aspect of establishing and maintaining a scheme. No scheme ever had to re-invent the wheel.

As a UK wide organisation, rather than planning in advance each year, we would review our resources, and increase them only in order to respond as effectively as possible to known growth and needs.

By the early 1990s though, funders began to ask us for our 'strategic plan'. Home-Start had become recognised as part of the mixed economy of care, so we had to commit ourselves in writing to the services we would provide.

We were, as always, very clear though, that the words we used must reflect our values and beliefs. To produce a 'strategic' plan sounded too military, with all the 'targets' involved. A business plan did not reflect the voluntary sector. So we settled for a 'Five Year Plan', with a series of 'Annual Plans', building on the needs of the schemes, the families and the professionals we served, up to the year 2000.

ANNUAL APPRAISALS

Each member of staff had an annual appraisal, which was always a good opportunity to praise all. My own was undertaken by the chairman at the time. We simply considered together and then recorded the results of our discussion on:

1) Job satisfaction
2) Position responsibilities
3) Possible problems and difficulties
4) The future, including the individual needs of the member of staff
5) Anything else.

AUTHORITY

I have always been wary of hierarchical systems and power-based relationships within them. I am more comfortable with the concept of authority, which I consider to have more subtlety. It can be both given and taken, and should be there to serve. In Home-Start, relationships of authority can shift between the people involved, when appropriate to do so.

BEFRIEND

Being a friend, is what Home-Start is all about. Befriending sounds rather like "doing to" someone, rather than being alongside, offering friendship.

CAMPAIGNING

Home-Start supports families, rather than being a campaigning organisation. After many discussions, for example, we agreed not to take a campaigning stand on issues such as anti-smacking. It is crucial that we do not alienate parents who may need our help. Instead, we can strengthen parents' relationships with their children, and build their self-confidence, finding alternative ways together, to defuse difficult situations.

CAPITAL PROJECTS

Investing in large capital projects, such as a building, was generally discouraged as being too time-consuming to fund-raise, house-hunt, decorate, furnish and then maintain. We suggested to Home-Start schemes, that all their focus and energy should go into supporting more and more families and volunteers locally, from rented accommodation. Of course though, the final decision always rested with the management committee of each scheme.

However, having discouraged the others, we actually bought the property at 2 Salisbury Road, Leicester ourselves. It was ideally situated for the train station. Almost daily we had visitors from around the UK and from other countries. The mortgage turned out to be lower than the rent for a similar sized property. So our trustees, glad of more security with a capital investment, gave us the go-ahead to buy. Miraculously, within 18 months of fundraising, the Baring Foundation agreed to pay off the outstanding balance of the mortgage.

CARDS

Cards abounded in Home-Start in the first 25 years, each one a sign of friendship and affirmation. They expressed gratitude, invitations, and acknowledged celebrations.

Our first Home-Start Christmas card was special. It was designed by Don Sinclair, whose wife Peggie was first a volunteer and later on an organiser with me in Leicester. The card was a 3 dimensional Christmas tree. Perhaps we should produce it again.

Over the years, many other contemporary artists generously donated their artwork free of charge, to produce cards for general use and to mark seasonal festivals.

Andy Goldsworthy, artist and sculptor, donated the picture of his Ice Sculpture for the 1990 Christmas card. The Department of Health ordered hundreds of copies to be sent out on behalf of the Social Services Inspectorate, providing yet another wonderful opportunity for publicity.

Each year, the staff at Home-Start UK, personally signed and sent around 500 Christmas and greetings cards to schemes, their committees, funders, colleagues and government departments. They were sent with sincerity, but also proved to be a good public relations exercise.

CELEBRATIONS

Celebration alongside innovation has, I believe, always been a part of the culture of Home-Start. First with the families we visited, we always remembered birthdays and other significant dates. We shared food, enjoyed one another's company, and often had a lively time together. This carried over to special occasions with our family groups, volunteers and staff.

Once we had established the national organisation, the celebrations continued. Arrivals, departures, seasonal festivities, significant funding and birthdays, were all marked.

Whenever Home-Start people met, it seemed that celebration was in the air, even at the national study days. Staff produced skits and sketches, making us all roar with laughter, as our personal foibles and working practices were exposed. Some of the titles included When We're Old and Grey, Carry on Consultancy, The Charge of the Home-Start Brigade and This is your Life. We even performed for each other outside our rented office on pedestrianised New Walk, Leicester, where people passing by, would stop and join in the fun. Somehow too, the sun really did always shine.

CHAIRMEN and CHAIRWOMEN

Every three years, Home-Start Consultancy/UK had a new chairman or chairwoman. Looking back, I realise how fortunate we were to have individuals, each from such different worlds. These included the Department of Health Inspectorate, Management Consultants, Charity funders, the Army, Law and Medicine. My last chairman, who carried over the organisation to my successor, had built up his own very successful national business.

CHARITY OR INCORPORATION?

As a voluntary not-for-profit organisation, we were a charity and not a company limited by guarantee.

Over the years, usually with new incoming chairmen, we would re-consider, whether it was in their interest, and the long-term interest of future trustees, for Home-Start to become incorporated. Of course they were concerned about their own financial liability under charity law. But having read all the pros and cons, the trustees and I were convinced each time that there could be the same risks, whether a voluntary organisation or a company. In practice, the only way that trustees can reduce these, is to be vigilant about all aspects of Home-Start's finances and administration.

So why change when we were really a not-for-profit charity? We didn't. Whenever possible we always adopted the simplest structure or method, so that our energies could be focused on work and living. Charity begins at home!

Even as recently as 2002 my successor, Brian Waller stated:

> ***"We have examined the pros and cons of Home-Start staying as a charity or becoming a company limited by guarantee. The latter route is one that seems to be increasingly pursued by some of the larger voluntary organisations. What Trustees have found is that the safeguards apparently presented by the company route are largely illusory and that it is perfectly feasible for Home-Start to remain a charity without taking on the added bureaucracy that comes with company registration. Staying as a charity also has the rather splendid advantage of keeping Home-Start as simple and straightforward as possible – and absolutely in keeping with its ethos and principles."***
>
> **Brian Waller, Chief Executive, Home-Start.**

I was saddened recently, at a long-standing scheme's AGM, when the chairman announced with considerable pride, that they were about to register as a

Company limited by guarantee. Legislation had changed, he said, and they needed to guard their financial and employer's liability. How far removed that felt, from a charity working through trust.

I believe that Home-Start has the unique opportunity to stay on course, holding onto our charitable aims and holding out against the constrictions of a fear-full society.

I remain indebted to Albert Clark, our volunteer legal adviser, who was always prepared to guide us in finding ways which were both unique and legal, to establish our constitutional charitable status and structure.

CHARITY FRANCHISING

In 1990, the Directory of Social Change held the first ever conference on Charity Franchising. The aim was to enable the voluntary sector to find out how franchising could be used, as in some businesses, to extend their projects to other locations.

At the time, we were informed that Crossroads Care and Home-Start, were the only two charities which had developed a successful replication model. We were surprised, but delighted to be invited to present our methods at the conference. Our way of working had evolved quite naturally over the years. But it was reassuring to know that, with our common constitution and the Policy and Practice Guide, we really were ensuring that schemes were providing the highest quality support to families wherever they were in the United Kingdom.

COMMUNICATION

Our aim always is for all relationships both within and outside the organisation, to be based on good, open communication.

> ***"What Home-Start provides, above all, is meaningful communication based on acceptance, understanding, listening and talking, and in so doing opens up many other channels of communication – a simple response to a basic need."***
>
> **Beryl Riley, Organiser of first Ripley, later Cambridge Home-Start.**

CONFERENCES AND PARLIAMENTARY PRESENTATIONS

We were always delighted to be invited to contribute to a very wide range of conferences. Some were for health visitors, GPs, the army, psychologists and psychiatrists; some were on crime prevention or child protection, and many others were held by a wide range of government departments and national statutory and voluntary organisations. Home-Start, it seemed, had relevance to them all.

We held national conferences in each of the UK nations over the years, highlighting the holistic, informal approach of Home-Start to supporting families.

One which was held in Kensington Town Hall, focussed on The Family: A Cycle of Courage. Chaired by Herbert Laming, then Chief Inspector of Social Services, it proved truly to be a most unusually creative event. Dr.Larry Brendtro from the USA, explained that the word 'courage' stems from the French 'Coeurage', coming from the heart. We identified many parallels between Home-Start and his working practices with Lakota native Americans.

Memorably we were told that they have no word for 'child', but that until the age of 11, each is called a 'sacred being'. How much better it sounds to say "Larry, you are behaving like a sacred being", rather than "Larry, you are behaving like a child"!

Dr. Margaret Oates, from Queen's Medical Centre, Nottingham, shared her experience of using Home-Start volunteers in her work with mothers who had post-natal depression. She was unequivocal in her praise, stating " Home-Start is good for your health."

Then in the afternoon, Andy Goldsworthy, artist and sculptor, presented a slide-show of his work with natural materials in nature, such as icicles, stones or leaves.

> ***"When I work with a leaf, I work with the summer it has grown in, and the tree it has grown from, and the place in which it is found. This is why I must work with the materials at their source".***

So many parallels with Home-Start. He starts with what exists, in its own surroundings, emphasising place and time. He too cares deeply, drawing out beauty and potential. An example of his creativity is the dry stone wall in Dumfriesshire, requested by a farmer who wanted to keep another's sheep off his land. Andy, typically creative, designed an S shaped wall, so that each farmer's sheep could feed off the other's land, where the grass is always greener.

Live music was played, by a busker friend, as people arrived and during the lunch break, providing a relaxed, welcoming atmosphere in which to be together.

In Scotland in 1993 Home-Start held a conference for policymakers and practitioners in every field of child care, with the theme A Good Start in Life, chaired by Angus Skinner, Chief Inspector of Social Work Services at the Scottish Office. It positioned Home-Start as a major contributor to family support, north of the border.

Two Parliamentary Presentations were held in London, to inform Members of Parliament about Home-Start's support for families in their constituencies all over the United Kingdom. They were then encouraged to visit their local scheme. In many cases, this really helped with funding, publicity and volunteer recruitment.

CONFLICTS

When difficulties or tensions occur, I am inclined to face them immediately, if allowed to, with the person(s) concerned, to defuse or try to understand the problem as soon as possible, rather than letting it rumble around. Listening, caring, understanding, empathising or being willing to change things, have always proved important to the well-being of all of us in a values-based organisation.

There is a lot of wisdom in the old Chinese saying that in any disagreement, "the one who is most playful wins."

CONTAGION

"There is something about Home-Start that is highly contagious, affecting everyone it touches......It is the essential idea that communicates so well", writes Tony Crispin a volunteer from Dunfermline, who helped the scheme to establish itself locally with high-quality publicity material and documentation. He had caught the bug from his wife Christine, who was involved as a volunteer on the management committee. As Chairperson Christine stated, "There is absolutely no truth in the rumour that I have prowled the aisles of Marks and Spencer, recruiting unwitting friends and acquaintances for the management committee. I sometimes went to get the shopping!"

Their daughter sang a solo at the Carol Concert in Perth, then referred a young friend in the South to the local scheme there, and sometime later, Christine's 86-year-old mother was enlisted. "In the early days, she would tell our family about her own mother who had brought up no fewer than eleven children at the turn of the century 'without this Home-Start nonsense'. Yet, affected by the 'contagion' at 86, she volunteered to abseil down Fraserburgh lighthouse in aid of schemes in north-east Scotland. A field-day for the press!"

Friends and friends of friends and professional colleagues (including a retired chartered accountant, a lawyer and an educational psychologist) all contributed their skills to enhance the scheme, once the contagious ideas had reached them. "Ten years of purposeful 'contagion' suggest that Home-Start Dunfermline can look forward confidently to the next ten. And I am sure that is also true of other schemes," writes Tony.

CO-OPERATION WITH OTHER VOLUNTARY AND STATUTORY ORGANISATIONS

Home-Start is not an organisational silo. Its strength lies in its ability to draw on the expertise of other organisations, to co-operate with them and form good relationships, so that rather than duplicating or overlapping their work with families, Home-Start can genuinely plug the gap in those parts of family life which other organisations simply cannot reach.
The Big Five, – Barnardos, The Children's Society, Save the Children Fund, the NSPCC, and the **National Children's Homes** (as they were then called) were all well established (over 100 years), well known, and focussed on children. As Home-Start developed nationally, there was talk sometimes about "The Big Six", but Home-Start was different, having been established from the beginning to work specifically with and through parents, for the benefit of their children. Every £1 we raised was used either directly or indirectly to support our work with young families, with no publicity consultants and just one fundraiser towards the end of the 1990s. Other voluntary organisations often spent literally thousands of pounds annually on advertising and fund-raising. Certainly they were better known than Home-Start. . . . .!

Relationships between Home-Start and the others were usually supportive and friendly. In the early 1980s the NSPCC drew heavily on our Policy and Practice Guide in their endeavour to prevent cruelty to children, planning to work in homes as well as in centres. I was constantly frustrated though, and told them so, that Home-Start was always omitted from the "useful contacts list of other organisations" on the back of their regularly produced public leaflets and literature.

In various areas of the United Kingdom over the years, there have often been representatives from one of the Big Five child care organisations on a local Home-Start committee, to the mutual benefit of both.

There were even difficult times during the first 25 years when our Home-Start UK Trustees considered asking the Big Five for financial help. But the feeling always went away, as soon as another funding source became available to us in the nick of time!

Home-Start UK staff regularly used residential accommodation in London, provided at modest prices by NCH Action For Children (as it is now called) for our meetings.

Quite often we shared the platform with others from the Big Five at national conferences.

Barnardos' last two Directors – Mary Joynson and Roger Singleton - were particularly supportive over Home-Start's international development and occasionally did trouble shooting on our behalf in England.

I wish to record here other voluntary organisations with which we enjoyed close, supportive relationships over the years. Hoping that none is forgotten, I begin (appropriately!) with the Alzheimers Association. Then also with the Belfast Voluntary Welfare Society, British Association of early Childhood, British Association of Adoption and Fostering, The Association of Boards of Prison Visitors, Carer's Association, Charities Aid Foundation, ChildLine, Community Education Development Centre, Co-operative College, Cope, Crossroads Care Attendant Schemes, Directory of Social Change, Family Service Units, the Mental Health Foundation, National Children's Bureau, National Childbirth Trust, National Council of Voluntary Organisations, National Council of Voluntary Child Care Organisations, National Marriage Guidance Council/Relate, National Association for the Welfare of Children in Hospital, OMEP, Open University, Organisation for Parents Under Stress, Pre-School Playgroups Association /Pre-school Alliance, SSAFA, Voluntary Organisations Liaison Council for Under Fives/Early Years Network and the Volunteer Centre.

We are also indebted to the Statutory sector, their Associations for Health, Social Services, Probation, and Education, as well as to individual professional people within them, throughout the country.

COSTS

Home-Start is FREE for families. As such, it is priceless.

The essential costs of the organisation are simply there to release the huge generosity of human spirit.

In the not-for-profit sector, it is important to keep all costs low but fair. There are nearly always creative ways to solve a problem, for which the solution is not always more money. Sharing responsibility, delegating more, being heard, having time out, building morale, e.g. a one month sabbatical (for staff and volunteers alike), can all regenerate energy - often miraculously.

DECISION MAKING

In 1993, the Citizens' Charter was created to empower people to have a greater say over the decisions, which affect their lives. This is a shift from organisations being service-led, to being consumer-led. Home-Start had already been practising this, responsively, and with a genuine personal touch, for 20 years previously.

DEVELOPING A NATIONAL ORGANISATION/ MANAGEMENT ISSUES.

"She's running it like a family. It's big business now!" So said some of our staff in 1995, doubting that our simple structure, based on relationships within the organisation, could continue for much longer. We needed proper management techniques, they suggested.

Some Home-Start organisers even began to call themselves managers.

Charles Handy in his book The Elephant and the Flea, (Hutchinson 2001) has called our type of voluntary organisation - a 'federation', or 'community', in which the old language of business structure is inappropriate.

> ***"Communities have to be led, influenced and persuaded, rather than commanded. Their citizens demand a voice in their future, want to be trusted and need to be given opportunities to grow."***

Fantastic! Why didn't I have this information to quote then? The aim has always been to provide paid Home-Start consultants, who are close to the schemes in their regions, so that trusting relationships can be built, where people can meet, individually, or in groups to discuss and to learn together.

Our freedoms and mutual responsibilities were clear. We had created independence, yet recognised our interdependence. The sense of belonging to Home-Start, was both inclusive and exclusive. In the words of Montefiore:

"We are worth what we are willing to share with each other."

As stated in **Chapter 5,** with three years to go to my retirement, Rosemary Jackson, from Coverdale Management Consultants, undertook an independent review of every part of Home-Start. She listened to the views of staff, volunteers, management committee members and trustees throughout the UK, but obviously did not necessarily agree with all she heard. She was fair and detached.

To my relief, Rosemary wholeheartedly endorsed our lack of centralised control. By avoiding becoming a monolithic organisation, she told us that people felt safe and valued, able to share their experiences and feelings. The independence of local schemes ensured immediacy with flexibility in supporting families. The whole emphasis could be on local outcomes. This, she told us, simply does not happen with a centrally managed organisation, which is often more concerned with covering its own back, rather than truly working with and through families.

Rosemary did though, advise that we should ensure the future maintenance of common standards throughout the organisation. This led to the development of the Agreement Among All in Home-Start, outlined earlier.

She also recommended that in future, all senior staff should be based in a central office, to ease communication and to deputise for each other when necessary.

DIRECTOR

When, at a management committee meeting in 1988, it was suddenly decided to call me Director, things were never quite the same again. In Rogerian terms, the whole idea in Home-Start had been to be 'alongside' other staff, building partnerships, nurturing individuality. Once I had been given the rather didactic title of director, it sometimes felt as if petty jealousies, resentment and anger were beginning to creep in.

I was always keen for all in Home-Start to know that I could be contacted directly anytime, even though a scheme's regional consultant or other organiser, were really the nearest points of contact. People often expressed surprise in those days, when I answered the phone myself – something which seemed perfectly natural to me.

It is often said that parking is the biggest cause of friction in an organisation. Fortunately I had found a secret parking space round the corner from the office, which meant that even when I was there (because three days out of five I was generally out) someone else had room for their car.

DIVERSITY AND UNITY

Living in Leicester, we enjoy a significant 45% non-white population in our multi-cultural city. Since the tensions of the early 1970s, when so many Asian people arrived from East African countries, there has been much hard, effective work here by the Race Relations Council, Housing Associations, the Council for Voluntary Service (now Voluntary Action Leicester) and local government.

That is why, when Home-Start began in 1973, we stated genuinely, that we existed to support any parent with at least one child under five, and anyone with parenting experience could volunteer. We quickly realised though, that volunteering was considered by many Hindus, Sikhs and Muslims to be menial work for people who were not adequately qualified.

We promoted opportunities in Home-Start, for people from different cultures to meet each other in a non-threatening, friendly relationship. Much of this revolved around sharing food, clothes and problems. Often visits to one another's homes and places of worship were arranged. By celebrating parenthood together, we found we could harness human qualities, irrespective of culture, religion or ethnic differences.

On our courses of preparation for new volunteers, we had sessions on volunteering in a multi-cultural community. Later, it was considered that this did not go far enough, for it was important to increase volunteers' awareness and understanding of racist remarks, language and behaviour.

Many lessons were learned, especially in matching volunteers to families. Was it appropriate to match a Sikh parent with a Hindu volunteer, or a Muslim parent with a Jain volunteer? We quickly found that this was sometimes unacceptable. Even linking people from the same religion caused difficulties because of confidentiality within their places of worship. Confidentiality was also sometimes difficult in a small minority neighbourhood, where so often everyone knew each other. Just as with our work in small rural communities, or army garrisons, an Asian family would often prefer a volunteer who did not live nearby.

> **There was, for example, a young woman from Pakistan, referred to us by her health visitor, who told us she was agoraphobic. She had two young children and simply never went out. Very quickly, the volunteer learnt that the baby had been born with a large birthmark over his cheek, which the woman had been told was a manifestation of past sin and should be kept hidden. The local Home-Start volunteer was quite natural in simply accompanying the young mother and her children to the health centre, the park, the library, or into town. The young woman really began to renew her confidence and to live again.**

We always felt it was easier to face difficulties and tensions as they emerged, rather than pre-empting them, or trying to solve them once they had gone badly wrong. By talking together, being willing to understand differences with tolerance and humour, we found that newly formed attitudes had the most amazing potential to spread.

In the 1980s we devised a short, practical Equal Opportunities statement, for inclusion in our Policy and Practice Guide. So I was rather dismayed when, by 1995, there was so much more emphasis on being universally friendly, that we had to add a whole list of anti-discriminatory practice, instead of simply ending our statement as we had before, with the words "against any form of discrimination".

Diversity makes a garden beautiful. So do people of varying cultures, colours, ages, stages, ideas and energies. They all contribute to a vibrant community.

ECOLOGICAL CONNECTIONS

Home-Start has always grown organically. The first scheme in Leicester was rooted in the needs expressed by local parents. Each subsequent new scheme, was germinated by an individual local person or organisation.

The fact that each local Home-Start scheme is autonomous is a graphic reminder that plants in individual containers need less water. Like local funding, it can reach the roots directly, rather than also feeding a redundant mass of supporting soil. Far better to keep the Home-Start central organisation in a pot of its own too, but with branches linking it to all the schemes, through regionally based staff.

The earth, it is said, is like a family – an ever-active system, which is never as well ordered as one might wish – thank goodness! But all good earth relies on good composting, most often with the nutrients coming from surrounding elements. So too, parents and children are dependent on the nurture of supportive networks of family, friends and services within their community. An extra flow of energy, from a Home-Start volunteer, another parent, often an earth mother, can be infused, stored and then released when necessary. If only each community would act as an extended family!

EMPLOYMENT ISSUES

Over the years, some difficult issues have arisen. These were often uncomfortable to tackle, and with more experience and hindsight, might not have occurred in the first place.

One memorable incident was when a man applied for the job of organiser. Though numbers are relatively low, there have always been some excellent male organisers. This one though, was not short-listed, because it was learned that he had broken confidences in a previous job. After demanding to know all the details of those who had been called for interview, he then took us to a two day Industrial Tribunal. It was eventually accepted that the grounds had been the applicant's lack of understanding of the importance of confidentiality, rather than discrimination. The Tribunal held against the applicant.

Some of the most difficult situations involved colleagues who had done wonderful work within Home-Start. Some took it personally when they applied for promotion, but were not after all appointed to the new job, on which they had set their hearts.

Painful and time consuming as several incidents were, I am convinced that where people and relationships are involved, one can neither legislate nor train to prevent all human misunderstandings or frustrations.

ETHOS THROUGHOUT THE ORGANISATION

Home-Start is a values-based organisation, where we try to convey our ethos through language, style and manner. It is as much in the heads and hearts of those involved, as in any written guidelines. It can show in our administration, attitudes and approach. All are interdependent.

In 1996, schemes were asked to let us know what they considered to be the essential elements of the Home-Start ethos, both for schemes and for Home-

Start UK, past, present and future. They presented us with over 100 concepts, from 'acceptance' to 'whole family'. Those which were most frequently emphasised were:

> **Choice, empathy, encouragement, energy, flexibility, friendship, fun, generosity, happiness, hope, humanity, informality, joy, kindness, laughter, love, mutuality, openness, reciprocity, respect, responsiveness, sharing, simplicity, spontaneity, trust, truth, understanding and welcoming.**

Finally, everyone agreed that human attributes and attitudes become very potent when expressed in the privacy of the family's home. Ethos is about feelings, and feelings transcend language.

EVENTS

Over the years we had some wonderful events, due to the generosity and foresight of many of our trustees and outside supporters. They included lunches and launches, receptions and celebrations.

1981 Reception at 10 Downing Street

The Prime Minister, the Right Honourable Margaret Thatcher, held a reception for representatives from key voluntary organisations in the field of health and social welfare. It was there that I first met Sir Patrick Nairne, then Permanent Secretary at the DHSS, who, with his wife Penny, was to help Home-Start so wholeheartedly during our crucial, formative years of UK-wide development.

> ***"I came away firmly convinced that, if ever a valuable voluntary initiative deserved government encouragement and support, Home-Start did."***
>
> **Sir Patrick Nairne.**

As I left the reception, I enquired about Denis Thatcher's back, which I knew he had recently injured. It was good to see the compassion in Margaret Thatcher's eyes, as she told me all about it.

1990 Pop Art Exhibition at the Royal Academy

Bankers Trust International sponsored a special evening of a Pop Art exhibition at the Royal Academy to enable invited representatives from the corporate sector to learn more about our work.

1992 Joseph and the Amazing Technicolour Dreamcoat

Home-Start families and volunteers were invited to a Gala performance of Joseph at the Coliseum in London, due largely to the generosity of trustee Chris King and his wife Charlotte.

1992 10th. Anniversary Celebration in Northern Ireland

Lady Mayhew, wife of Sir Patrick, then Secretary of State, spoke supportively about how she would have welcomed visits from another parent, when her own children were young.

1994 Channel Tunnel Walk.

Just before the channel tunnel finally opened in February 1994, charities were invited to sponsor walkers through the tunnel. Our own intrepid Chris King, trustee and later chairman of the management committee, undertook the training and final walk on behalf of Home-Start. Our staff ensured he had a miner's lamp, Kendal mintcake and a survival kit. He was amongst the first to step out into the sunlight, on this side of the channel, with Ulrike Jonsson at his side. The money he raised was distributed to schemes towards fun and celebrations for families that summer.

1994 The London Marathon

Baring Brothers entered a five-man team, raising over £11,000 for Home-Start.

1994 A Boat on the Thames

Our 21st anniversary annual meeting was held with lunch on the HQS Wellington on the Thames, thanks to the personal generosity of Richard Macaire, another of our trustees. Many of our colleagues from other voluntary and statutory organisations joined us.

1994 Kensington Palace Reception

Hosted by Princess Diana, to mark the International Year of the Family, 12 representatives from Home-Start were invited, along with people from the other children's and family charities of which she was the Patron.

1994 onwards Annual Carol Concerts in The Guards Chapel, London

Ginny Evans, and (Lady) Juliet Cooper, both military wives and staunch supporters of Home-Start, initiated a most successful annual fund-raising event for Home-Start, by organising a carol concert in the beautiful Guards Chapel in Birdcage Walk. Together with a committee of friends and with television presenter Alastair Stewart, hosting it, this has raised around £60,000 each year. It continues to be a sell-out feast of music, with celebrity readings, flowers, candles and the most amazing generosity.

> ***"I had no idea what Home-Start was, when asked by my boss Michael Green, Chairman of Carlton Communications, to be master of ceremonies at the first Home-Start Carol Concert. I embarked on a splendid journey of discovery. Home-Start and I have become firm friends. Seven years on and I have rubbed shoulders with so many great names of the TV and theatre world who came to read at our carol service. And I have performed before and been introduced to several members of the Royal Family, not least Her Majesty the Queen at our very special Jubilee Year concert.***
> ***I have been so happy to help and so happy to have squirreled away all those happy memories. It's just as well I didn't tell Michael Green I was too busy!"***
>
> **Alastair Stewart, TV Presenter and Home-Start Vice-President.**

1995 Anna Scher Theatre Group

These young people, some of whom were themselves 'at risk', made a spontaneous, enthusiastic, thoughtful and thought-provoking presentation at the end of one of our conferences in the Friends Meeting House in London. This memorable act put us vividly back in touch again with communication and relationship skills. We all left the conference re-energised.

1995 The Chippendales – Yes, the Chippendales Shows

During a run of their concerts, Home-Start collected literally buckets full of money at their shows. Even Ruby Wax and Alan Rickman made an appeal with them on behalf of Home-Start. This fundraising ploy, through the daughter of a member of our staff who worked with the group at the time, was not universally acceptable, but it seemed to create a lot of fun.

1996 The Co-operative Wholesale Society Ball

The Co-op was celebrating its 100th anniversary and asked us to encourage someone from the Royal Family to attend their celebration at the Dorchester Hotel, London. If we succeeded, Home-Start would receive a substantial donation – well worth the extra effort involved. It was to be in August, when no members of the Royal family would be in the capital, except for Prince and

Princess Michael of Kent, who graciously accepted. Several of our trustees, with Basil and me, were invited to attend.

1996 Carol Concert in Birmingham Cathedral

Peter Dallow, who chaired a significantly multi-cultural Home-Start scheme in Birmingham, took it upon himself, to organise a carol concert for schemes in the Midlands. For two years running, this was a major, extremely successful undertaking.

> ***"The Cathedral was full on both occasions, it seemed that everybody sang their heart out, even those of other faiths, who had learnt carols at school."***
>
> **Peter Dallow, Home-Start Saltley.**

When we acknowledge volunteers in Home-Start, so often the unsung heroes and heroines are those who are peripheral to the actual work with families, but who, like Peter, contribute in a major way to our committees.

1997 Princess Diana's Funeral

After the shocking sudden death of our much loved Patron, Her Royal Highness Diana Princess of Wales, Home-Start was invited to send five representatives to walk behind her coffin in the procession to Westminster Abbey. Selected volunteers and parents each carried a lily on the day. It was Diana's favourite flower. Basil and I had the privilege of attending the funeral itself in Westminster Abbey.

1997 St. James Palace Reception.

In December, our new Patron, Princess Alexandra, held a reception for our newly appointed Vice Presidents, funders and other supporters. On this occasion, Cherie Blair, the Prime Minister's wife turned up unexpectedly. There was no name badge for her, but she shrugged it off with "I don't think I really need one of those!"

1998 This is Your Life

When Alastair Stewart's life was presented on television, I was invited to represent our charity, to which he contributed so much over so many years. He is a Vice President of Home-Start.

1998 The Jubilee Ball

The Silver Jubilee Ball was held at the Dorchester Hotel, in London. It raised a considerable sum of money as well as the profile of Home-Start. The organisation of the event, was a model of goodwill and generosity by all involved. One member of the organising committee took half her garden by car, to arrange the flowers at a fraction of the commercial price. Marbeth Tobin, a Home-Start chairwoman and volunteer fundraiser, with sheer nerve and charm, elicited the most amazing prizes and gifts, which enabled Jeffrey Archer to raise over £50,000 for us in a 20 minute auction.

1998 House of Lords Reception,

In 1998, to celebrate Home-Start's Silver Anniversary, Home-Start Vice-President Baroness Brigstocke, held a reception for 150 supporters from within Home-Start throughout the UK, as well as colleagues from other related organisations. All the people present had contributed to building the success of Home-Start during the first 25 years.

> ***"It was a glittering evening with many celebrities all buzzing with enthusiasm for the success of the simple idea that is Home-Start."***
>
> **Libby Lee, Home-Start Bristol.**

FUNDERS

In our experience the majority of our funders, - statutory, corporate and Trusts, were generous and often movingly committed to our cause. For Home-Start schemes and Home-Start UK our funders often performed for us, the task of affirmation, filling us with hope through their acknowledgement that our approach to supporting families was indeed worthwhile.

Occasionally though, there are funders who can literally and subtly change the focus of the organisation, by their demands in return for their cash. This was the prime reason why the Home-Start constitution states that no scheme should be chaired by a member of its primary funders.

FUNDING

In 1984, guidance to the voluntary sector from the National Council for Voluntary Organisations, stressed that

'Each voluntary body should seek, both in its funding strategy and in its financial dealings with government, to ensure that its dependence on government finance is compatible with its basic independence as a voluntary body'.

The Department of Health and Social Security had actually asked us whether they could contribute up to 49% of our expenditure, after the first prolific year of Home-Start Consultancy's national existence in March 1982. They wanted to be supportively linked to our family support work. However, this percentage gradually dropped over the years to 11% of our total funding needs. "You simply can't develop, Margaret, at a time of constraint and consolidation", I was told.

Every year, from the early 1980s, each of my chairpersons and I met a senior civil servant at the Department of Health, almost literally to beg for our next year's funding. One particular occasion remains vividly in my memory. For once I did not bubble about all that Home-Start volunteers achieve, but sat in silence, waiting for the usual civil servant to take the lead. We sat literally for ten minutes, in silence. Then, rather questioningly I thought, he suggested that we really needed to prove Home-Start's worth by "saturating an area with family support, whilst simultaneously researching the results". Two weeks later the Government announced its Family Support Initiative, of which Home-Start was a leading recipient.

Every year, applying for government funding presented the same challenge: How to be a new initiative each time, while still conveying the basic, unchangeable messages implicit in our Home-Start work with families?

Other government departments were not allowed to co-fund us. So although the Home-Office was in tune with our contribution to crime prevention and a caring society, they were unable to supplement our grant.

Throughout my time with Home-Start, I had many meetings with government ministers and civil servants, often along with colleagues from other voluntary organisations, urging for secure funding for known effective practice. We also always emphasised the need for a coherent national strategy to support family life.

To no avail. It was only as I retired, and the new Labour Government came to office, that employment, education, health, housing, juvenile justice, economic and social policies for families, began to be co-ordinated across the boundaries of local and national government departments.

The year-end 1989/90 was potentially terminal for our thriving organisation. We had realised that our funding would run out completely by the end of February, one month before the end of the financial year. For the first and only time in my career, our committee talked seriously about taking a decision to issue redundancy notices to Home-Start Consultancy staff. The trustees had previously requested papers on the 'worst case scenario'. Yet we knew we already had other grants from April, secured for the following financial year.

I vividly remember talking to the Tudor Trust, which had been the most supportive and generous to our national organisation as well as to individual schemes for very many years. Would it be possible for us to receive their next year's grant a month early, I asked tentatively?

"Yes"! was their miraculous reply.

That time was certainly a turning point in Home-Start Consultancy's existence. We continued into the following financial year, determined to remain buoyant and optimistic, based on our continuing hard, effective work.

In support of the Home-Start Consultant for Northern Ireland, I visited Stormont Castle outside Belfast several times. The N.I. office of the DHSS was housed there. The meetings were memorable, not only for the beautiful setting, with the long drive up, but also for the warmth and enthusiasm with which I was always received. One of their staff, Victor McElfatrick, was on our Home-Start Consultancy committee.

The Ministry of Defence gave direct and adequate funding to Home-Start with service families in Germany, Cyprus and Gibraltar. We had to ensure though, that the female Home-Start staff received fair wages for their work.

Many local schemes, when offered a pot of funding by social services on a county wide basis, always really impressed me, by their willingness to work co-operatively with one another, to decide on equitable distribution. Issues sometimes arose over higher travelling costs in rural compared with city areas, but often they resolved simply to divide the money according to their numbers of volunteers.

FUND-RAISING

Fun-draising can be a lot of fun!

This was a creative aspect of our work, which I really enjoyed. It took me literally into other worlds, of business, banking, supermarkets, trusts and commerce. I usually relied on introductions, often from those I met, such as when the chairman of Tate & Lyle, signed letters of introduction to 10 of his colleagues, including Tesco, Inchcape, GEC and Lehman Brothers.

Lord Joseph, who had become a very staunch supporter of Home-Start , both for what we were doing for families, as well as for developing a national voluntary organisation, introduced me personally to colleagues of his, in his capacity as non-executive director of Bovis. These included Michael Green (Carlton), Bernard Taylor (Medeva), Garry Weston (Allied Foods), Stanley Kalms, (Dixons Group), Lord Wolfson (Next Plc), Lord Peyton (Barclay Brothers) and a business man, Harry Woolf. Some provided substantial grants. Others gave us office accommodation and administrative facilities for two London-based offices – one for a fundraiser, the other for a Home-Start Consultant in London.

During my years as organiser of Home-Start in Leicester, I had always enjoyed the matching process, of finding the most suitable volunteer for a particular family by identifying something they had in common. The same, I found, also applied to fundraising. From Barclays Bank to the Sainsbury Trusts, often a good relationship based on mutual interests – art, travel, gardening, music - was quickly established at the beginning with the person I was meeting. Once trust had been established, (very many told me they were not interested in meeting professional fundraisers), only then would we talk together about the funding needs of Home-Start, to support families. I was also able to clarify their wish for public acknowledgement or not.

All this, I later learned, is actually known as 'Relationship Fundraising' – a donor-based approach to the business of raising money. It suited my instinct well!

Occasionally there were ethical dilemmas, including the discovery that many local authorities which fund local Home-Start schemes, invest in defence and the arms industry. With our trustees, management committee members and the staff, we discussed our concerns together, including the line we should take with a possibly unacceptable donor.

As a result, with the fundraiser Glyn Berwick, who we had just appointed at the time, we produced a Fundraising Policy for Home-Start based on that of the ICFM (Institute of Charity Fundraising Managers), which stated that

> **'Home-Start will accept money from any source or activity, except where the activity is itself illegal, in direct conflict with Home-Start's aims, or where the acceptance**

of cash is deemed to be counter-productive'.

Our greatest funding allies over the years, were Charitable Trusts, such as Carnegie, Gulbenkian, Hayward Foundation, J. Paul Getty Jnr, Lankelly, London Law Trust, Norton, Sainsbury Family Trusts and Tudor. There were times when, without their reliable support, we might well have given up.

"The work of Home-Start was a perfect fit for the Trust's objectives as set out in their Deeds, which included the relief of distress of mind or mental illness of children and young people, caused by family break-up, bereavement or other kinds of social deprivation".

Georgina and Conrad Natzio, The Norton Trust.

Over the years, with ever more growth, we gradually conceded that we needed to appoint a fundraiser. We did so on three separate occasions. What a delicate balance it was, appointing another member of staff on a full-time salary, who would have to raise so much more than their own costs.

The first one left after six months. It was her first job after university, and she realised the enormity of the task. The next felt that she was up against our over-high expectations of quick results, which, combined with our lack of a high profile, was indeed daunting. She left after 18 months. The third lone fundraiser, before a team was appointed after my retirement, was more successful, though never, I thought, given the back-up he needed from some of the staff, who resented his higher salary. This had happened in other voluntary organisations too. We had to succeed in our fundraising in order to survive at all. He left shortly after I did, two thirds of the way through the Silver Anniversary year.

GOVERNMENT

For 18 of the first 25 years of Home-Start's existence, there was a Conservative government under Margaret Thatcher and John Major. In 1997, only a year before I retired, Labour was re-elected under Tony Blair. We always had a good relationship with the Liberal Democrats. We were keen to work with politicians from any party, most of whom told us of their commitment to supporting family life.

INTERVENTION

A definition of intervention is an 'interference in the affairs of'. Not a word to be associated with Home-Start.

LANGUAGE

In Home-Start we have always been mindful of our choice of words, since values and attitudes are conveyed in our use of language. We talk about families, not cases or even case-loads (what a burden!).

There is always a pressure to be drawn into the current language fashion. In the 1980s, this was the language of business, so marketing, selling the scheme, business plans all came to the fore. In the 1990s, the language of bureaucracy took over – accountability, monitoring and evaluation, meeting targets (whose targets?). I believe it is important for Home-Start to remain true to its own values system, rather than being seduced into the current vogue, whatever the pressures from funding agencies. At all times we need to continue to respect the dignity and autonomy of families and their right to make decisions about their own lives. We must continue to support them in the unique Home-Start way.

LEADERSHIP

Surrounded by staff with immense talents, I often balked when I was acknowledged as the leader. We were very definitely a team of leaders, each contributing our own particular expertise.

Early on, when we first had regular senior staff meetings, I would chair them and take notes, mindful that the others had had to travel to Leicester from all over the UK. Then one day, the bubble burst and we decided that each of us should chair or take notes in rotation. This meant that I was free to contribute to the meetings along with the rest.

I was teased that whenever someone made a good suggestion, I'd say "What a great idea. Do it!"

Sometimes I was criticised for working too hard. "You'll make it too hard for someone to follow you, Margaret". I'm still confused about this. Should one hold oneself back, or should one do what is comfortable, necessary and usually enjoyable? It certainly made me consider whether I might be neglecting my own family, but they were definite that I wasn't. Somehow Home-Start's development fitted ideally with my husband's career and the ages and stages of our three children. It was developing locally when Jane, David and Clare were at their primary and just into secondary schools; then nationally at secondary and university stages; then internationally when they had left home and my husband Basil had retired, so was often free to travel with me.

The worst aspect of leading a growing voluntary organisation, was being constantly challenged from within, about the structure and style of management. So at one stage, I took myself away from the situation to talk the whole thing through individually, with a management consultant, a spiritual leader, and the head of a national voluntary child care organisation. Each was a person whose judgement I trusted. Each, after listening intently and then discussing seriously various issues, wholeheartedly endorsed the path we were on, giving me the confidence to continue.

We also went through times when people inside as well as outside Home-Start Consultancy/UK, quoted how "charismatic" leaders should start an organisation or movement, and then get out, leaving others to set the structure and manage the growth. It hurt. I have never ever considered myself to be charismatic, nor in any way different from the rest of the hardworking staff. I have never led from the front and have very much enjoyed involvement in the administrative side of the work too. Anyway, surely Home-Start was about drawing out the potential in everyone, for the common good of families. This always included volunteers, staff and. . . me too please! Fortunately, the people making such suggestions were not the trustees, or close members of staff. But of course I did check it out with them from time to time.

Staying in touch with families, has been important throughout my time with Home-Start. How could I write reports, give talks or discuss our needs with potential funders, if I was out of touch with the actual daily needs of the parents and children with whom we worked. In Leicester, some of the original families kept in touch with me quite naturally through all their ups and downs. Some, like Tony Davies, turned up every year with flowers on my birthday (1st. April, so how could they forget?) Throughout Home-Start in the UK, I always took every opportunity to meet and to talk with families and volunteers.

The other significant challenge, was knowing the concept that many religions have gone from inspiration, to communication to dogma. Now, of course Home-Start is not a religion, though I am amused very often to hear people saying "we believe in it". The inspiration of course, was the families themselves. The communication happened quite naturally, as all of us involved shared the approach and the passion together. But the dogma stage, I always believed, had to be avoided at all costs. We had produced written guidelines on every aspect of establishing and maintaining a scheme and about the process of our work in partnership with others. But there was never any dogma. Nor hopefully, will there be in future.

The art of knowing when to go, or "quitting at your peak", I gather is sometimes difficult for a leader. However, I had decided quite definitely with my family, that I would leave on my 60th birthday. This happened to coincide with the beginning of the new financial year for Home-Start and was also during the Silver Anniversary Year – a good time for my successor to come in, during a period of celebration.

What I had not anticipated, was that this time would also coincide with our first ever, very major government grant of over £1million, including more cash for local schemes and a new emphasis from central and local government, on the need to support the whole family and not just to focus on the needs of children. 25 years after we began Home-Start, some of our successful ways of supporting families were being acknowledged at last. Anyway, I knew I was definitely leaving on a high.

LOGO

In the early days of national Home-Start Consultancy, the trustees and I discussed the need for a logo. Fortuitously a friend had sent me a greetings card, which had on the front the Ancient Friendship Symbol. The words by Susan Polis Schutz read:

> ***"When a person has a real friend, he learns not only to appreciate another human being, but he also learns to understand himself better".***

That seemed to describe our aim in Home-Start. Friendship is, after all, at the core of our work, pervading our approach throughout the organisation. It represents our side-by-side, person-to-person approach, with neither one above nor below the other. The symbol might relate equally to the relationship between volunteer/family, organiser/volunteer, organiser/organiser, statutory/voluntary, Home-Start Consultancy/each Home-Start scheme......all truly in partnership with each other.

After a thorough search into ancient runes and copyright requirements, we adopted it as our logo. At first we presented the friendship symbol in dark brown on our cream stationery, which even photocopied well. Some people interpreted it as trees, but that was alright, because after all, trees only grow from their roots too.

> ***A portion of your soul has been entwined with mine,***
> ***A gentle kind of togetherness, while separately we stand,***
> ***As two trees deeply rooted in separate plots of ground,***
> ***While their topmost branches come together,***
> ***Forming a miracle of lace against the heavens.***
>
> **Janet Miles, Winona, Minnesota.**

Later on in the development of the organisation, we were encouraged to re-present the logo in a red circle, with the friendship symbol itself in clear white – so that it looked more vibrant and up-to-date. The circle is the symbol of the sun and of the earth and of the universe. It is a symbol of wholeness and of peace. The unbroken circle holds the Home-Start logo - the symbol of friendship, the partnership of equals – within it.

Like the Red Cross logo, we agreed with all the organisers one year at the study days, that our logo would, in due course, become recognised because of the work we were undertaking. Some of the earlier Home-Start schemes had devised their own local logos – ducks on ponds, or teacups in hands. But we planned that by our 21st Anniversary in 1994, the ancient symbol of friendship would be used by all Home-Start schemes . . . . . and it was!

The logo was registered at the patent office, along with the name Home-Start.

MANAGEMENT COMMITTEE MEETINGS

Management committee meetings, though absolutely essential to keep the staff focussed and to time, are immensely time-consuming, generate ever more work, and should I believe, be kept to a minimum.

In Home-Start Consultancy/UK, we had a separate multi-disciplinary management committee, comprising senior people with national experience drawn from the public and private sectors in each of the UK nations. Members of our senior staff attended each meeeting, as did two Trustees, a Department of Health observer, and two scheme organisers.

> ***"As a representative organiser on the management committee of Home-Start UK, it gave me a new interest and a wider perspective on the many new schemes that were being established in all parts of the country. We had stimulating debates on current issues of development."***
>
> **Libby Lee, organiser Home-Start Bristol.**

The management committee met with me four times each year to discuss specific everyday and development issues in depth.

For the meetings to be as effective as possible, knowing that many people had travelled long distances, paperwork was meticulously prepared in advance and was brief and lucid, so that decisions could be taken and the work of Home-Start proceed quickly and efficiently.

Until my final year, I got away without producing a written 'director's report'. This was never requested. There were always written reports from the regions, nations of the UK, or from training. These allowed me the freedom to add additional up-to-date points, and to share future plans. I suspect this added variety to the form of presentation.

Home-cooked lunches were a welcome feature of all our committee meetings. For the first few years I produced these myself. Then for several more years my secretary Heather, who worked hard with us all day, produced the meals with amazing professional flair the night before, charging only for the ingredients. When she emigrated to New Zealand – yes, that far away – we found a vicar's wife and later the friend of a friend, who continued the tradition of home-cooked food for us.

MANAGEMENT COMMITTEE CONSULTATION DAYS

In 1990, the development of Home-Start was at a stage, which was both crucial and exciting. The organisation was evolving rapidly. It was therefore essential that together we were clear about how all existing Home-Start schemes could maintain close links both with Home-Start Consultancy and with each other, to ensure that Home-Start in the 1990s would be as effective as possible in supporting families.

At a lively, constructive day in mid-June a hall full of management committee members from all over the UK, met with our own staff and committee members, to discuss the following:

- The services provided by Home-Start Consultancy;
- How income and expenditure related to growth;
- Issues relating to the structure of Home-Start Consultancy, a charitable trust;
- Issues and ideas from the schemes, including how they were raised with Home-Start Consultancy.

This was the first of what became our annual Management Committee Consultation days, subsequently held regionally and nationally throughout the UK each autumn. At each meeting, there was the opportunity for feedback on what had been done with the issues raised the previous year.

Residential days for management committee members were pioneered in idyllic Dartington Hall in South Devon, England. Unfortunately, though well attended, they proved too costly in expense and also time, for the management committee volunteers, most of whom also worked full-time.

MANAGERS

Recently I listened as a newly appointed scheme 'manager' talked of her experience. The local scheme had grown so big previously, she told me, that one of the experienced members of staff had been divested of her direct work with families and volunteers, so that she could focus on all the administrative tasks. That had been alright, because she had experienced the whole process of Home-Start previously. The needs of families she had met and the volunteers who had contributed to their lives, were still in her head and her heart.

When this 'manager' had left, the present one was appointed (significantly none of the other staff members even wanted to apply for the job). She had brought with her, excellent administrative skills, but with no experience of Home-Start's support to families. Just recently, because another member of staff had left, she had had to take on some of her "caseload" (not a Home-Start word!) and only now was she becoming familiar with the work with families. This experience, she said, was proving crucial to her wholeheartedly carrying out the administrative tasks for which she had been appointed.

MINISTRY OF DEFENCE (M.O.D.)

In chapter 5 I have described the way in which Major-General John Page introduced the Home-Start approach to the Ministry of Defence and also to

SSAFA (Soldiers', Sailors' and Airmen's Families Association). Learning about rank structure, the role of wives and how both these related to their husbands' positions was a new world for the majority of us, and alien in Home-Start, where each person is valued both as an individual as well as for what they contribute. Somehow though, both the MOD and Home-Start understood each other's positions, respected the differences, yet acknowledged the value of an informal, human approach. In due course, families, volunteers and professional welfare staff all came to appreciate our joint work.

In addition to Home-Start, the MOD initiated HIVEs (Help, Information and Volunteer Exchanges), the equivalent of the voluntary workers' bureaux in the UK. These provided the first focus on voluntary welfare work in a military setting.

As we developed our informal yet structured support for Service families, there were several memorable events and experiences along the way.

At the Berlin annual conference for all SSAFA health visitors and social workers working in Germany, I vividly remember being told by one officer, that if Home-Start were to succeed in a military setting, then all our staff and volunteers would have to wear uniform. We didn't - and it still worked.

The RAF felt at first that their families were too intelligent to use Home-Start. But that quickly changed, as RAF wives expressed their pleasure in becoming involved in voluntary work, or receiving support themselves. We worked with them in bases in the UK, as part of the local community, but also exclusively in RAF stations in Germany and Cyprus.

One memorable opportunity fell to me to speak at SSAFA's 100th Anniversary celebrations, held in Berlin. Together with their Patron, Prince Michael of Kent, I was flown to Germany on the Queen's Flight. Unusually, I had to speak at the Conference before him. When I had finished, he followed immediately by stating that the last time he had been in Berlin, he had visited a motorcycle factory. "So you might say, it has been from Kick Start to Home-Start!"

The army accepted the Home-Start approach with enthusiasm, encouraging us to work closely with their Families' Officers and Welfare Assistants for family referrals. Confidentiality was the greatest potential difficulty, but after many meetings, we agreed that we would work through SSAFA on a strictly "need to know" basis. I am not aware that this ever presented problems for families, or for the chain of command.

A Bridging Committee was established, to consider civilian and military needs in a Service setting. This met in Germany twice each year, and was attended regularly by Sue Everitt, a senior member of Home-Start UK staff.

In the early days, after I had sent letters about annual statistics to the Home-Start schemes working with British Forces in Germany, I was severely reprimanded that I should have communicated through the MOD or Joint Headquarters. It felt as if all our meticulous negotiating for our freedom with Home-Start schemes was being undermined. We took several steps backwards, re-negotiated, and were able to agree a mutually acceptable way forward in future.

Each year I was invited to the Adjutant General's Conference in London. Sir David Ramsbotham, who was AG and later became Chief Inspector of H.M. prisons, requested Home-Start support for 'his families' in both positions.

On one agonising occasion, I was invited by the MOD to speak to approximately 100 of their grey suited medical staff in their formal forbidding Institute of Medicine. At the end of my presentation, there was a deathly hush. Then eventually one lone Sloane voice suggested that our organisation should be re-named Up-Start!

In Cyprus, we launched Home-Start with ease in the Western Sovereign Base Area, but were constantly rebuffed by a colonel in the Eastern Sovereign Base Area. Home-Start there lagged badly behind, and I was constantly frustrated at being prevented from offering our form of support to their many very young and lonely families.

Experience with the Royal Navy proved enlightening, but hardly successful. A Home-Start scheme began in Gibraltar, but lasted only about three years, as naval staff were moved to Cyprus. In Faslane, Scotland, the Admiral's wife had been keen to embrace the Home-Start approach, but eventually it was decided that the navy could adapt Home-Start to support naval families themselves, without having to fund an actual scheme. Many of the wives were already involved in the local scheme in Dunfermline.

A great advantage of Service wives involved in Home-Start was that they moved so often that they sometimes joined or even started another Home-Start scheme themselves, wherever they happened to be.

"I am proud to have been one of the first volunteers in British Forces Germany and very pleased now that I am back in England to be a senior organiser in Salford".

Grace Kay.

The best measure though, of Home-Start's acceptance in a military setting, must be that even since draw-down began in earnest, in the last few years of the 1990s, our voluntary organisation remains an important source of continuing support to Service families.

MODELS WITH SIGNIFICANT RELEVANCE TO HOME-START

Two particular models that I learned about in the course of developing Home-Start, significantly influenced my approach to families, volunteers and schemes.

1) Psychologist Ann Dally, in her book **Mothers: Their Power and Their Influence,** which Willem van der Eyken had brought to my attention in his Four Year Evaluation of Home-Start in Leicester, suggests that children go through three stages in their development:-

   a) **Enclosure** from 0 - two years old, when they are totally dependent on a caring adult, usually their parent.

   b) **Extension** when the child is influenced by other people and the world all around. (I am convinced that as we extend our children, they too extend us.)

   c) **Separation** when the child seeks independence and separates physically and emotionally from the parent.

BUT! Ann Dally suggests that if we get it right, then throughout our adult lives, we each will continue to need doses of all these three stages at different times. We each need a partner, parent or friend on whom we can totally depend when we need to. We all need to be extended with new opportunities and experiences and we certainly all need our independence.

The way this model seems to apply to Home-Start, is that as a family is referred, they are usually in need of a period of enclosure again, - dependence on a caring adult - in our case, a Home-Start volunteer, who will share the strain and responsibility with them. Then, they are 'extended' as they begin to regain control over their lives, possibly with a network of family or friends of their own. Finally then, the Home-Start volunteer 'separates'. But if, as often happens at a later date, a family needs a bit more dependency because of another bad patch, then a volunteer is reintroduced for as long as is needed.

This model has considerable significance for Home-Start organisers, as they support their volunteers. Recognising the stages the family has reached, can really help to determine when to end formal visiting, or suggest that the parent might wish to become a Home-Start volunteer herself. At this stage the volunteer is released to support another family, beginning another cycle, whilst remaining open to supporting the parents again if ever necessary.

2) **The Circle of Courage.** Larry Brendtro, spoke with conviction and vision at a Home-Start conference about what he had learned from working with Native Lakota American people. Their Circle of Coeurage, illustrates how every person, needs the following in their lives for wholeness:

   a) The spirit of Belonging;

   b) The spirit of Independence;

   c) The spirit of Mastery; and

   d) The spirit of Generosity.

When the circle of courage is broken, lives are no longer in harmony and balance.

In other settings, the above have been called Attachment, Autonomy, Achievement and Altruism.

The reason why I am particularly drawn to this model, is that it can be applied in at least four aspects of our work.

   i) It relates to the lives of each one of us, including the parents we support, who choose to become volunteers themselves.

   ii) It can illustrate the relationship between a volunteer and family she supports. She belongs to them, yet is independent; she aims for competence for herself and for the family, all with a spirit of generosity (which incidentally, is infectious).

   iii) It is also a significant model for the 'community' of Home-Start, both nationally and internationally. Each scheme, wherever it exists, has chosen to belong to Home-Start. It is independent, based locally. Each strives for mastery or quality. Each is generous within the community and to each other.

iv) And finally, the spirit of generosity pervades the whole organisation, from the moment a person becomes involved, in whatever capacity. People so often comment that they find everyone in Home-Start to be generous in sharing their time, caring, resources and experience, whilst also being open to the generosity of learning from each other. There is a good deal of interdependence.

We did not work consciously to this model as Home-Start developed, but with hindsight I can now see clearly why, in my experience, the organisation has become balanced and harmonious.

MONITORING, EVALUATING AND STATISTICS

Of course national standards need to be monitored and applied. BUT…when all the focus is on targets, achievement and assessment, it damages the system. People show their reluctance to fill in too many forms, by failing to do so. Or they leave.

There has to be a balance between measuring and doing; of keeping enough facts, being in receipt of public money, and a necessary minimum of record-keeping.

A person is so much more than a statistic. We always said, "Don't just count people - Count **on** people." Counting numbers rather than success stories of the families themselves, means that we have lost the plot – for ourselves and for our funders. I am deeply concerned when people talk of little other than measuring, rather than about their involvement in the job itself and how families have benefited.

There is also, I believe, an important difference between promoting best practice and insisting on accountability throughout an organisation. The first is dependent on trust, which of course, will occasionally be breached. But the alternative is immensely more costly, time and paper-consuming, proving an unnecessary burden to the people who conscientiously seek to comply. Their time could be better spent working directly with families. Anyway, are those who oversee performance, necessarily always effective themselves?

Hopefully, Home-Start will never become like so many of the high-cost statutory services, for which monitoring and evaluating are a public necessity – but I can't help feeling that the scales of balance are tipping too far in

Home-Start's direction.

NAME CHANGES

In 1988, when there were around 100 schemes, we wrote to them all asking whether we should change the name Home-Start at that stage. 80% replied decisively "NO". They were too well identified locally and had all their stationery printed. 10% thought it would be a good idea, but only three schemes had alternative suggestions. The final 10% were undecided. So we kept the name and decided it was up to each of us to emphasise how we begin with families at **home**, at the **start** of their children's lives. We would build on our reputation.

In 1993 our trustees accepted the advice, that Home-Start Consultancy should change its name from Consultancy to Home-Start UK, as outlined in Chapter 5.

ORGANISERS/CO-ORDINATORS/MANAGERS

I was the first organiser of Home-Start in Leicester. Quite simply the term implied that there was organising to be done behind the scenes, to enable the volunteers to support families at home.

Then eventually, as new schemes developed throughout the United Kingdom, and particularly in Scotland, the word co-ordinator crept in. That was great! To co-ordinate behind the scenes is a lovely lateral approach, which is key to the way Home-Start works.

More recently however, and I think it is a big mistake, many now call themselves managers.

We say we aim to work in genuine partnership, with parents and with professionals. This does not mean that we have to use public or private sector language to perform our voluntary service function. Becoming a manager usually implies more time for more meetings and paperwork.

OVERNIGHT ACCOMMODATION

Partly because of lack of money, but also because it was a pleasant way to spend time together, members of staff stayed in one another's homes when visiting schemes or areas of the country. Similarly we had open house at our home, for staff or visitors when they came to Leicester. Many summer evenings were spent chatting and laughing together in the garden. Ronnie Highmore, consultant for Scotland, was particularly memorable for her cartwheels and handstands. In the winter, we would sit round the fire, drinking (whatever) and sharing our stories.

My own most memorable stay in an organiser's home, was in Sheila Withnell's converted chapel in Essex.

PARTNERSHIP

In the early 1970s, 'partnership' really was a new concept, which we used in our work with families and with other agencies. The Volunteer Centre used it, when they reviewed Creative Partnerships in Leicester, between the statutory and voluntary sectors. From the beginning of Home-Start, we always talked about partnership with parents and with professionals.

Partnership is such a good way of describing a relationship, in which each partner has experience and expertise to contribute. Neither is more important than the other. Their needs and skills are complementary. Together they can create a whole.

PATRONAGE OF HER ROYAL HIGHNESS THE PRINCESS OF WALES and HER ROYAL HIGHNESS PRINCESS ALEXANDRA

Patronage was a whole new concept to me when it was suggested by people helping Home-Start to raise its profile and to raise more money. Should we try for Royal Patronage and if so, should it be for the future King or the future Queen?

It was decided that for a family organisation, it would be more appropriate to ask Her Royal Highness, The Princess of Wales, as she had worked for some years with young children herself. We sent a formal letter to the Palace, but simultaneously several personal approaches were also made.

We were delighted to learn that the work of supporting families was very close to Princess Diana's heart and that enquiries by her office, about the standing of Home-Start, had endorsed our work and credibility.

Princess Diana attended many functions on our behalf, in all countries of the United Kingdom, as well as with British Forces schemes in Germany.

It was a disappointment when she wrote to us, along with her other charities, stating that she was giving up most of her charity work. It was a huge shock and deep sadness, when she died so suddenly in the road crash in 1997.

Towards the end of that year, to our great pleasure, Her Royal Highness Princess Alexandra, the Hon. Lady Ogilvy, GCVO enthusiastically undertook to become our new Patron. She told me she was very willing to do this, as she had a real interest in supporting families.

When I retired, Her Royal Highness invited Brian Waller, my successor, and me to tea for the handover. She also attended the Home-Start carol concert in The Guards Chapel.

POLICY AND PRACTICE

Sue Everitt, who was the first organiser of Home-Start in Royston and later an assistant director with Home-Start nationally, with special responsibility for the Policy and Practice Guide remembers:

> ***"When I had my initial induction with you in Leicester Margaret, I came back with 10 sheets of paper in a buff square cut folder – this was all that was written down in 1983. Subsequently Marie Forsyth developed the first guidelines packs on every aspect of Establishing and Maintaining a Home-Start scheme. She learned from the existing schemes at the time and made the file informative, readable and colourful, with 10 colour-coded sections. This was updated over the years and evolved as the Home-Start Policy and Practice Guide in 1997, just before you retired."***

The Guide was based on the good practice of Home-Start schemes during the first 25 years and remains a testament to their willingness to build best practice of the Home-Start ethos and approach, on the constitution, with its standards and methods of practice, on the agreement among all in Home-Start, on the equal opportunities policy statement, on employment law, monitoring and evaluation, and child protection. There are sections on Home-Start in the community, Home-Start UK, resources, Home-Start and other agencies, funding, finance, and of course Home-Start volunteers and support for families.

Having all the above for ready reference when needed, freed the staff, management committee members and volunteers of individual schemes, 'to get on with supporting families at home with their unique spontaneous, flexible and creative flair.

POLITICIANS

With Conservatives in government during most of my time with Home-Start nationally, I naturally had most contact with Tory politicians. Of these, retired **Lord Joseph** was the most significant supporter. It was many years since he had retired from life in government. He had remained passionately concerned about family life ever since the early 1970s, but it was only once his own thinking was converted to understanding the difficulties of parents, as well as being concerned for their children, that he became seriously committed to the work of Home-Start. He wanted to help us in our holistic approach to meeting the needs of families.

Keith Joseph promoted Home-Start in the House of Lords, introduced us to potential business funders, including his own company, Bovis, of which he was non executive director, and to politicians and other titled colleagues. Having become a friend, I was touched to be invited by Yolanda, Lady Joseph, his widow, to speak at his memorial service at All Souls in Oxford. I took great pleasure in mentioning that Keith had been a chocoholic.

Other politicians who have been significantly involved in supporting Home-Start over the years include:

David Blunkett. We first met in Sheffield, at a Home-Start AGM, then at a Home-Start Parliamentary Presentation, followed by many meetings when he was MP and then Minister in different government departments. It was delightful, when as a family man himself, he brought along his sons to one of our Home-Start receptions.

Oliver Letwin was introduced to me proudly by Lord Joseph, as "our future prime minister". Time will tell.

Peter Bottomley For several years, I had served on Peter's Family Forum Board. Later, when his wife was Health Minister and due to speak at a Home-Start conference, he came in her place on the day and really spoke from the heart. Whenever we met, he was encouraging and supportive of our work. On one memorable occasion he had been keynote speaker at a national conference held in the Royal College of Medicine. After his contribution, he leapt energetically up the steps to leave, caught sight of me in the back row, clambered over several people and planted a kiss firmly on my cheek. He then clambered out again and left, leaving me blushing but elated at his endorsement of Home-

Start once again. "It was the Windmill Theatre in reverse," he joked, when I mentioned I would include the incident in this book.

Virginia Bottomley, as Minister for Health, and an ex-social worker, promoted Home-Start and the need for family support on many significant occasions. Occasionally she sent us small personal donations, which were fees for her articles or speeches. She visited our office in Leicester, and included me in meetings at the Department of Health, whenever appropriate.

Tessa Jowell, who had also been a social worker and understood the needs of families, took a personal interest in Home-Start not only in her constituency of Southwark, but also considerably helped to raise our profile nationally in her speeches. She once told a Home-Start meeting in Southwark, that wherever she met people from Home-Start in different parts of the UK, she knew that she would have welcomed any of them to support her and her family if necessary. "You must continue to sprinkle your magic" she told the volunteers.

Michael Howard, as Home-Secretary and MP for Folkestone, attended the launch of Home-Start in his town. It coincided with his birthday, so we all sang Happy Birthday and he cut the cake produced for the double celebration. He also invited me to speak with him privately in his office in Westminster, when he was Home-Secretary. Unfortunately, at the time, despite being immensely supportive of all Home-Start was achieving, the Home-Office was unable to provide national funding.

Glenys Kinnock was extremely supportive to Home-Start in Wales, spoke at some of our AGMs there, and helped us to pursue EU funding. She is patron of Home-Start in Cwm Rhymni Valley.

Margaret Thatcher, encouraged by Lord Joseph, invited me to 10 Downing Street to discuss charity work in general, but Home-Start in particular. Despite her pressure of work, she gave me her undivided attention for 40 minutes, indicating that the needs of families were high on her agenda. She insisted in the long-term though, that the voluntary sector should be sustained by tax benefits and grants from businesses. In the meantime, she gave Home-Start a generous donation from her personal trust.

Gillian Shepherd first introduced herself when, as MP in King's Lynn, she attended several of their AGMs. Later as Secretary of State for Social Services, she spoke at one of our London conferences and then involved me in some of her meetings about lone parents. She then requested information about the funding plight of individual Home-Start schemes, which she followed up positively on their behalf.

Rhodri Morgan, now First Minister of the Welsh Assembly, was formerly president of Home-Start Ely, in Wales.

PROFESSIONALS

Baroness Wootton once announced that professionals were people who were better at their job, than anyone else. I was always pleased when Home-Start was described as a professionally run organisation. 'Professional not Amateur' was the phrase at the time.

PUBLICATIONS

Home-Start Consultancy's first published book, was 'Home-Start: A Four Year Evaluation' by Willem van der Eyken. We had to learn about obtaining ISBN numbers and anticipated the actual publication date with eager anticipation, not knowing quite what would happen. Nothing did – no media interviews, no accolades for Willem, no queues of people to purchase his work - nothing.

In 1982/3, we produced our first guidelines on different requirements for launching a Home-Start scheme, such as Why is Home-Start Voluntary; Appointing an Organiser or Secretary; Costings; Launching Home-Start; and Appointing a Management Committee.

Albert Clark, former Head of Law at Leicester Polytechnic, produced the first papers for schemes on Insuring your Home-Start; Conditions of Service; Disciplinary Action; and Adopting the Home-Start Constitution and Registering as a Charity.

A key role of ours was to keep abreast of new legislation and changes in society on behalf of all Home-Start schemes. Through a process of consultations, Home-Start Consultancy Staff, with representatives from schemes, produced guidelines on:

Home-Start and the Children Act 1989;

Home-Start and the NHS & Care in the Community;

Home-Start and Child Protection;

Home-Start and Equal Opportunities;

Home-Start and HIV Infection; (this was offered as a model to its members by NCVCCO)

Home-Start and Service Agreements;

Home-Start and Quality Assurance: The relationship between Home-Start Consultancy and each autonomous Home-Start scheme.

In 1990 and again in 1997, Home-Start UK staff re-wrote and updated the full Home-Start guidelines pack on Policy and Practice – i.e. every aspect of establishing and maintaining a Home-Start scheme.

Reports were produced for the Department of Health on their various funding initiatives, - Under Fives, Inner Cities, and Family Support. Home-Start Consultancy/UK administered the Small Grants scheme, in which we were able to distribute up to £1,000 each per annum, to local Home-Start schemes in England and Wales for specific projects.

In 1994 we published Dr. Sheila Shinman's Family Album in celebration of our 21st. Anniversary. In 1996 we published Sheila's Family Health and Home-Start, which provided information for commissioners and purchasers of family support services.

In the same year also, the research findings by the University of Leeds about the experience of the Comprehensive Home-Start Initiative for Parental Support (CHIPS) were published in a book Negotiated Friendship – Home-Start and the Delivery of Family Support.

PUBLICITY and the MEDIA

Looking back over the Diary of Development kept from early 1981, I am amazed how much we did with and for the media. Personally I neither wished for, nor sought publicity. However, whenever asked for comments, or to promote the work of Home-Start, I was always glad to affirm our approach, or endorse the work of the thousands of people all over the country, who were making Home-Start work successfully for families. If a broadcast or interview were called for, I would usually choose to delegate the opportunity to an enthusiastic, capable member of staff.

Several of us wrote articles in health and social work journals, and contributed to various books on the need to support the family as a whole.

Throughout the first 25 years, we had a wide range of articles in the broadsheet press, a 'tame agony aunt' in one of the tabloids, and colleagues in various journals and magazines. In 1997 Good Housekeeping Magazine adopted Home-Start as its charity of the year.

In 1990, we produced a video with an accompanying booklet on Home-Start: A Gift of Time. It showed how a Home-Start volunteer offers her time to a family through a period of stress and difficulty. It showed volunteers at a preparation course, listening to an organiser outlining her work for the week, and accompanied families who were attending a Home-Start family group. There was a special section on fundraising and the cost effectiveness of the Home-Start approach. The video proved useful for training, general information and attracting funds.

Mindful that we needed a Home-Start image in addition to our logo of friendship, Lynsey Mitchell aged five from Bassingbourn Primary School in Hertfordshire, drew what we called our 'Little People'. They were adults and children in all shapes, colours and sizes, with character, humour and vitality. In her pictures, the sun was always shining, or the stars were out. We used her illustrations widely in our publicity materials, including the Guidance on the Children Act. Her simple, spontaneous approach, attractively enlivened some rather serious topics.

In 1993, in anticipation of the International Year of the Family, which coincided with Home-Start's 21st anniversary celebrations, Workhouse Design in London, which had already previously designed our annual reports and stationery for several years running, again supported our work in kind, by helping us to produce a Publicity Manual for each scheme, to ensure that throughout the organisation we were speaking with one voice, and that we had a united image.

When schemes and members of the general public bewailed the fact that Home-Start was not better known, we emphasised that we had existed for less than 25 years, with no surplus cash to advertise. We always encouraged each scheme to have a high profile locally if they wished. When this was combined with over 200 other schemes doing similarly, we found we had stumbled on an inexpensive and successful marketing medium.

Knowing that we lacked marketing materials, one of our creative regional consultants, Jenny Hurkett, persuaded a local firm in Kent to produce a range bearing the Home-Start logo, including key rings, tea towels, playing cards, book marks, mugs, tee shirts and beer mats. At our last Parliamentary Presentation in 1997, Jenny handed a beer mat with the Home-Start name, logo, and byline 'Supporting Families', to each participant as they left. She had no doubt that it was this which led to the £1million government grant the following year!

QUALIFICATIONS

Voluntary work, it is said, is at the heart of a civilized society. People caring about each other.

> ***"We are all made for community, for caring and for love. If I value you, I hope you will value me and that sets up all sorts of repercussions".***
>
> **Archbishop Desmond Tutu**

I remain confused. Many parents who consider themselves to be "just a mother"- as I myself do first and foremost - are now volunteering in Home-Start and benefiting from NVQs (National Vocational Qualifications). This shift in motivation could well be significant, the more it happens. Whose needs are we serving? During the earlier days, the fact that someone had been a Home-Start volunteer was often itself instrumental in getting them a job interview. The Home-Start courses, support and voluntary work with families, were often considered experience enough for a volunteer to be accepted for professional training or paid employment. Would that this could continue.

REFERENCES and POLICE CHECKS

Because of the death of a child at the hands of a probation service volunteer, in the 1980s, suddenly the whole of the voluntary sector was encouraged to take up police checks in addition to personal references, on all volunteers. This was to be done through the DHSS, the Volunteer Centre, local social services departments and the police, who, at the time, were not even indemnified, to release confidential information.

This process continues to incur considerable expense, both in terms of cost and time, yet does not, in itself, offer 100% certainty. To my mind, the system is still open to abuse by a person who is committed to offending.

Police checks, I am told, do not necessarily reveal a conviction for an offence such as sexual abuse. In some instances, this may be a reflection of the low percentage of sexual offences that are disclosed in the first place, and also, the low percentage of these that actually result in a conviction. In other cases - depending obviously on the nature of the offence - I firmly believe that a previous conviction should not always be an insurmountable obstacle to someone ever being trusted again.

Recognising these qualifications, I believe implicitly though, that everything must be done to safeguard children and their parents.

In the normal course of our involvement, Home-Start volunteers would not have substantial access to children alone, since our focus is on working with the parents and their children together. We do, however, have substantial access to the home-visiting volunteers themselves, through our meticulous Home-Start process of recruiting, preparing and training, matching and supporting them, throughout their involvement with families.

RESEARCH

> ***"Margaret, why do you need to do research on Home-Start, when you know that the families want it, the professionals use it, and it is growing and developing so naturally and cost-effectively?. . . What more do you want to prove?. . . .At what cost?"***

Yes Thijs Malmberg. I agreed wholeheartedly. He was the Director of Social Policy in the Ministry of Health, Welfare and Sport in the Netherlands, and his words resonated with my own feelings towards research at the time.

Of course, it is essential to have outside validation of an organisation, but it is too easy to become swamped by all the administrative details, so that subliminally, the emphasis shifts from serving the families, to re-assuring the funders.

Willem van der Eyken carried out the first qualitative study of the first four years of Home-Start in the late 1970s, through the Social Science Research Council. After my initial fears that he would find nothing to research, given our intuitive, individual approach to families, (each of which is unique, as is each volunteer), he proved me wrong. After many meetings with parents, and everyone involved in Leicester Home-Start, he gave us real insights as to why our informal approach was succeeding.

We were working with people, rather than doing to them. We were not a treatment model. We focussed on each family member as a person, rather than just on their problems. We built on strengths, rather than focussing on weaknesses. We built on true partnership with statutory agencies. We appreciated that support precedes the effective take-up of other services; and we were offering the hand of friendship, which could miraculously expand and extend a person's social network.

"Home-Start: A Four Year Evaluation", Willem's descriptive study of the formative years of the first Home-Start scheme, immediately sold 2,000 copies. It was distributed to libraries and social services departments throughout the UK, widely influencing policy, practice and ideology.

Possibly because it was one of the few pieces of research which had proved to be so readable, another 1,000 copies were re-printed in the 1990s.

Most importantly of all though, the book was distributed to volunteers and even to the families who had participated in the discussions. In my experience, that was most unusual, as most research is produced for – and disseminated amongst - other academics.

In the early 1990s, two eminent researchers, Mog Ball and Dr Sheila Shinman, together with Home-Start staff and trustees, produced Home-Start's Research Policy Guidelines. These considered how we should assess research proposals, the methodology to be used, its framework and ultimate ownership. Guidelines were included, on protecting Home-Start's interests – i.e. the ethos and the families.

I was relieved, that we would only get involved in 'cooperative enquiry' in the style of Peter Reason from the Marylebone Health Centre and then Bath University, by working *with* people. There would be absolutely no sense of 'intervention' or of 'control groups'. These are still complete anathema to me, when human relationships are involved. Even when more gently called 'comparison groups', I consider these to be contentious.

There was much subsequent research on Home-Start, including that by the National Institute of Social Work, the Department of Health, the Universities of London, Brunel, Leeds and Queen's Belfast. It felt as if Home-Start was the most researched voluntary organisation in existence at the time. On the other hand, we were well aware that when good qualitative research is carried out sensitively and with understanding, it can of course contribute substantially to everyone's knowledge.

Sometimes I felt like a parent attending her own case-conference, when faced with a team of researchers, amazed at the amount of time, expertise, and money being spent on assessing Home-Start. I was mindful of the language used by the researchers, and was relieved when they concurred that it should be neither intrusive nor invasive. Some proposed a closer inspection of the volunteer/parent relationship. I still believe that such 'intervention' would be death to the magic of Home-Start.

Would I like my own friendships to be analysed, or our own children's family lives to be monitored and evaluated after their babies were born? When our daughters became parents, what they valued above all else, was the opportunity to rest, to have a meal prepared for them and to be given praise and recognition for all they had achieved. Occasionally they needed breathing space away from the children, to do something other than child care. It was their friends and family members who provided these opportunities, so that refreshed, they could again respond to the endless demands, which all young children make on their parents' emotions and energies. In the absence of these, they would have welcomed the support of a Home-Start volunteer.

For parents referred for support to Home-Start, who most frequently feel isolated and overwhelmed, Home-Start volunteers can step in, responding to whatever the parent needs on a particular day. They need to be equally free to do so, spontaneously and flexibly, unimpeded by a whole background of bureaucratic requirements.

Put simply, do we really need an on-going flurry of expensive research to deliver a smile, some eye-to-eye contact, and some practical help to a young family, when we know that it helps everyone involved, including the professionals who made the referral in the first place?

When he was chairman of the Trustees, John Page acknowledged the need to assess the effectiveness of Home-Start, but was clear that this should in no way

> ***"jeopardise the simplicity and personal relationships at the heart of the Home-Start concept. Organisers must not be side-tracked from their aim of helping families".***

SABBATICALS

Wishing as we did, to reward our valued staff in ways other than salary increases, beyond what we could afford, it was decided that Home-Start Consultancy senior staff and consultants should have a one-month sabbatical during their fifth year. It was also proposed that if, during this time, a member of staff undertook any work which would benefit Home-Start, they should be awarded a £500 grant in addition to their normal salary, towards such a project.

Sue Pope, Consultant for the West/South West of England and Wales, was the first to be granted such a secondment, to review the implications for Home-Start of the new Children Act 1989. The leaflet, which she produced for parents, was purchased in large quantities by the Department of Health, the magistracy and the voluntary and statutory sectors. Quite an achievement!

SAFETY

While it is right to do everything possible to ensure the safety of everyone within Home-Start – organisers, volunteers and families – it is equally important to keep things in perspective.

- Families need to know that the stranger coming into their home can be trusted. Necessary checks must be made (references, police checks etc.) but these are only supplementary to the organiser getting to know the volunteer well on the course of preparation and during regular support sessions.
- Volunteers need to be assured that their safety has been taken into account and should work within clear guidelines.
- Similarly, organisers need to feel secure in their work, with safety policies which are implemented, and clearly defined open lines of communication.

An unjustified pre-occupation with safety may heighten our level of anxiety, which actually serves to increase our vulnerabiltiy - like shouting to a child on top of the climbing frame "watch what you are doing" – the child is distracted, loses confidence and falls off – "see, I told you so". People need to be reassured that Home-Start is generally a safe place to be.

"In all the 20 years I was with Home-Start, I never felt threatened, though undoubtedly organisers and volunteers have felt so. It is a question of keeping a sense of reality not hopping on to every media bandwagon that is passing. Also we must not allow current obsessions with Health and Safety procedures to pervert the essential work of Home-Start or to ferment a sense of anxiety which in itself saps confidence, distracts, and increases risk."

Beryl Riley, Ripley and later Cambridge organiser.

SALARIES

We decided from the beginning, that salaries should be on a recognisable scale, so we used local authority 'spinal points in the purple handbook'.

The salary structure in Home-Start Consultancy/UK, it was agreed, should be as flat as possible, in recognition of the essential qualities and contributions of every member of our able staff.

SEMINARS

One of the pleasures of being involved in organisations and opportunities beyond Home-Start, throughout the 25 years, was that I met people who could extend and stimulate our thinking.

Among those who came and inspired us with their work, was Professor Alice Honig from Syracuse, New York, who spoke amusingly to around 100 organisers gathered in Leicester, about the development of humour in young children. Similarly, a few years later, Maria Aarts from the Netherlands moved us to tears with her pictures and stories about her work with families, using the Video Home-Training approach.

To mark Home-Start's 25th Anniversary, and during the three months before I retired, we ran 14 seminars across the United Kingdom. Our focus was on Strengthening Families to Build Strong Communities - Working Together.

These were attended by over 500 elected members and senior managers from local and central government: health, probation, education, social services and housing; community police and architects, academics, the media, faiths, and the voluntary and corporate sectors. A distillation of the key messages was then sent in a report of the seminars, to politicians, policy makers, managers and practitioners who were directly or indirectly responsible for the welfare of parents and children across the UK during 1998.

SENIOR STAFF

Margaret, Sue, Sue and Maggie. We were the first 'staff team' in Home-Start Consultancy in the mid '80s. When Maggie dyed her hair fair to match the rest of us, this caused considerable teasing.

As other staff joined us, from all parts of the UK, it was clear that together we could really make Home-Start and its development succeed. Their good humour and hard work really amazed me. They too, were all dedicated parents, who put their own families first, but still contributed unstintingly to the spread of our Home-Start support for others' families.

We were a strong, usually mutually affectionate, senior staff team. When, in the course of our fast-moving, detailed monthly staff meetings in Leicester, one person would express concern about the way something was being handled, then we would all screech to a halt and really discuss the issue properly. Occasionally, when we couldn't agree, one or two of us would be left feeling a little raw. Certainly I sometimes found it frustrating, when something seemed obvious to me, but the others just wouldn't agree. Then, either I had to hold back, or sometimes concede to the other annoyingly wise and capable women. I'm sure that each of them felt the same way at times too.

We worked genuinely alongside each other, honouring our respective leadership qualities. It was neither necessary nor worthwhile to appoint a Deputy, as each member of senior staff could deputize. Responsibilities were essentially shared. Salary levels were flat, hierarchy kept to a minimum and affirmation to a maximum.

Although there were times when we really struggled, memories of our unity and sense of common purpose generally, are ones, which still cause me to smile with pleasure.

STAFF

Home-Start is essentially about the human spirit – caring spirit, team spirit, entrepreneurial spirit, inspiring spirit. It must never be eroded. Franklin D. Roosevelt once said that:

> ***'Happiness lies in the joy of achievement and the thrill of creative effort'.***

I know it. We had it.

This was supported by the staffing structure being as flat as possible, including salaries, responsibilities and lines of communication. We all made each other coffee, or produced lunch. We tried to leave parking spaces for those who had travelled the furthest or needed the convenience of office parking. My office was often used for meetings by various groups of staff in my absence.

All the staff met the management committee members and trustees at our Annual Meeting, so that everyone could put a face to one another's names. We also felt it was important to prioritise opportunities for all regional consultants and central staff to meet each other at least three times a year for training and to exchange ideas face to face, ear to ear.

I remember learning an important lesson, which I now know is referred to as the horseshoe effect, which applies to most jobs, marriages and even parenthood. They all start on a high, then begin to dip, until just as they seem to hit rock-bottom, things start to improve again for those who have stayed with it, even ending again for some, on a high. There is often a mismatch between those who are on the ascendancy while others are still heading downwards. This image was helpful to me in understanding staff, who sometimes in their second and third years, would begin to dip.

Secretaries are one of Home-Start's greatest resources. They are pivotal in all communication and are responsible for presenting an efficient, yet caring image. Every year, we had an opportunity for all Home-Start UK secretaries to meet, to share experience, to learn new skills and to recognise those to whom they often spoke on the phone.

One amazing coincidence in our central office, was when another secretary joined our team. Angela, my personal assistant, thought she looked familiar. One lunchtime she joked that a free gift in a gardening magazine she had bought, looked like a gun. The new secretary turned pale and explained how she had once worked as an Au Pair girl in Canada, when one evening, when she was alone with the children, a man had burst into the house and held her up with a gun. Shocked, she had left the job and decided to return to England. "Was that on a train to Toronto in 1973?" asked Angela. "Because I now remember sitting next to you on that train when you told me your story." Goose pimples!

I felt genuinely, that friendship pervaded our organisation. There were opportunities for all of us to celebrate, to have fun and freedom, as well as working very hard together. I was privileged to work with so many like-minded, creative, energetic and enthusiastic staff.

STAFF APPOINTMENTS

I still believe that it should be written into the Job Description of every member of Home-Start staff, whatever their position, that they should support a family themselves. They need to feel, smell, see, hear and generally stay in touch with the needs of families, as a motivating foundation for their daily work. Often, when I felt bogged down by paperwork, I would track through for myself mentally, how what I was doing could ultimately help a family in a practical way. It always did, so I always kept going.

When appointing staff, I followed the advice of a University Vice Chancellor colleague. He suggested that in shortlisting and interviewing, one should look for the person with a demonstrable track record. When appointed, the member of staff should be given the best possible resources and support back-up that the organisation can afford and provide.

We learnt an important lesson, about how not to appoint or promote staff, when Valerie McGuffin in Northern Ireland, who had set up and run the first scheme in Belfast, was given the job of the first Consultant for Northern Ireland. It had seemed obvious to the trustees and the senior staff, including me, that she was our first and only choice. But Valerie herself told us afterwards, that she felt she had never been through a formal interview, there had been no competition and that she had not 'earned' the position. She was right, and we never did it that way again.

Twice I had to tell a new member of staff that his/her initial six month probationary period would not be renewed. This was painful for us both.

STAFF SUPPORT

I always thought of our regular support sessions as Support and Encouragment, rather than Supervision. Each member of staff was trusted and valued. If they tackled an issue differently from my approach, we discussed this openly. The likelihood was that they were right anyway. But I do remember vividly, the handful of times when we disagreed and it was very difficult to handle.

I always gained so much from our one-to-one meetings as well, in terms of support and encouragement. It was good to be able to share my load with close colleagues too.

STRUCTURE

I remember reading that there are two relevant paradigms: the dominator model and the partnership model. Western civilisation, despite its professed democracy, has the former. The only true partnership model, is one in which each person has an independent voice and is heard; where choice and autonomy are real.

People need the opportunity to make a phone call, write a letter, or stand up and make a statement themselves, rather than feeling represented by someone else all the time. This is why Charles Handy has called our type of organisation a 'community'. Hence the flat and lateral structure of Home-Start, which makes it possible to focus on the individual - be they parent, organiser, volunteer or member of staff, and the choices they make. Keeping schemes small and local for the families, or in touch with one another regionally, endorses the principle that small really is beautiful.

In 1987, Beryl Riley, by then the organiser of Home-Start in Cambridge, sent out a questionnaire to 70 Home-Start schemes and had a 100% response. In her conclusion she wrote:

> ***"The relationships working within Home-Start, from families through to Home-Start Consultancy, form a chain of reciprocal relationships, based on openness and trust, rather than a hierarchical pyramid of authority or bureaucratic mode of operation. This has contributed to the opportunity to review and question practice issues in a healthy way."***

STUDY DAYS, FOCUS GROUPS AND ROADSHOWS

Our first study days for all organisers, were held in the National Marriage Guidance Council offices in Rugby. It was refreshing even then to consider together such issues as family stress, case studies, supporting volunteers, Home-Start's public relations role, child abuse and Home-Start in the national context of child-care and the welfare state. As the number of schemes increased, we moved our venue each year, until we alighted on Swanwick, Derbyshire, a not-for-profit centre for the not-for-profit sector.

Oganised by Maggie Rowlands, in beautiful surroundings and comfortable accommodation, these were our most memorable opportunities to be together, from all over the United Kingdom.

> ***"As the Co-ordinator of the second Home-Start scheme in***

> ***Scotland – Leith and North East Edinburgh – I have fond memories of our early trips to Home-Start training days down South. We met other co-ordinators/organisers from all over the country and shared our experiences, recognising our differences and offering support to each other."***
>
> **Wendy Brownlee, Leith Home-Start.**

The energy level in Swanwick, could have lit up the United Kingdom! These were special days for extending both our hearts and our minds.

Anthony Douglas, Assistant Director Children and Families' Services, in Hackney Social Services, commented after his visit to Swanwick, that he noticed the:

> ***"lightness, joy and fun, which occur mostly where women are together, with their aspirations, visions, difficulties, hopes and dreams."***

From 1990, organisers who had been in post for over four years, were given the opportunity annually, to meet for two days at Launde Abbey – a beautiful Diocesan retreat house in Leicestershire. They enjoyed rest, refreshment and stimulating seminars together.

SURE START

During my last year, 1997/98, I was involved in meetings with other related voluntary organisations, politicians, and the Social Exclusion Unit to consider ways of reaching the most vulnerable families in our society. Various new government initiatives were being planned, including the Children's Fund, Safer Cities and Sure Start.

When I retired, Tessa Jowell, who was then Minister for Public Health, sent me a handwritten card, saying, "I hope that you will watch what we are doing and can see your inspiration, particularly in Sure Start". This was indeed an accolade for all that everyone in Home-Start had achieved.

BUT! Would Sure Start, which was to be top down and government led, at enormous cost, with all the related accountability, contracts, control, performance indicators, targets, and measurement of outcomes, be able to co-exist with Home-Start? Or would Sure Start gobble us up? Fund us? Manage us? Change us?

For Home-Start, it is vital to grow organically, from within a community. We work alongside families through unpaid volunteers offering friendship, with no specific goals, either for the families or for the organisation itself. By existing, listening and responding, we can genuinely meet the needs expressed by those we serve, at the time that they need us. We have proved we can raise morale, just by building on a family's enthusiasms and strengths. We can kindle kindness, pass on passion, reward responsibility and love laughing together. It's as simple as that.

In the 60 areas of the country initially designated as most deprived by Sure Start, Home-Start was already in 49 of them. Significantly though, we were equally available to any family in the wider area, and not just to those on run-down council estates. We work responsively from within, rather than pro-actively from without.

I recently attended an AGM in one of the Home-Start schemes in England, for which I have great respect. Glad that Sure Start now provides them with extra funding and extra paid staff, I listened with keen anticipation to their joint presentation. But I was bewildered by what I heard, for in the same breath and the same sentence as they talked about the friendship they offer families, they also talked about the forms they fill in with the families for funding the scheme. Fffff! Would you do that to a friend?

In the meantime, our organisations will complement each other, with respect for the differences, for the sake of the families we serve.

> ***"It is heart connections not political or economic reform that will transform our society"*** **said E.F. Schumacher in 'Small is Beautiful' .** ***"And"*** **he said,** ***"the work begins at home".***

TALKS

Did you know that some people consider that when really geared up to giving a successful talk, a woman's nipples should be erect? No? Neither did I. But having been told that, the staff often gave each other knowing winks before one of us had to speak.

One year, at the Study Days for organisers, I decided to feed back all that they, as well as Home-Start volunteers, give to young families, in terms of human qualities, and emotional support. I presented these in alphabetical order, as much for my own benefit in presenting them, as for the timing. After that, I often used all or part of the speech when talking to groups of volunteers or at AGMs.

Always, I was asked by someone for a copy. So it is included in **Appendix II**.

> ***"After all these years, it was so good to hear, in spite of all the changes in Home-Start both nationally and locally, the ABC for volunteers is still the most relevant set of values and principles underpinning the Home-Start ethos".***
>
> **Philomena Gray, Chair Home-Start Stoke-on-Trent.**

TIG (Training Information Guidance) FEE

In 1992 the Department of Health told us that their grant to Home-Start Consultancy would be cut, unless schemes contributed to the costs of the central organisation. Reluctantly, we agreed to charge each 1% of their statutory core funding. This method of bringing in additional income, was much simpler than costing the consultants' time for training, travel or guidance.

TITLES

Receiving an honour from Her Majesty the Queen is never for the work of one person alone. In the case of Home-Start:

OBE stands for On Behalf of Everyone, and 'Ome-Start Benefits Everyone.

CBE was our Combined Brilliant Effort.

Thank you again to each person who contributed to the success of Home-Start.

A TRADING COMPANY

Although we were advised to form a trading company – Home-Start (UK) Ltd - for funds raised through corporate or promotional sponsorship, we never ever reached our trading limit for VAT exemption - £37,000 in the 1990s.

TRUST

Clive Bate, a management consultant of high repute, who chaired both the management committee and the trustees for three years, left us with acknowledgement of the secret of Home-Start's success:

> ***"Home-Start thrives because of the energies and dedication of those who become involved in it. It will continue to thrive particularly because of the trust that is communicated between each Home-Start scheme and Home-Start Consultancy. Those of us who have become involved have experienced the amazing strength of people who believe in each other".***

Home-Start will do well to remain based on relationships of trust, not truss. Trust, like hope, is an orientation towards the future.

TRUSTEES

The biggest trick of all in a voluntary organisation, is to have trustees who trust! Miraculously, we had! With their backing, we were able to develop rapidly, creatively and effectively, knowing that we were fully supported and wisely guided by them. Not only was each of our trustees prepared to contribute his or her expertise individually, but they always worked supportively as a team. They told me that our meetings were also a lot of fun.

For ten years we had only four trustees; then eight. Records show that we had 100% attendance at our meetings always. Once numbers exceed ten, I believe people begin to think it doesn't matter if they miss a meeting. Personally I still consider the cell-of-seven to be the ideal number for a group.

UMBRELLA ORGANISATONS

Home-Start schemes which began under an umbrella organisation, like NewPIN, (New Parent Infant Network), which was built on Home-Start principles, but developed through Guy's Hospital, and Home-Start schemes developed by Children North East, in Newcastle, eventually presented us with difficulties. At first, in the mid 1980s, we took them as a compliment, as Elizabeth Bryan, chairwoman at the time, indicated in the annual report:

> ***"One of the most gratifying signs of success for any organisation, is when other people begin to see it as a potentially useful model for their own work, or ask advice about common concerns. The Consultancy is receiving an increasing number of requests for information and advice, both from voluntary organisations and statutory bodies."***

With the needs of families uppermost on our minds, we always supported other organisations wishing to establish the Home-Start approach themselves. It was only when another charity used our name, but ceased to contribute to- or avail themselves of- Home-Start services and resources, that we asked them to change their name. I had experienced a difficult workshop at a national conference, when the chief executive officer of an umbrella organisation which had developed Home-Start schemes, but had refused to pay our Training, Information and Guidance fee, and chose to "go it alone", began to talk about

her "five Home-Start schemes". Then, when it was my turn to be introduced, I talked about the 150+ Home-Start schemes in existence at the time. After all, they did not **belong** to Home-Start Consultancy, but instead were each locally independent.

Soon afterwards, our trustees insisted that Home-Start schemes, which either of necessity or choice began under the umbrella of a parent body, should work towards autonomy, within three years. It fell to me and my chairman to be firm on several occasions, which was hard but necessary.

At least though, this ensured that everyone in Home-Start was working to the same constitution, firmly rooted and well-connected to a wide range of other agencies within their local community through their own multi-disciplinary management committee. All then shared the same approach to supporting families and each other, throughout Home-Start.

VALUES

Together, our values and ideas shape our relationships and vice-versa – a cycle which is fundamental in Home-Start.

VOLUNTEERS

The very heart of Home-Start is its team of volunteers, wherever and whoever they are. They are the most valuable resource we have. Home-Start volunteers are members of local management committees and support groups, sharing their professional expertise. They are the home-visiting volunteers whose relationships with each family they visit, benefit the families and Home-Start as a whole. The mystery and magic of Home-Start are rooted firmly in those relationships

Volunteers are friends who show a remarkable willingness to stay with a family for as long as they are needed. They share their humanity and their knowledge, as an informal source of information, until the parents are coping and even enjoying life again. They lend their strengths, until a family finds its own.

Some volunteers see their involvement in Home-Start as part of their wish to build a better world. It can be so important to begin locally, perhaps with a family from a very different background or culture. They can learn together about peaceful co-operation and understanding within their non-threatening relationship. Many volunteers are aware of the reward of having created an atmosphere of reliability, stability and honesty for a family. It is their gift of truth, which goes with trust, which can make family members feel more like relatives.

It has been said that the ultimate cure for one's own stress, is helping others. Arguably, there is no such thing as altruism, so it can be important to identify what each person gains. All the annual reports from Home-Start schemes in many different countries, contain testimonies from the volunteers themselves.

- It's nice being of value to others.
- I was new to the area and now I have made a lot of like-minded friends.
- After I retired, I found it hard to get out of bed in the mornings. Now I can't wait to pop round again to my Home-Start family, who, I know, really love me.
- I have had some of my most profound learning experiences through the family I visit.
- With no money, you are vulnerable and dependent on developing a special relationship with a family, learning from each other about ways of life, culture and ideas.
- Human problems need human qualities – you can't use a tank to mend a marriage.

But what do the parents and children say about their volunteers? Dr. Sheila Shinman, in Family Album, Snapshots of Home-Start in Words and Pictures (Home-Start UK 1994) reports on a study, which distils parents' descriptions of volunteers under three clusters:

1. The fun factor
   Volunteers are Cheerful – Fun to be with – Bright - Exciting – Smiling – Laughing – Shares jokes – Outrageous – Outgoing – Bubbly – Absolutely Brilliant – Absolutely wonderful – Can't wait to see her – Great – Positive.

2. Volunteers explain and are not authoritarian
   Asks – Explains – Involves – Doesn't push – Is easy to talk to – Takes your mind off things – Will talk you through things – Puts you in a better mind – Allows you to talk – Makes conversation easily.

3. The volunteers' qualities
   Friendly – Warm – Approachable – Caring – Kind – Nice – Pleasant – Easy going – Happy – Affectionate – Loving – A special friend – Thinks of you – Likes you for what you are – Respects you.

The parents in the study clearly perceived their volunteers as positive, caring and approachable people, prepared to share their time and their humanity.

In **Appendix II**, I celebrate, what for me have always been, the essential qualities of our Home-Start volunteers in their relationships with parents and children.

In Darwin, Northern Territory of Australia, they celebrate and commemorate ordinary people who have made a difference to Darwin, by naming them on paving stones around the town. On that basis the streets of so many places around the world now, would be paved with Home-Start volunteers' names, memorialised forever.

APPENDIX II

THE IMPORTANT ROLE OF HOME-START VOLUNTEERS WHEN SUPPORTING FAMILIES WITH YOUNG CHILDREN AT HOME

Alphabet Speech For Volunteers and Schemes Between 1993 – 1998

The Home-Start approach draws on human qualities for which, I believe, one can neither legislate nor train.

Human attributes and attitudes become very potent when expressed in the privacy of the family's home – Home-Start!

Thinking through these qualities, I have decided to offer them to you in alphabetical order, partly for my ease, but also for your sense of knowing when I shall end!

A. Affirmation
Amazement – We affirm with amazement how so many families cope in the most daunting circumstances.

B. Being with, rather than doing to
Behaviour "Behaviour can be seen; experience cannot." Ronald Laing. We have a responsibility to make each other's experience of life as rewarding and positive as possible.

C. Care/Confidentiality/Celebration/Co-operation

D. Development of self and others

E. Energy – We can help turn apathy to energy.
Encouragement – encouraging parents' strengths and emotional well-being and encouraging families to widen their network of relationships and resources.
Earth – Home-Start grows organically, from the very roots of a community. Anagram Home-Start/Most Earth.
Emotion – We give emotional support.
Enthusiasm – has the most amazing power to spread.

F. Friendship/Fun/Flexibility to take account of different needs.
Food – never underestimate the value of eating or cooking together.

G. Generosity - of spirit and of sharing oneself. e.g. the parent who was living in extremely poor circumstances, and under severe stress herself, who sorted out clothes "for the poor kiddies".

H. Happiness/Home/Hope – "Hooray, Here Comes Tuesday!" "Out of happiness" wrote Vaclav Havel, "all good affections grow". This is a challenging thought in a world where the remedy for ills is so often punishment.
Heart – at the heart of Home-Start. Anagram Home-Start/Most Heart.

I. Information – provide it or seek it for a family as necessary.

J. Joy – spread it.
Judgement – we say we are non-judgemental, but in practice, we make positive judgements all the time with and on behalf of a family.

K. Kindness – is composed of thoughtfulness, gentleness, tolerance and a respect for the dignity of others. E.g. remembering the birthday or providing a bunch of daffodils in a vase, because the likelihood is there may not be one.

L. Love – Quite simply, if it is genuine, it can change the world.
Laughter – really is the best medicine.

M. Mothering – According to Anne Dally, mothers are natural therapists. 'At Mother's is another anagram of Home-Start.
Men – There are many involved, either as sons, husbands, partners of the female volunteers, or as part of a male/female partnership visiting a family together, or as male Home-Start volunteers. Sometimes it is hard to place them with a family that might prefer a mother-figure.

N. Need to be needed – We all do, don't we?

O. Offer – we have no authority to do anything but 'offer' as volunteers in Home-Start.

P. Power of powerlessness
Practical help
Person, rather than problem-oriented.

Q. Quality – to which we all aspire.

R. Rights – The right of every child to have a supported parent.
Relationship/Respect/Reciprocity/Reassurance – reassuring parents that difficulties in bringing up children are not unusual.

S. Support/Start/Simple/Spontaneous/Self-esteem
Smile – the power of a smile. I am sad that so often for a volunteer to deliver a smile into the home, it has to be backed up with a scheme with a Service Agreement back at the office.

T. Time – to be there, to listen and to care
Touch – physically and emotionally.
Trust – not truss.
Truth – Vaclav Havel said "Truth and love must triumph over lies and hatred."

U. Us/Understanding/Um el Fahm – the Arab community in Israel where Home-Start exists.

V. Volunteering – Volunteers are not conscripted – volunteering engenders choice.
Value/Valued/Valuable

W. Work – at its best, is love made visible – we work at a marriage, work in Home-Start, work bringing up the children.

X. X-Ray Art – i.e. the Aboriginal cave paintings, where there is the skeleton of a fish, for children to learn the structure, before putting on the variations of flesh, size, colour – like our basic structure with the variations of Home-Start schemes.

Y. You – Thank You!

Z. ZZZZZ – Falling asleep.

We are extremely aware, that without Home-Start volunteers, Home-Start could not exist. After all, it is the volunteers who work directly with the families. We thank you for choosing to belong, yet we value your independence. Together we strive to make Home-Start as effective as possible for families. Thank you for all your kindnesses and for your personal generosity.

APPENDIX III

HOME-START UK

1. STANDARDS & METHODS OF PRACTICE OF HOME-START SCHEMES

HOME-START STATEMENT OF PRINCIPLE

HOME-START is a voluntary organisation in which volunteers offer regular support, friendship and practical help to young families under stress in their own homes helping to prevent family crisis and breakdown.

****

The following Standards and Methods of Practice are included as a Schedule to the model Constitution agreed by the Charity Commissioners. They must be followed by all HOME-START schemes.

1. HOME-START works with families who are experiencing difficulties or suffering stress and who have at least one child under five years of age. These families are offered support in their own homes by volunteers for as long as is necessary.

2. Each HOME-START scheme is an independent voluntary organisation which works towards the increased confidence and independence of the family by:-

   - offering support, friendship and practical assistance
   - visiting families in their own homes, where the dignity and identity of each individual can be respected and protected
   - reassuring parents that difficulties in bringing up children are not unusual and emphasising the pleasures of family life
   - developing a relationship with the family in which time can be shared and understanding can be developed; the approach is flexible to take account of different needs
   - encouraging the parents' strengths and emotional well-being for the ultimate benefit of their own children
   - encouraging families to widen their network of relationships and to use effectively the support and services available within the community

3. The Management Committee of each HOME-START scheme employs the staff and is responsible for the effective management of the scheme including funding, insurance and premises. The Committee members ensure that proper links are developed with the statutory caring agencies and with other voluntary organisations within the community.

   No representative of a funding agency is eligible for election as the Chairperson of HOME-START.

APPENDIX III

4. At least one salaried Organiser is employed who has relevant training and experience, and whose duties include:-

   - the administration of HOME-START to ensure conformity with the Standards and Methods of Practice

   - the preparation and support of volunteers

   - liaison with other voluntary and statutory agencies working with young families

   - the initial visit to each family. Careful attention is paid to matching volunteers' skills and experience to the needs of the families.

5. Organisers and volunteers are normally parents themselves or have had parenting experience. Volunteers are supported by HOME-START Organisers and other HOME-START volunteers. Support from other professional workers associated with the families is available to the scheme.

6. All volunteers attend an initial course of preparation and receive additional information and support to meet the needs which develop in the course of their work with HOME-START.

7. The range of referrals or self-referrals accepted are not limited, except where the resources available to HOME-START are not adequate to meet the number or complexity of cases.

8. All information about parents and families is treated as confidential, to be discussed only as necessary with the Organiser in support of the volunteer and to assist the family. Any disclosure of the confidential information to any other person may only be undertaken with the expressed permission of the parents for the purpose of assisting the family, except where it is considered necessary for the protection of a child when information shall be shared with the appropriate authority.

9. All members of Management Committees, staff and volunteers, must be aware of the HOME-START Equal Opportunities Policy and its implementation. They must also be sensitive to race, class, gender, sexual orientation, religion and disability.

10. All HOME-START schemes retain close links both with HOME-START UK and with other HOME-START schemes and avail themselves of the training and information provided. The shared experience of each HOME-START scheme and of HOME-START UK, regionally and centrally, ensures that the development of HOME-START nationally is as effective as possible to the ultimate benefit of the families.

1/28.07.93

APPENDIX IV

START DATES AND FOUNDER ORGANISERS

START DATE	NAME OF SCHEME	FIRST ORGANISER
1973	Leicester	Margaret Harrison
1977	Hinckley	Ann O'Neil
1978	Charnwood	Kay Hancock
	Nottingham	Jill Manning-Press
1979	Ripley & District	Beryl Riley
1980	Bristol	Richard Sykes
1981	Harrow	Ruth Dale
	Herefordshire	Sue Pope
	Melton & Rutland	Christine Tracey
1982	Bassetlaw	Ruth Glover
	Hull & East Riding	Susheela Lourie
	Northampton	Pauline Pearson
	Sheffield	Margaret Jackson, Maggie Rowlands
	Swindon	Linda Wright
1983	Armagh & Dungannon	Anna Logan
	Braintree & Witham	Sheila Withnell
	Conwy	Margaret Sewell
	Dukeries	Barbara Phillips
	East Belfast	Valerie McGuffin
	Havant	Valerie Norman
	Mid-Suffolk	Caroline Tisdell
	N.W. Leicestershire	Erica Whayman
	Royston & South Cambridgeshire	Sue Everitt
1984	Bolsover District and Claycross	Lynn Glover
	Chelmsford	Annette Fagge
	Dacorum	Veronica Wellman
	Doncaster	Glenys Hall, Margaret Kennedy
	Harborough & District	Elaine Dilleigh

	King's Lynn	Clare Cooke, Charlotte Mannion
	Leighton Linslade	Susan Welch
	Lincoln	Jackie Dunmore
	Newark	Jenny James
	Perth	Sue Gamwell and Judi Sutherland
	Reading	Pam Cooke, Annette Hendry
	Shrewsbury	Fiona Sibbick
	Stoke-on-Trent	Glyn Chapman
	Sutton	Marian Moss
	Uttlesford	Jo Moody and Linda Robinson
	Worcester	Wendy Collier
1985	Peterborough	Stella Kempsell
	Rhymney Valley	Merryl Roberts
	Swadlincote & District	Pat Petty
1986	Banbury	Kathy Goodey
	Breckland	Doreen Martina
	Dundee	Julie Robertson
	Exeter	Anne Laws
	Leith	Sybil Brown
	Mansfield	Barbara Davies
	Milton Keynes	Margie Charlewood
	Stamford	Jill Haigh
	Wisbech	Margaret Rouse
1987	Bedford	Jenny Magee
	East Fife	Martha Simpson
	Fenland	Sheila Tooke
	Leeds	Anne Pemberton
	Maidstone	Sue Long
	Marlborough	Jenny Poole
	Medway	Jenny Hurkett
	North Belfast	Hilary Smyth
	North Herts	Charmaine Rogers
	Nuneaton	Ann Rowe
	Rotherham	Liz Thompson

	Scunthorpe	Margaret Bird
	South East Essex	Peggy Church
	Thanet	Gwen Kidd, Janet Moran
1988	Ashfield	Wendy Haynes
	Ashford	Bob Travers
	Bolton	Pat Clark
	Clackmannanshire	Anne Dornan
	Harlow	Ina Quig
	Hastings &Rother	Barbara Mullen
	Lorn	Bette Graham
	Mastrick	Gill Parsons
	Oxford	Lynne Lawrence
	Ross & Cromarty	Marie Macintosh
	St. Helens	Elaine Appleton
	Surrey Heath	Carol Gibbons
	Telford & Wreakin	Cherida Fletcher, Maggie Powell
	York	Celia Harris
1989	Bexley	Pat Pitcher
	Cambridge	Beryl Riley
	Croydon	Sophie Cottrell
	Down District	Deidre Brady
	Erewash	Sue Belcher
	Hackney	Thelma Stephens
	Newham	Sheila Kataria
	Newry & Mourne	Jane Elliott
	North Down	Heather Knox
	North West Kent	Liz Garsed
	Redditch	Chris Wilkinson
	Saltley	Rajvinder Nepal
	South Shropshire	Paula Spencer
	South Oxfordshire	Karen Salmon
	Stockland Green & Erdington	Kate Batchelor
1990	Antrim District	Margaret Thompson
	Barnsley	Jackie McCudden
	Central Fife	Margaret Campbell
	Dunfermline	Maureen Trumper

	Epping Forest	Christine Chapple
	Selly Oak	Valerie Green
	Sudbury	Jane Arkell
	Teignbridge	Jo Bickle
	Torbay	Annie Morris
	Wakefield	Sheena Bell
1991	Blackburn	Sally Collins
	Brentwood	Cathy Burton
	Castle Vale	June Mountney
	Wrexham	Gillian Cutler
1992	Canterbury & Coastal	Sari Sirkia-Weaver
	Castleford	Gaynor Annesley
	Colchester	Linda Watts
	Cymorth Ceridigion	Delyth Jones
	Ely (Cardiff)	Janet Child
	Gainsborough	Carol Vessey
	Greenwich	Rikki Adam
	Hemsworth & South Elmsall	Caroline Longhurst
	Levenmouth	Janet Blues
	Lisburn	Jackie Valentine
	Pontefract	Dawn Covey
	Portsmouth	Mandy Lindley
	Preston	Helen Walsh
	Rhondda	Melanie Andrews
	Tunbridge Wells	Rachel Ferguson-Gow
1993	Merton	Barbara Cluer
	South Sefton	Deborah Woof
	Sutton Coldfield	Celia Kelly
	Watford & Three Rivers	Vivienne Davies
1994	Angus	Julie Thomson
	Bracknell	Tania Honey
	Camden	Myra Farnworth
	Corby	Mary Champion
	Dearne Valley	Rita Hodkin
	East Herts	Vanessa Rogers
	Eastleigh	Sandra Lawton
	Kirkcaldy	Eleanor Thomson
	Kingston	Valerie Markwick

	Redhill, Reigate and Horley	Julie Bezzina
	Sittingbourne & Sheppey	Laura Jobson
	South Cumbria	Jean Sadler
	West Tyrone	Pauline Rice
	Woking	Eddie Ross
	Wycombe	Ruth Court
1995	Ammanford	Jayne Davies
	Bournemouth	Wendy Staples
	Brent	Angelle Bryan
	Caerphilly	Lynda Kelly
	Causeway	Ann Laird
	Derby	Debbie Smith
	Dover	David Rains
	Dudley	Gail Howden
	Ealing	Liz Foreman
	Flintshire	Sandra Hughes
	Garioch	Barbara Foad
	Goole & District	Gill Pirt
	Gosport & Fareham	Sue Gillard, Kathryn Wood
	Great Yarmouth	Laura Cary
	Kettering	Lynn Chapman
	Kincardine	Isobelle Maloney
	North East Aberdeenshire	Linda Chambers
	North East Lincolnshire	Lesley Whittaker
	Northfield	Jill Shepherd
	Richmond	Anthea Cameron
	Runnymede	Liz Fox
	Rushmore & East Hart	Pat Nield
	Sedgemoor	Julia Setter
	Shepway	Maggi Frize
	Sleaford	Linda Nixon
	Southwark	Sherri Pickles
	Spellthorne	Amanda Groves
	Wellingborough	Janet Sanders
	West Devon	Julie Meakin
	Wyre Forest	Ellen Dolphin, Sheila Lockwood

1996	Ash & Guildford	Patricia Borthwick
	Basildon District	Geraldine Evans
	Blackpool	Carmen Conquer
	Chorley & South Ribble	Carole Lee
	Daventry	Jean Miller
	Epsom, Ewell and Banstead	Carole Goldsborough
	Harwich	Laura Garnham
	Isle-of-Wight	Jill Wade-Smith
	Islington	Libby Spring
	Mid Argyll, Jura, Islay & Kintyre	Jackie Fulton
	Molesey	Fran Buckley
	Slough	Maureen Kiffin
	South Downs	Tina Jackson, Vivienne Singer
	Stafford & District	Ralph Lilburne
	Wokingham	Angie Mycock
	Ynys Mon	Liz Gilham
1997	Ards	Terri Cochrane
	Barnet	Julie Phillips
	Bridgend	Tania Treble
	Crawley & Horsham	Michaela Richards
	East Cambridgeshire	Sue Wilson
	East Northamptonshire	Katrina Rodden
	Enfield	Gillian Antoniou
	Farnham	Taryn Lawrence
	Glenrothes	Jan Marshall
	Manchester Central	Kathy Shaw
	Newcastle-under-Lyme	Liz Watson
	North Shropshire & Oswestry	Elaine Griffiths
	Rugby & District	Rosemary Tipping
	Shipley	Eileen Broomhead
	Stockport	Jo Speakman
	West Berkshire	Megan Danvers, Lyn Hancock
	West Lancashire	Linda Chambers
	Winson Green/Handsworth	Wendy Millichamp
1998	Bridlington & Driffield	Jackie Pockley
	Butser	Kath Shaw

	Central Cheshire	Sheila Deaville Lockhart
	Craigavon	Siobhan Wallace
	Kirklees	Jill Long
	Louth & District	Sue Bourne
	Meon Valley	Gloria Russell
	Ribble Valley	Sylvia Wyatt
	Sandwell	Judith Smith
	Speke	Sophie Howe
	Staffordshire Moorlands	Louise Walker
	Torridge & Taw	Ali Bellamy, Sue White
	Walton, Weybridge & Hersham	Debbie Johnson